Reincarnation
is Making
a
Comeback

THE INS AND OUTS OF
THE HUMAN SPIRIT

Dan S. Ward, Ph.D

Cover Design by Bob Boberitz.

Library of Congress Number: 90-63688
ISBN: 0-924608-07-2
Manufactured in the United States of America

The following publishers or authors have generously given permission to use extended quotations from copyrighted works. Text from *Into the Unknown*, copyright © 1981 The Reader's Digest Association, Inc. Reprinted by permission. Excerpts from *The Unquiet Dead*, by Edith Fiore copyright © 1987, and *Nostradamus & The Millennium* © 1987, by John Hogue. Used by permission of Doubleday, a division of Bantam Doubleday Dell Publishing Group, Inc. From *Introduction to Yoga Principles and Practices*, by Sachindra Kuman Majumdar, reprinted with permission by Citadel Press, Carol Publishing Group. *Man and The World in Light of Anthroposophy*, Stewart C. Easton, reprinted with permission by Anthroposophic Press. Writings from William J. Baldwin, Ph.D. of Carmel, California. Reprinted with permission of the author. From *Death to Rebirth*, Manly P. Hall, reprinted with permission from Philosophical Research Society. From "Parapsychology Review", May/June 1979, reprinted with permission from Parapsychology Foundation, Inc. From *After We Die, What Then?* George W. Meeks. Reprinted with permission of MetaScience Corporation. Sylvan Muldoon and Hereward Carrington, *Projection of the Astral Body*, © Sylvan Muldoon, 1969, (York Beach, ME: Samuel Weiser, Inc., 1973), used by permission. From *Wounds of War*, Herbert Hendin and Ann P. Haas, © 1984 reprinted with permission of Basic Books, Inc. From *Proceedings of the Symposium on Consciousness and Survival*, Rupert Sheldrake and Jacqueline Damgaard, excerpted from *Global Mind Change*, reprinted with permission by Institute of Noetic Sciences. From *Emmanuel's Book*, by Pat Rodegast. Copyright © 1985 by Pat Rodegast. Reprinted by permission of Bantam Books, a division of Bantam, Doubleday, Dell Publishing Group, Inc. From *Strangers Among Us*, by Ruth Montgomery, reprinted with permission of Coward, McCann & Gehegan, Inc., Putnam Publishing Group, Inc. From *Memories and Visions of Paradise*, by Richard Heinberg. Published by Jeremy P.Tarcher Inc. Reprinted with permission of the author. From *The Road Less Traveled*, by M. Scott Peck, M.D., reprinted with permission of the publisher, Simon Schuster. From *Whirling Darkness*, by Mary Kay Rae, reprinted with permission of the author. From *The Man Who Wrestled With God*, by John Sanford, reprinted with permission of Paulist Press. From *The Power of Myth*, by Joseph Campbell, reprinted with permission of Doubleday, a division of Bantam Dell Publishing Group, Inc.

Published by Whitford Press
A division of
Schiffer Publishing Ltd.
1469 Morstein Road
West Chester, Pennsylvania 19380
Please write for a free catalog.
This book may be purchased from the publisher.
Please include $2.00 postage.
Try your bookstore first.

Contents

Acknowledgements

No book is ever written in isolation (which if they were, would constitute a pretty dismal situation). Instead, innumerable friends, associates, authors, teachers, and editors interact with an author and ultimately contribute in a substantial way to the finished product. They also occasionally serve to keep the author sane during the process. To all of these people (and/or entities), the sincerest gratitude is extended, particularly to those who don't actually get mentioned by name here.

Particular thanks go to Maurice Albertson, who first whetted my appetite for the subject, and who, along with Ken Freeman, allowed the use of the first versions of the text in a series of reincarnation classes offered at Colorado State University. Thanks also go to the members of SPRE, a strange group of people with some of the most outlandish ideas ever heard (most of which have turned out to be amazingly accurate), and to William Baldwin and Gloria Sutton, for some of the most incredible and loving demonstrations in metaphysics I've yet witnessed.

Editorial and critical reviews have been generously provided by many friends and associates, and while these terrific people can't be held responsible for the final text, nevertheless they deserve credit for many of the good portions. Particular thanks go to Mary Herrick, Karen Christophersen, Margie Butts, Cheryl Herzig, Carolyn Duff, Cathy Graepler, Mark Sloniker, Louise Thornton, Mary Kay Rae, Olivia Rud, Rakel Sayre, Lon Spencer, Judy Turner and Kate Taylor.

To all the authors, thinkers, teachers, healers, and metaphysicians that have added to my thoughts, experiences, and understanding, I am particularly indebted. They often do not get mentioned in an author's acknowledgements, but inasmuch as they have shaped so much of my work, they deserve my special thanks.

Finally, my love and heartfelt thanks go to my family, and particularly my children, Scott, Shari, and Kelly, for their unconditional love and support throughout the entire process.

Preface

Reincarnation is making a comeback. Routinely accepted by a majority of the world's population, reincarnation and related psychic phenomena have never been given their due in the western world. Western science, religion, and the news media have gone out of their way to ignore even the possibility of reincarnation. Ordinary citizens, however, have begun to sit up and take notice. Hundreds of thousands are actively studying the subject, reading books on a variety of related topics, changing their lives to reflect their new beliefs, and, for the most part, acting as if reincarnation was an established fact.

With all of this energy being expended by those who believe in reincarnation (or who find it difficult to simply dismiss it out of hand), millions of other rational, acceptably normal humans are beginning to wonder about what's causing all the commotion. The sheer volume and clamor of activity has attracted the attention of others, who are simply curious or who are willing to look for an alternative way. Suddenly reincarnation has become an idea that the Western mind accepts as a legitimate topic for discussion.

Purpose of Book

What will be attempted in the following pages is the bringing together of the relevant facts, opinions and claims concerning reincarnation and related psychic phenomena. Heavy emphasis will be placed on objectivity, as we attempt to explain, as concisely as possible, the various aspects or areas of interest in reincarnation, and to comment on or discuss the extent to which these various aspects are verified or supported by case studies, experiment, and/or other forms of evidence.

This is, quite obviously, a challenging task. Reincarnation and the related topics being explored in this book, constitute nothing less than the whole of life and are potentially without limit. George W. Meek, in his book, *After We Die, What Then?*, has noted that three psychical research libraries in the United States alone, list more than 100,000 books on the broad subject of life after death.

Clearly, this book which you now hold in your hands must be viewed as a terse but objective introduction to the subject. By organizing the myriad aspects of reincarnation and related paranormal phenomena into an intelligible whole and placing each of the strange phenomenon in its appropriate cubby hole, the author hopes to facilitate the reader's understanding of each aspect and at the same time allow for a better overall appreciation of the combined subjects.

What this book will not attempt to do is to overwhelm the reader with massive amounts of evidence supporting any particular point of view. Instead, the weight and breadth of evidence will be noted, along with its significance. The challenge of convincing the reader of a specific idea will be left to others. It is not the intent of this book to sell anything, or attempt to convince the reader of any specific idea, but merely to offer ideas and possibilities.

Organization of Book

The book is organized into four sections: Basics, Experiences, Possibilities, and Implications. The basics include discussions of reincarnation, karma, soulmates, and other topics which seem intrinsically tied to the subject of reincarnation. The second part of the book deals with birth, near-death, and out-of-body experiences as well as regressions to the state between lives and the possibility of "earthbound spirits". The experiences section of the book provides detailed information about the specifics of reincarnation theory, derived from a diverse group of unique and significant experiences. These experiences may be considered as supporting evidence for reincarnation theory.

The third part of the book begins to consider some of the possibilities arising from reincarnation theory. These possibilities include the possible need for changes in the way we view the universe, ESP, time, dreams, divination, channeling and near-term prophecies (as well as a few other subjects). Many of these subjects are not obviously related to reincarnation, but they are often discussed in the same context. Connections between the various topics do exist, however, and while they may be tenuous, they are important to an overall view of life and death. In many cases reincarnation is an essential ingredient in the validity of that subject. In other cases the connection is more circumstantial.

The fourth part of the book deals with the inherent implications of reincarnation theory. This includes how an individual's acceptance of reincarnation might influence that person's life and beliefs, and an attempt to consolidate the diverse evidence into a consistent and all-inclusive theory of reincarnation, which can then be either accepted or rejected.

Questions

An essential aspect of this book is to ask questions. Not just the ones with quick and clever answers, but ones such as: Why are we here, what is the basic purpose of life on earth, is there an overall pattern, and are we involved in some sort of journey or evolution of the soul? If there is a single question that will appear more than once in this book, it will be: Why? Many answers or alternatives will be provided by the author, but it is emphasized that an understanding of reincarnation will evolve only by the reader's own questions. In Voltaire's words: "Judge a man by his questions, not his answers."

I trust you will have some excellent questions ready, once you have finished reading this book.

Chapter 1:

Reincarnation:

The Basics

Kelly had always had a fear of heights. This was not your ordinary, garden-variety style of acrophobia. Kelly's fears were much more specific. Flying in airplanes, for example, never bothered her, nor did she have any compunction about a tour of a wire-enclosed observation deck of the Empire State building. Kelly even lived on the fourth floor of her apartment building, complete with an often-used balcony.

On the other hand, Kelly's balcony was enclosed by a heavy concrete railing. Take away the artificial walls, which kept the open space at a distance and afforded a convenient handhold in "emergencies," and Kelly would feel more than a queasiness; Kelly would become abnormally worried about falling to her death.

Her phobia had never ruled her life, but it did on occasion provide her with an embarrassing moment or two. There was the time she and her fiance, Frank, stopped off at the Black Canyon of the Gunnison. The Black Canyon is a sheer-walled canyon in the San Juan Mountains of western Colorado, formed by the Gunnison River. The river has cut nearly vertical walls of several thousand feet and exposed rock from virtually every geologic time period from the present back to and including pre-Cambrian time.

At the first stop along the canyon's rim, Kelly and Frank hopped out of their car to walk out on a small finger of rock to an observation area neatly provided by the National Park Service. Frank strolled ahead with complete abandon and eager anticipation. Kelly was much more aware to the possible dangers, however remote they might have been.

At first her attitude was merely cautious. Then she found herself reaching for the bare comfort of a low ledge of rock, anything to keep her in touch with terra firma. By the time she reached the observation area, she was nearly crawling. Still five feet from the precipice, she sat down on a very solid and (hopefully) very secure rock. She had begun to sweat profusely.

A small boy, the offspring of another family, arrived at about that moment. Young and eager, he ran down the path to the observation area while his parents followed along unconcerned. When the youngster leaped up on the rock ledge to look down into the canyon, Kelly very nearly swallowed her heart. She was certain that the boy was about to take his first and only flying lesson. Reaching out toward the boy, Kelly croaked out an unintelligible warning. The youngster never noticed her, but her fiance of only two months did!

Frank was a nice fellow, but he couldn't help but laugh at his petrified sweetheart. She did, in fact, look rather absurd as she hung on to her rock. Seeing Frank watching her, Kelly realized how she must look. She quickly became aware of her perspiration, her apparent weakness, and her complete inability to talk (much less, laugh it off). She knew she looked to be the prize fool of all time. And in front of Frank! It was blatantly obvious to her rational mind that there was no danger, and yet she was weakened and very nearly ill simply due to the proximity of the canyon's vertical walls.

Suffice it to say that Frank became very gallant and Kelly became very embarrassed. By the time she was back in the safety of her car, she had made up her mind to do something about her "idiotic phobia."

Kelly decided not to go to a psychiatrist, she figured she was not that crazy, at least, not yet. But she had to do something, if only to encourage Frank to stop his occasional "cute" smiles. So she went to a hypnotherapist.

Kelly's therapist was very understanding. He smiled reassuringly as she described her ordeal. Then using a hypnotic regression technique, he asked Kelly to go back to a time that was important to Kelly's fear of heights. Immediately, Kelly visualized a stark peak against a background of low-lying clouds. The peak was only a few hundred feet higher than her own vantage point, but on all sides of the mountain vertical cliffs fell a thousand feet to the rampaging river below.

In her visualization, Kelly was running down the path atop a ridge that connected her village to the mountain's peak. In her hypnotic state, she sensed a panic; not for herself, but for someone else. She scrambled furiously up the switchback path leading to the peak's summit. She began breathing hard from the exertion and running, despite the fact that she was accustomed to high-altitude breathing.

Finally she reached the top, but only to see her lover, a "prince of her people," being thrown from the mountaintop. Her lover made no sound, as if he was oblivious to the danger. The scream came from Kelly, startling the two behemoths who had so casually thrown a prince to his death. (Her scream startled her therapist as well.) The killers quickly ran to her, grabbed her by the arms, and virtually by reflex carried her to the ledge. Shocked and horrified at her lover's death, she forgot her own danger. Then suddenly, she, too, was thrown into space and to the river below.

Kelly had visualized "her death." The therapist was only slightly surprised, while Kelly was stunned. Once out of the hypnosis, she could only exclaim, "What was *that*?"

The therapist smiled as he answered her, "You recalled a past life in which you were murdered by being thrown into a vast canyon. It was that memory of your "death" that affected you when you found yourself in a similar environment at the Black Canyon."

Kelly raised an eyebrow. "Are you serious? Another life? It's not some childhood trauma?"

"A childhood trauma was certainly a possibility. But think about it. If a near brush with death when you were a child could traumatize the mind, wouldn't a terrifying and very real death traumatize it even more, and thus be more lasting in your memories?"

"But death is the end!"

"It is of that life, but you are carrying the memories and trauma from it with you today."

Was he kidding? Aren't past lives just a figment of the imagination? Aren't they something from "reincarnation"?

Reincarnation

Certainly there are those who would have us believe that "You only go around once in life, so you have to grab all the gusto you can." For recipients of such sage advice who find gusto-grabbing to be one of the lesser rewards of heaven, there is an alternative. Perhaps instead of a single tenure of one life to live on this earth, each of us has (or will have) many lives. As a result, each and every one will have a whole slew of opportunities to reach, grab, or otherwise attempt to acquire the gusto. (Assuming of course, you're into gusto-grabbing.)

The most fundamental aspect of reincarnation is the belief that a single soul will be incarnated in more than one body. By definition, reincarnation is the doctrine of the soul incarnating or reappearing after death in another and different bodily form. Furthermore, this rebirth of the soul in another body can occur numerous times (some believe reincarnation can involve hundreds, if not thousands, of different lives).

To the Western mind reincarnation is often thought of as a product of certain Eastern religions, such as Hinduism or Buddhism. While reincarnation may be considered to be an essential part of these religions, it is not necessary to accept any of the other tenets of these religions in order to believe in reincarnation. As a matter of fact, it should be noted that reincarnation has a long and honorable history in Christianity, Judaism, and Islam as well as the Eastern religions. These religious connections and implications will be discussed in Chapter 2. Suffice it to say for now that any acceptance of reincarnation as a realistic or factual possibility carries with it *no* obligation to accept any established religion, cult or spiritual standard. Reincarnation is a theory that may be considered separately as an independent and alternative way of thinking about life and death.

Déjà Vu

Déjà vu is typically defined in the dictionary as "the illusion that one has previously had an experience that is actually new to them."[1] Typically a person finds himself, for the first time, in a place he recognizes. He might remember specific streets, landmarks, or buildings, but he is equally certain that he has never been there. At least not in this life.

For example, consider a hypothetical American mathematician, wandering around the lesser-known parts of Budapest and finding himself familiar with his surroundings. With no previous visits to Budapest, Hungary, or even Europe; with no Hungarian ancestry in his background; and with no previous interests in either Budapest, Hungary, or goulash, the man is amazed to find a particular house with which he feels an immediate and intimate familiarity. He senses that he grew up in the home, but he is certain he has never before seen it in this lifetime. How can he explain to his highly analytical mind his strange but apparently strong feelings of attachment?

If reincarnation is a reality, then the explanation for the mathematician could be simply that he lived a prior life in Budapest, Hungary. The explanation is simple and to the point.

But if this explanation is insufficiently logical to our arithmetic specialist, he might turn to other possibilities. One alternative answer is precognition, the ability of someone to foresee an event or activity. Unfortunately, precognition, is generally no more acceptable to modern science than reincarnation. Modern psychology, finding neither the idea of reincarnation nor precognition acceptable, has instead coined its own neurological term by which it can explain the phenomenon. This is a clever tactic, inasmuch as naming something typically tends to take the mystery out of it.

Some psychologists describe the phenomenon of recognizing a place or person without ever previously having seen it as the "Ah ha" problem. These psychologists theorize that the perceived information is traveling through different neurological pathways; an introhemispheric synchronicity, in which the subconscious mind sees something just prior to the conscious mind seeing it. Then when the conscious mind does see it, it is recognized as familiar because it is "remembered" by the subconscious. Unfortunately, from an objective viewpoint, it is arguable that this explanation may actually be more esoteric than the idea of reincarnation.

In another instance, a young Nebraskan on her first sailing trip becomes unaccountably proficient at getting her "sea legs," hoisting the mainsail, and accomplishing other seafaring tasks, as if she had done this many times before. It becomes even more incredible as she realizes that she knows how to do things she has never done before or even known of before. Everyone else naturally makes the assumption that she's been sailing many times and has

---

[1] One can question why the dictionary used the word "illusion" as opposed to "feeling" or "sense." "Illusion" implies the feeling cannot be real, whereas "feeling" makes no judgment either way.

been less than forthright in describing herself as a rank amateur. But Miss Nebraska knows better, and her abilities, that she can't account for as learned in her lifetime, lead her to the feeling of having done all of this before . . . perhaps in another lifetime?

So how does one explain it? The dictionary terms the feeling "déjà vu" and then quietly moves on to the next word, "deject." For the average person, merely giving a name to a strong and unsettling feeling is seldom sufficient to alleviate the feeling, Webster notwithstanding. Accordingly, it seems reasonable to consider other explanations.

Reincarnation would suggest that Miss Nebraska had perhaps been a sailor in a past life. The mystery is thus solved very simply.

However, for those not willing to admit to reincarnation and having no other ideas to explain Miss Nebraska's apparent skills and knowledge, these skeptics will often take the position that Miss Nebraska is not what she claims to be. Again, we find a rather simple answer: The lady is lying.

Skepticism is certainly not to be easily dismissed. Hopefully it can be tempered with an open mind, but the right to question must be retained at all times. Thus it is entirely reasonable to doubt the veracity of both Miss Nebraska and our mathematician. Unfortunately for the detractors of reincarnation, skepticism is less defensible where very young children are involved.

In one case, as a young girl first learned to talk, she began to tell about her life as Fred Thompson, the wife of Mary and the father of three children. Her parents' reactions were understandably skeptical until the young girl described her death in a motorcycle accident in such vivid detail that the parents were forced to take her seriously. The fact that the girl was also unusually afraid of motorcycles only strengthened her parents' interest.

Subsequent investigation allowed the parents and independent researchers to take the young girl to Fred Thompson's hometown in an effort to verify or dismiss the apparent evidence. The girl was, in fact, able to take them to Fred Thompson's former home, and there meet his mother. Even the very skeptical Mrs. Thompson eventually accepted the young girl's story and became convinced that the three-year-old was indeed the reincarnation of her son, who had died in a motorcycle accident.

The cause for skepticism is dealt a heavy blow in this case. The forthrightness of a three-year-old girl is simply harder to discredit. While it is, of course, plausible for the parents to have concocted some nefarious scheme in which to prove something (reincarnation or whatever), their motives for doing so are not readily apparent. Even in the event the parents did attempt to perpetrate some form of fraud, it would be difficult to train a three-year-old girl to maintain the "act" that she did in front of trained and skeptical investigators.

Into the Unknown, a book published by *Reader's Digest*, notes that:

> There are constants in the field, elements that occur with near universality and suggest to some researchers that the body of reincarnative lore, even without conclusive proof or a good chance of obtaining it, reflects common human experience

and thus cannot be ignored. Such recurring features include the extremely early age (two to four years) at which many subjects express their feelings about apparent past lives, the age (five to eight years) at which they tend to stop such communications, and the intensity of memories related to the death of the alleged previous personality.

It is Fred Thompson's case, and others like it that for many scientists make the subject of reincarnation fraught with difficulty. One might always explain any of our three cases mentioned above as reincarnation or simply dismiss them as a lack of memory or honesty on someone's part. From a scientific point of view, however, the better solution would be to conduct an experiment to determine which answer is more justified.

Unfortunately, the evidence of Miss Nebraska's seafaring skills, our mathematician's familiarity with Budapest, or a young girl's memories of a motorcycle accident fall under the category of irreproducible results. For science, evidence or experimental results that cannot be reproduced by others is invariably suspect. For the most part it is simply ignored.

Because déjà vu is inherently a one-time event, proving its reality by scientific means is more than just a challenging task, it is a virtually impossible one.

Prodigies

The inexplicable does not end with déjà vu. If we carry memories from a past life, is it not possible to carry a great deal more? Could we carry over skills or knowledge from a previous life as well?

Consider, for example, world-famous eighteenth-century composer Wolfgang Amadeus Mozart. At the age of four, he wrote a piano concerto, a sonata, and several minuets. His compositions were anything but simple but were nevertheless technically accurate. Think about that for a moment: four years old! By the age of seven, he had composed a full-length opera. So what has your child been doing lately?

How does one explain Mozart's genius, particularly at such an early age? Genetics? Do we carry genes that determine how well we can compose or play the piano or violin? Do genes carry the "blueprints" via DNA for a myriad of other talents, or is there a source of intelligence, skills, and knowledge from which someone like Mozart can tap?

Reincarnation might suggest that Mozart in a prior life was a musician and composer. This type of reasoning would say that Mozart already had accomplished much of the necessary groundwork for his skills and genius, and that when he was born Wolfgang Amadeus Mozart, he was well primed to begin work at a very early age. Hey! that was easy! Reincarnation thus "explains" or offers a theory to justify this musical phenomenon. It may or may not be true, but the theory does have more appeal than to simply dismiss the existence of this child prodigy by merely saying that he had been blessed with innate genius or natural ability. Why, for example, should anyone be "blessed" prior to her or his birth?

Xenoglossy

"Xenoglossy" is the term given to the utterance of a language unknown to the speaker. The term seems somewhat superfluous if we quite rationally reject the idea of someone conversing in a language he doesn't know. Unfortunately for our rationality, we are now routinely presented with subjects reliving past lives under hypnosis and speaking in foreign languages–languages of which they have no knowledge in this lifetime. To further emphasize the inexplicable, some of the languages are now so rare that it takes an exhaustive effort just to find someone (scholar or linguist dealing in very rare languages) to interpret what they are saying.

Joel Whitton and Joe Fisher, in their book *Life Between Life,* point out that xenoglossy cases have been investigated by researchers such as William James and Ian Stevenson as well as numerous past-life therapists who have considered the growing incidence of trance subjects speaking in foreign tongues. These languages, to which they had no previous exposure in this lifetime, have included everything from modern European languages to ancient Chinese and jungle dialects.

Perhaps we can challenge some claims by pointing out that modern languages can often be learned very quickly with modern techniques. Furthermore, any interpretation of the long-dead languages spoken by subjects may be suspect because the experts often are unaccustomed to hearing the language. For example, how many people regularly converse in Old Norse, the language of the Vikings and the precursor to modern Icelandic? Come to think of it, how many people regularly converse in modern Icelandic?

Unfortunately for such doubters, we also have examples of xenography, the writing of a language unknown to the "author." One of Dr. Whitton's subjects, for example, while reliving a life in seventh-century Mesopotamia, was able to put down on paper what amounted to doodles. Upon close examination, these doodles were interpreted as an authentic representation of the long-dead language called Sassanid Pahlavi, which was used in Mesopotamia between A.D. 226 and 651 and bears no relation to modern Iranian.

Prejudices and Phobias

What about intuition? Is it, in part, based upon information or beliefs from a former existence? Have you ever met anyone whom you instantly disliked? Reincarnation would suggest that perhaps you had met this soul in a former lifetime and had had experiences that were not pleasant. Modern science would probably say that you met in this life, and because of the disagreeable nature of the meeting, you blocked it out of your mind. Alternatively, modern science might think that you were just being obnoxious or antisocial.

Clearly, prejudices and phobias are often carried throughout one's life. But could they be carried from life to life, and is this perhaps, at least in some cases, a better explanation? For example, does a person with acrophobia have this irrational fear of heights because of having fallen to her death in an earlier lifetime? Does the person suffering from severe claustrophia have a skeleton in the closet from a past life, one who perhaps suffered a traumatic event related to being closed in or buried alive?

Dr. Edith Fiore, a practicing psychologist, has often asked her patients to recall previous events that were causing present symptoms. These recollections under hypnosis have resulted in the removal of many of the symptoms. Dr. Fiore has now become convinced that many problems have their roots in past lives. In her own words:

> I have found past-life regression consistently helpful, often resulting in immediate remission of chronic symptoms that do not return, even after months and years.
>
> I now find that almost all patients with chronic weight excess of ten pounds or more have had a lifetime in which they either starved to death or suffered food deprivation for long periods . . . Cravings for particular foods have also been traced back to past lives.

Dr. Fiore has found the causes of phobias, fears, and even aversions to be rooted in a traumatic event of a previous life. Fear of the dark, insomnia, headaches, pains, disorders and some forms of physical weakness have been traced back to a past life. "Some recurring nightmares and pleasant dreams are actually flashbacks to experiences in a previous life."

Reincarnation thus gives a simple answer. A particular fear or phobia often derives from a traumatic experience and, in some cases, the experience was during a past life. Modern psychology, on the other hand, suggests that a forgotten childhood experience was the ultimate cause of the phobia.

It is undeniably true that people often suppress traumatic events and simply forget things that have happened in this lifetime. This ability of the brain to prevent the recall of such unpleasantness is actually a basic part of one's survival instinct. Unfortunately, not all phobias ever find a cause in this life despite a massive amount of psychological counseling and searching. Perhaps more importantly, there are some recollections or prejudices that do not carry with them the strong motivation to forget; in other words, there is no attached trauma.

For example, have you ever enjoyed the warmth and comfort of a fireplace? If you're a typical American, you will probably have sought out the opportunity to relax with a roaring fire either in a fireplace or while on a recreational outing. Have you ever wondered why?

That may sound silly. But if one objectively considers the advantages and disadvantages of a fireplace, one is inevitably led to the realization that there are no advantages, i.e., there are no reasons for our emotional attachment to fireplaces. As a system for warmth or heating, it cannot compare with modern heating methods. Fireplaces cause pollution, ignite occasional fires in the wrong places, and generally create a mess from ashes, wayward embers, wood leavings, and the like. So what's the appeal? Why do people not only enjoy fireplaces, but relish them to the point of paying a considerable amount of money and putting up with a great deal of inconvenience in order to have them?

If reincarnation is a reality, then it is quite reasonable to assume that in previous lives we have enjoyed the warmth and light of a fireplace–not to mention the relative safety from animal predators. In fact, this enjoyment might be more likened to a question of dire need and/or survival. In prior lives the roaring fire may have been one of the most important aspects of surviving in a cold world. Is it any wonder that such memories might make the presence of a roaring fire more than just a case of nostalgia?

Reincarnation, therefore, explains a great deal concerning our mental and emotional ties to the realities of our current lives. There are alternative explanations to these diverse events and feelings, and in some cases these alternatives to reincarnation make more sense. But equally true is the fact that many occurrences and emotional responses are not easily explained without recourse to reincarnation.

Effects of Past-Life Regressions

In addition to countless case studies of various people knowing things not learned in this lifetime, many others have discovered past lives under hypnosis. In many cases these discoveries have been totally unexpected.

Consider, for example, the case of Ernie Meadows. Ernie had an unaccountable fear of heights as well as a strong but equally irrational fear of rainstorms. His phobias were strong enough to justify psychological counseling. The therapist assumed the possibility of a traumatic experience in early childhood that could account for these problems, and he attempted to regress Ernie to his early years in an effort to uncover the source of the problem. Such regressions are common and are typically done with the use of hypnosis.

One aspect of a person under hypnosis is that the subject tends to take anything the therapist says in a very literal fashion. If, for example, a therapist instructed the subject, "Call me Friday," the subject might well turn to the therapist and say, "You're Friday." If a subject was regressed to age ten and then told to go further back to an important rainy day, that subject might go *much* further back.

As it turned out, this was Ernie's case, and the therapist suddenly found Ernie talking as if he were someone else, living in the past century and involved in repairing a cathedral in France. It was a windy and rainy day, and it was necessary for Ernie to leave the safety of the cathedral and venture out on its wet and slippery roof in order to make an emergency repair. Not only did Ernie remember the events, but over the course of several therapy sessions, Ernie literally relived the moments when he slipped on the wet roof and fell to his death.

The noteworthy factor of this case was that experiencing the fatal incident under hypnosis was real enough in Ernie's mind that, thereafter, his fear of heights and rainstorms virtually disappeared. In effect the therapist had regressed Ernie in psychological counseling's normal fashion to relive a traumatic event in order to alleviate a current fear. The therapy worked. But in the process, the therapist was confronted with Ernie having lived a prior life instead of the expected childhood trauma.

Kelly's case, with which we began this chapter, had similar results. After several sessions with her hypnotherapist, Kelly's fear of heights slowly disappeared. To make this fact clear, she took Frank back to the Black Canyon, strode boldly up to that same observation spot and, standing with one foot on the rock ledge, serenely looked out over the magnificent view. She looked much like a victorious mountain climber. Frank, needless to say, was thoroughly impressed, and maybe even a little convinced.

Does this prove reincarnation? No. Kelly may have had a much more traumatic event in her childhood and her mind subconsciously fabricated the prior life in order to avoid reliving the childhood trauma. It's hard to imagine how the childhood experience could have been more traumatic than dying in a sudden and homicidal fall, but one should never sell the mind short in its ability to protect itself.

On the other hand, the past lives Kelly and Ernie remembered may very well have been true. This possibility is given credence by the fact that literally thousands of other people have been regressed to past lives (sometimes inadvertently and sometimes intentionally), and in the process of reliving experiences from the past have come to grips with today's previously unresolved problems, phobias, and prejudices. Such cases have been recorded by numerous therapists who find reincarnation a bitter pill to swallow, but who continue to utilize the method of past-life regression simply because it cures the patient. In their view the reality of past lives may be in question, but the therapeutic method is not!

In *Twenty Cases Suggestive of Reincarnation*, Dr. Ian Stevenson, of the University of Virginia, has found numerous cases of death in a previous life by violent means. According to Dr. Stevenson, such cases may lead to a desire for revenge within the same society and place where the previous life had been lived. Dr. Stevenson has also noted that genetics alone cannot explain some specifically located birthmarks, but that reincarnation might. As many as 200 birthmarks found on subjects' bodies have been examined by Dr. Stevenson, who has suggested that these birthmarks are where fatal wounds had been inflicted in the previous life which the subjects seem to remember.

There are many traumas that might result in psychological problems after the fact, but clearly, violent death would be high on the list of major and/or intense ones.

Proving Reincarnation

From a scientific point of view, past-life regressions seem to offer a potential test of reincarnation. If it is possible to regress someone to a past life, would it not be possible for that person to provide information on that past life, which could then be verified by other means? Furthermore, if the person regressed did not have access in this life to the evidence that was used to verify the information gained from the past-life regression, couldn't this be used as proof?

This method of "proving reincarnation" has been the subject of numerous books, scholarly papers, discussions, and debates. If one is to believe the proponents on either side of the question, the answer has been determined innumerable times. Particular case histories have been exhaustively examined from both points of view and, inevitably, opposite results have been obtained. Proponents have searched for conclusive cases that are beyond reasonable doubt, and opponents have continued to try to pick apart those cases with meticulous glee.

One such contrary view is that of Jonathan Venn, who in his article, "Hypnosis and the Reincarnation Hypothesis: A Critical Review and Intensive Case Study," challenged the reincarnation idea. His objections to the large number of published case reports were that few had been exhaustively researched, few were based on extensive hypnotic interviews, and few authors had reported negative as well as positive findings. Instead, Dr. Venn conducted sixty hypnotic interviews with a single subject and concluded that modern psychological arguments were entirely sufficient for the particular case under review. Unfortunately (or fortunately, depending upon your point of view), his negative finding in one case does not contradict reincarnation as a reasonable explanation in other cases.

Considering the amount of data and information recounted by persons undergoing hypnotic regressions, it would appear that the sheer volume of data would strongly support reincarnation. At the same time, there is no conclusive evidence in any past-life documentation that cannot be accounted for by some form of deceit or tricks of the mind that as yet are not fully understood. After examining over 1,600 claims of past lives, Dr. Stevenson has concluded that conclusive evidence for or against the theory of reincarnation never will be obtained. In his view all cases have some flaws in them, but the improving quality of the cumulative evidence would certainly suggest that reincarnation is a viable theory.

Interestingly enough, the entire method of proving reincarnation with the use of past-life regression may be seriously flawed. If we assume the case where a person undergoing a past-life regression divulges information that no one could possibly have known before, does this prove reincarnation? Of course not. Reincarnation may turn out to be the simplest explanation, but it will almost certainly not be the only possible one. There is no assurance, for example, that a person describing in detail a past life on earth has in fact been reincarnated from that past life. The person may not be remembering, but rather obtaining the life information from another source–albeit the method of obtaining information from this other source may be, in and of itself, rather exotic. More on this later.

Similarly, if a case is demonstrated to be an outright fraud, such a negative will have no effect in disproving reincarnation. That case will simply be written off and all the other cases will have to be considered on their individual merits. Thus, the reality or fantasy of past-life "memories" will not prove or disprove reincarnation.

Populations, Past and Present

It has been noted by some opponents of reincarnation that whenever someone is regressed (hypnotically or otherwise) in an attempt to discover if they have any past lives, they invariably do. In fact virtually all of these people have a multitude of past lives. Is this perhaps a flaw in the theory? Are there enough past lives in our history to account for all the memories in current lives? In other words, are there enough former lives to go around?

Recent estimates of the number of former persons in recorded history places the number at about 113 billion. According to the *Atlantic Monthly*, in the April 1987 issue, the breakdown is approximately:

2.5 million years to 6000 BC	50 billion births
6000 BC to 1650 AD	42 billion births
1650 AD to 1962 AD	23 billion births
1962 AD to 1986 AD	3 billion births

Given that there are well over five billion souls currently on the planet, and allowing for a turnover time in the most recently departed, we might come to the conclusion that, on average, the players on the stage now could each have had over twenty prior lives. This would appear sufficient for most souls. However, nine of these lives would have been lived prior to 6000 B.C., leaving only about eleven or so lives each during recorded history. Since 1650 A.D., we would appear to have only four or five past lives available for every person now living on the planet. Is this enough?

Perhaps. But it is important to realize that the numbers quoted above are based on a simple mathematical formula and do not adequately account for worldwide catastrophes (such as the black plague of the Middle Ages). More importantly, they do not account at all for the possibility of past lives in Atlantis, Lemuria, Lyonnesse, Atland, and other lost, vanished, or possibly mythical lands. If these lands existed, then the population figures quoted previously may require revision upward. But they would not have to be revised by much–probably not more than an extra billion or two of past lives.

There is, however, one important statistic that does not require a belief in ancient, fabled lands. Dr. Helen Wambach, in conducting 1,088 past-life regressions (into well-established historical periods) has discovered that the described past lives accurately reflect current estimates of components of the world's population. Men and women, for example, were equally represented even when there were unequal numbers of male and female subjects being regressed. Socioeconomic data also corresponded to actual populations. Here, only ten percent of past lives described were from the upper class, whereas sixty to seventy-seven percent (depending upon the century being described) were of lower-class peoples, and in large numbers, farmers. Descriptions of the middle class varied, increasing as the centuries passed and the world as a whole became more prosperous.

The number of Dr. Wambach's past-life reports also reflected the gradual growth of the world's population. The world's population included only about 300 million from the time of Christ to the year A.D. 1000. Thereafter the population varied considerably up and down until 1750, when the population reached about 800 million. By 1800, the population had reached the one-billion mark. Since that time the world's population has increased dramatically.

Population	Year A.D.
1 billion	1800
2 billion	1930
3 billion	1960
4 billion	1974
5 billion	1990
6 billion	2000?

It is particularly noteworthy that Dr. Wambach's past-life reports reflected this growth. In her study past lives in the sixteenth century were twice as numerous as those in the first century, past lives in the 1800s were double those in the 1500s, and those in the twentieth century were four times as numerous as in the nineteenth century. Such numbers accurately reflect the growth of the world's population over these centuries.

If Dr. Wambach's numbers are accurate, this correlation between population growth and recalled past lives could be very important. Combined with the socioeconomic statistics, this evidence is very compelling. We would indeed have to bury our heads in the sand to dismiss these statistics by assuming that the subjects were merely imagining their alleged past lives.

Burden of Proof

Some have argued that since reincarnation cannot be proved, it therefore should not be considered as a viable theory. Such a view is also flawed, as there is no reason, a priori, to assume that a single life is more likely than multiple lives. To quote Voltaire: "It is no more surprising to be born twice than to be born once." If we consider the number of the world's people who accept without question the concept of reincarnation, it would appear that the burden of proof should be placed on those people who insist that only a single life is available to us all. Proving that is likely to be far more difficult.

In our discussions above, reincarnation has often been the simpler explanation for various phenomena. The simplicity of the explanation may not appear to carry much weight, but in the history of science the vastly complicated theories have usually been wrong. The Ptolemaic system of cycles and epicycles is a good example of a complicated system being surplanted by the comparatively simple relationship that describes Isaac Newton's gravitational theory. Consequently, the simple explanation has some appeal. Whether or not it is the correct explanation is still up for grabs.

Pros and Cons

Carl Jung, the Swiss psychotherapist and co-founder with Sigmund Freud of twentieth-century psychiatry, noted that the real problem is that doctrinairism and rationalism pretend to have all the answers, when in truth, our present, limited view is only approximate.

All too often, opponents of reincarnation have retreated behind the shield of doctrinairism to justify their positions, while proponents of reincarnation have seldom critically reviewed much of the alleged documentation on the subject. There is, for example, a noteworthy and strong tendency for the proponents of reincarnation to lovingly accept whatever comes down the pike and to avoid asking possibly embarrassing or discourteous questions of fact and credibility. This laissez-faire attitude probably derives from the fact that these same proponents have seen so many incredible things that they believe to be true that nothing seems beyond imagination or credibility. Such an attitude can be thought of as the opposite of doctrinairism. Neither position is all that defensible.

Chapter 2:

The

True Believers

"Care for some soup?"

"No thanks. I'm not that crazy about pea soup."

"But this is good stuff! It's Mama Tellurini's Favorite and Decidedly Luscious Pea Soup!"

"I think I'll pass this time."

"You realize, of course, that everyone in town is eating this pea soup now. It's the latest thing!"

"Really? Everybody in town?"

"Everybody."

"Hmmmm. No. Not now. Maybe I'll try it some other time."

"Did you know that Mama Tellurini's Favorite and Decidedly Luscious Pea Soup is Burt Reynolds' and Loni Anderson's favorite soup?"

"Really? In that case, got an extra spoon?"

One method of judging the veracity of a theory or point of view is to consider the popularity of that point of view. This takes on an added dimension when famous personalities or thinkers support an idea and, in effect, give the proposed concept greater credibility. It's as if we're hesitant to strike out on our own and much prefer that others do the trailblazing.

This is not an unreasonable position. Virtually no one has the time to try everything or to consider every point of view. Consequently, we often save time by eliminating numerous options by the simple expedience of not trying them, and try only those options with which we have a reasonable expectation of success. By relying on the opinions of others, we can more easily separate the wheat from the chaff.

Applying this method to the subject of reincarnation, we might first take a poll of our fellow incarnates (past and present). Hopefully, we can either establish that the subject of reincarnation is viable and at least worthy of our consideration, or we can write if off as a product of the lunatic, forty-percent fringe of society.

Opinions

In 1969, eighteen percent of the population of Great Britain believed in reincarnation. By 1980 this percentage had increased to thirty percent. By way of contrast, we can note that a Gallup poll taken in 1968 among members of the British populace gave the following responses: seventy-seven percent believed in God (eleven percent did not, twelve percent had no opinion); thirty-eight percent believed in life after death (thirty-five percent said no, twenty-seven percent had no opinion); and twenty-three percent believed in hell (fifty-eight percent said no, nineteen percent had no opinion). Apparently, for the British, hell was slightly more popular than reincarnation (at least in the late 1960s). In the same Gallup poll conducted in the United States, the results were ninety-eight percent believed in God (two percent did not); seventy-three percent believed in life after death (nineteen percent said no, eight percent had no opinion); and sixty-five percent believed in hell (twenty-nine percent said no, six percent had no opinion).

From 1982 until 1986, the percentage of the population of the United States believing in reincarnation had increased from twenty-four percent to thirty-seven percent. Of course, popularity can be a lousy indicator of truth. An even larger percentage of the American people believed there was no way the New York Jets could win Super Bowl III. (There are even a few people who still don't believe it.)

All kidding aside, it is difficult to dismiss out-of-hand the opinions of a third of the population, particularly when the opinions are shared by people for whom we have a great deal of respect. If such a view is applied to reincarnation, we find an impressive list of famous thinkers who believed and advocated the concept of reincarnation as a basic truth. We have already mentioned Voltaire, who appears to have accepted reincarnation as the more probable alternative to only living one life on earth. Other noteworthy members of the reincarnation fan club include:

> Aristotle, Plato, Socrates, Hume, Goethe, Schopenhauer, Emmanuel Kant, Friedrich Nietzsche, William Shakespeare, Henry David Thoreau, Walt Whitman, William Faulkner, John Greenleaf Whittier, Mark Twain, Henry Wadsworth Longfellow, Jack London, Edgar Allen Poe, Robert Burns, Charles Dickens, Oliver Wendell Holmes, Paracelsus, Charles John Lindbergh, Thomas Edison, George Patton, Frederick the Great, Henry Ford, Benjamin Franklin, Napoleon Bonaparte, Saint Augustine, Saint Justin, Saint Gregory, Saint Synesius, Saint Origen, and others.

These illustrious figures do lend credibility to a belief in reincarnation. While many of them thought that the earth was flat, it would be a mistake to dismiss the whole lot as a bunch of loonies. The fact of the matter is that many "great thinkers" did believe in reincarnation and clearly stated as much in their writings.

For example, Benjamin Franklin wrote that when he saw nothing annihilated, not so much as even a drop of water, he could not believe in the annihilation of souls, or that God would continually discard millions of minds and go to the continual trouble of making new ones. In Ben's view, if he existed in the world then, he would continue to exist in one form or another. Furthermore, despite the inconveniences of life, he would not object to a new edition of himself, hoping, of course, that the errata of his last edition would be corrected.

In his famous epitaph, written when he was only twenty-two years old, Dr. Franklin stated his view, perhaps more succinctly:

> The Body of B. Franklin,
> Printer,
> Like the Cover of an Old Book,
> Its Contents Torn Out
> And
> Stripped of its Lettering and Gilding,
> Lies Here
> Food for Worms,
> But the Work shall not be Lost,
> For it Will as He Believed
> Appear Once More
> In a New and more Elegant Edition
> Revised and Corrected
> By the Author.

Can we dismiss Benjamin Franklin's view because of the time in which he lived and the fact that he did not have access to our modern technology? It is possible of course, but very risky. It is not inconceivable that Ben might have known things that our society has long forgotten. It would be a mistake to dismiss his opinion simply because of his "antiquity."

The Ancients as Observers

Contrary to the modern view, our ancestors seem to have taken the concept of reincarnation as the natural state of affairs. Unfortunately for them, there is a tendency for people today to believe that ancient peoples were considerably less sophisticated than their progeny. This may stem from the fact that most sons believe their fathers to be incredibly naive and totally unaware of "what's hot and what's not." If sons are in fact more knowledgeable than their fathers and, if we assume that this has always been the case, then following this line of reasoning back through the ages generates the inescapable conclusion that our ancient ancestors must have been incredibly stupid! Not just slightly dumb, but ignorant in the extreme! One can easily visualize them walking around, stumbling over acorns, running into trees, and never, under any circumstances, having enough sense to get in out of the rain (except perhaps in the case of Noah–who had help).

An alternative but potentially radical position is to assume that the ancients were not blithering idiots, but were in fact quite intelligent *despite* the "disadvantage" of their not understanding modern technology. It is, after all, possible for someone to make intelligent judgments about observations even if these observations do not derive their data from sophisticated technology.

On this basis we can consider the possibility that all thoughts from antiquity are not flawed, but may in fact have some strong evidence in support of them. Because reincarnation appears to have been a viable theory from the earliest of times, it is just possible that it does indeed have merit.

Early Man

There are indications, based on ancient legends and myths, folkloric tradition, tribal memory, and certain archaeological discoveries, that suggest a belief in reincarnation may predate the establishment of the world's major religions. Incorporated in all such concepts, whether they be Eastern or Western, is a belief that some essence of individual life exists after death, that this same essence may leave the physical body that has perished, and that it may subsequently return to the known world in a similar or different guise.

Such beliefs may even have been included in Neanderthal societies, where artifacts dating back over 100,000 years provide the earliest known evidence for reincarnation. This evidence is circumstantial but derives from the discovery of remains of the deceased being found in forced fetal positions and placed in an east-west line. These discoveries suggest an understanding by the Neanderthal undertakers of an expected future birth, and also of an apparent recognition of the sun's daily birth in the east or death in the west (depending on your perspective).

One bone of contention was avoided in early Shamanic belief (dating from 25,000 to 15,000 B.C.) by the assumption that souls lived within the deceased person's bones, and that it was from these bones that new creatures were reborn. The Aztecs carried this concept further with the myth of their great god, Quetzalcoatal, whose blood would periodically combine with the ground-up bones of the dead to create a new human race. It is heartening to know that centuries ago the Aztecs were already heavily into recycling waste products.

Ancient Civilizations

Several ancient civilizations throughout the world include in their cultures and traditions a wide variety of expectations concerning reincarnation. The Chinese Tao suggests reincarnation by its relentless cycles of going and returning, while the four-armed Hindu god of creation and destruction, Shiva, has long been a symbol of death and rebirth.

Many of the ancient beliefs involve gods in the form of men returning to earth to assist humanity in some way. Egyptian pharaohs are perhaps the more obvious example, but even modern-day Tibetans have carried on the custom in their selection of their Dalai Lama. Diverse figures from Alexander the Great to King Arthur of Britain to the Hindu's Krishna are believed by some to be the reincarnation of a god.

Hinduism is preeminent among organized religions in its belief in reincarnation. Although the religion dates back to the fourth millennium B.C., reincarnation itself may have first originated in India as early as the sixth century B.C. (It may be comforting to know that the ancient Hindus took the trouble to think about the problem for two-and-a-half millennia before finally accepting the idea. Whether or not the necessity for this lengthy consideration bodes well for an acceptance of the concept by people today is another story.)

It is worth mentioning that Hinduism may not have been the original source. Older traditions concerning souls and the cycle of existence may have been adapted by the early Hindus, or they may have been handed down to the Brahmins by older races, notably the Egyptians or the Sumerians of the Tigris/Euphrates valley.

The Eleusinian Mysteries, from the city of Eleusis (near Athens, Greece), which date back as far as the fifteenth century B.C., appear to have included reincarnation as a central theme. It has been suggested by Robert Monroe, a preeminent researcher in the subject, that the extremely secretive rites of the Eleusinians involved out-of-body experiences (see Chapter 9), which served as a means of introducing a hint of the afterlife to their priestly neophytes.

Greek history continues to recall aspects of reincarnation in the Orphic Mysteries (seventh century B.C.). In the fifth century B.C., Pythagoras (of Pythagorean Theorem fame) is said to have told a man who was beating a puppy not to hit him because it was the soul of a friend of his that he had recognized when the dog/friend cried out. Well, let's face it, mathematicians can be a bit strange.

Plato's ideas on reincarnation (as exemplified in the Phaedrus) have been interpreted by Ducasse, such that the really honest ones come back as philosophers, artists, musicians, or lovers; the slightly less honest people return as righteous kings, warriors, or lords, the marginally honest ones as merchants, economists, or politicians; and the less-than-honest as physicians or gymnasts! The thoroughly bad ones return as tyrants. Obviously, Plato gave entirely too much credit to the economists and politicians.

Fifth-century B.C. Greek historian Herodotus attributed the Grecian belief in reincarnation to Egypt. The Egyptians in turn pointed to the east, where they believed the god Osiris had brought the knowledge from India to Egypt. As we pointed out previously, the Hindus suspected the Egyptians of being the original source.

Gautama Buddha believed that mankind was confined to a cycle of earthly existences on what he called the "treadmill of rebirth." Having allegedly lived over 500 previous lives over a period of some 25,000 years (or about one life every fifty years or so), it is perhaps not surprising that Buddha seemed to regard reincarnation as a treadmill. This concept, however, is echoed in the pervasive Hindu belief that all souls are held to a "Wheel of Life," which through its revolutions brings life and death over and over again.

Reincarnation crops up again in the myths and legends of European Druids, Celts, and Gauls. These people were so certain of reincarnation as a fact of life (and death) that they often rejoiced at a person's demise (and his return to heaven?) and mourned the birth of a child as a return of some poor soul to the trials and tribulations of earthly existence. The Druids even accepted the idea of borrowed money being repaid in a subsequent reincarnation. It is left to the reader's imagination (or some creative legal mind) as to the form and wording of a modern loan agreement that would provide for such contingencies. At the same time, I'm confident that your local savings and loan would probably be eager to loan money on some such basis. But then again, savings and loan executives are not necessarily that smart.

Religions

Lest we subscribe too much of a belief in reincarnation to the ancients, it must be stated that many modern-day religions continue to believe in the concept. Besides the obvious examples of Hinduism and Buddhism, other lesser-known religions accept reincarnation as an article of faith.

In 1933 one of the best examples of modern-day beliefs in reincarnation occured when Thupten Gyatso, the thirteenth Dalai Lama, died at his summer palace in Lhasa, Tibet. His death set in motion a long, sacred search for the child whom Tibetans believed would be born soon afterward as his reincarnate successor, the latest in a line that had continued uninterrupted since 1391. Using beneficial omens and visions, the sacred search reached the small village of Taktser, where a young boy, not quite two years old, was tentatively identified in 1936 as the reincarnated leader. The boy was subtly put through detailed and exhaustive testing. In one instance, for example, the boy readily went to and sat on the lap of the chief Lama of the search team, who had been disguised as a servant. The boy also seemed to recognize a rosary hanging around the Lama's neck–the rosary had belonged to the thirteenth Dalai Lama. In 1939, the child was finally accepted as the Tibetan leader and transported in royal fashion to Lhasa (after bribing the local Chinese officials). On the fourteenth day of the first month of the year of the Iron Dragon (1940), the child was placed on the Lion Throne.

Clearly many of the modern religions not only accept reincarnation but also go to great lengths to shape their lives from its basic assumptions. It has been estimated that eighty percent of the world's religions believe in reincarnation and the responsibility of each individual for his or her own life. On the other hand, modern-day orthodox Christian, Jewish, and Islamic beliefs continue to reject reincarnation as a viable theory. While there is always room for disagreement among religions, it is also obvious that some of these august bodies are wrong. With only two mutually incompatible alternatives, it is apparent that only one can be correct.

Admittedly, such an argument is like saying that a stopped clock is correct twice a day, but it does seem apparent that one body of opinion is wrong. If it is the orthodox Christian, Jewish, and Islamic religions that have been led astray, perhaps it is these religions upon which the burden of proof should fall.

But is this the case? Have the traditions of the Christian, Jewish, and Islamic religious faiths ever supported the doctrine of reincarnation? Consider the following quotations, taken from the the sacred writings of each of these orthodox religions.

Islam's Koran states:

> "And Allah hath caused you to spring forth from the Earth like a plant; Hereafter will He turn you back into it again, and will bring you forth anew" (Sura 71:17-18)

Judaism's Zohar, a Kabbalistic classic believed to date from the first century A.D., states:

> "The souls must re-enter the absolute, whence they have emerged. But to accomplish this end they must develop all the perfections, the germ of which is planted in them; and if they have not fulfilled this condition during one life, they must commence another, a third and so forth; until they have acquired the condition which fits them for reunion with God."

Christianity's Bible includes:

> "Him that overcometh will I make a pillar in the temple of my God, and he shall go no more out." (Revelation 3:12)

Authors, such as Joe Fisher in *The Case for Reincarnation*, interpret these statements to imply an early belief by each of these religions in reincarnation. Clearly the statements can be interpreted in this way, but are there other interpretations? Of course. There always are. Interpretation of biblical and other passages has always been a case of rushing in where wise men fear to tread.

But if we again rely on great thinkers to do our thinking, we will find it worthwhile to consult one of the greatest of the interpreters of Christian teachings, Saint Origen.

Early Christian Church Beliefs

Encyclopaedia Britannica considers Origen to be the most prominent of the church fathers with the possible exception of Augustine. Saint Origen was, in fact, accused of having advocated a variety of concepts at variance with established church doctrine, and one in particular was reincarnation. In *Reincarnation in Christianity*, Geddes MacGregor wrote that Origen may have been intrigued by the theory, but had some doubts with respect to certain forms of reincarnationism. At one point Origen apparently did refer to reincarnation as a false doctrine with respect to the transmigration of souls into bodies.

Transmigration, however, is not necessarily the same thing as reincarnation. It can refer to the passing of the soul from one body to another (as in possessing another soul's body), or it may involve reincarnating in an animal or plant after having been incarnated in a human body. The manner in which Origen used the term is not definitive. But in other areas it is clear that Origen's teachings were full of the preexistence of the soul and reincarnation. This would be surprising only if such ideas were contrary to the scriptures of the day.

Unfortunately, much of what we know of Origen is limited to what has come down to us in quotations of his words from his detractors. There is reason to believe, for example, that Origen inclined toward a more Platonic philosophy and did, in fact, agree with the Greek philosopher that the soul was cast into a corruptible body in order to prove itself superior to the failings of the flesh. Furthermore, Saint Origen wrote that the soul was worse off in the body than outside it, and that the importance of the body was only to meet the varying conditions required by the soul. Bodies, in fact, were merely vehicles for the reincarnation of the soul.

But Saint Origen is not alone. Saint Augustine may himself have questioned certain beliefs when he asked if his infancy succeeded another age of his that had died before it. In the Gnostic gospel, Pistis Sophia quotes Jesus as saying that "souls are poured from one into another of different bodies of the world."

When did the church and, ultimately, modern-day Christianity, turn away from reincarnation? Most historians see the crucial turning point in the Second Council of Constantinople (the Fifth Ecumenical Council of the Church) in 553 A.D., during the reign of the Byzantine emperor Justinian I. It was one of the council's fourteen anathemas, or denunciations, which stated that if anyone asserted the fabulous preexistence of souls and asserted the monstrous restoration which followed it, that person would be anathema.

There is considerable doubt among modern theologians as to whether or not the anathemas announced by the council should be considered binding on contemporary Christian denominations. This is due to the fact that the 553 A.D. council may have been illegal. At the time Pope Vigilius was clearly not in control of the situation and, in fact, was literally imprisoned by Justinian. There were apparently no Eastern bishops in attendance at the meeting, and there is even the possibility that the condemnation of reincarnation was not even an official part of the council (an early version of "back-room negotiations"?). This latter item is emphasized by the fact that it was not the actual writings of Origen himself that were condemned but those belonging to certain Origenistic sects. This sounds suspiciously like a compromise to condemn reincarnation but to avoid condemning a venerable saint who had lived 350 years before the council meeting.

What ulterior motive could Justinian and the Second Council have had in denouncing reincarnation? One thing is clear: Most people with a firm belief in reincarnation do not fear death, and because of this, they tend to fear little else. The absolutely fearless Celtic warriors are perhaps the best example. Reincarnation believers are also unlikely to be moved by threats of eternal damnation or swayed by the promises of priestly interventions on their behalf. Believers in reincarnation tend to be very self-reliant, intimately aware of their own very individual responsibility in developing their soul, and as a consequence make lousy subjects for edict-minded emperors. In *Patterns of Destiny* Hans Holzer wrote that the church needed the whip of Judgment Day to keep the faithful in line, and that it was even a matter of survival of the early church not to allow a belief in reincarnation to take hold among her followers.

Joe Fisher, in *The Case for Reincarnation*, places the charge more squarely against the empire-building emperor, Justinian, who in his zealous quest for cannon fodder and loyal troops followed up his ecclesiastical curses with tenacious persecution. But not all of the condemnation by the church can be ascribed to Justinian I. Over the course of the following millennium, the church's persecution against the doctrine of reincarnation became ever more extreme, with mass executions of peoples (the Albigensians of southern France, for example) and subsequent church councils (Lyons in 1274 and Florence in 1439) affirming that souls go immediately to heaven, purgatory, or hell.

During the tenth century, Bulgaria became the center of the Cathars. Following Gnostic traditions, the Cathars held that one should obtain direct knowledge ("cosmic-consciousness") of divine principles on one's own, rather than arbitrarily through churches and priests. The Cathars, who considered themselves to be the only true Christians, carried the struggle well into the thirteenth century, while mystical groups such as the Alchemists and the Rosicrucians managed to carry the belief into modern times.

Biblical Sources

Despite the church's holy war against reincarnation, the Bible remains the most notable "Achilles' Heel" of orthodox church doctrine. Admittedly, the Old Testament contains only peripheral references to reincarnation. But the New Testament alludes to the subject more often and more directly. Again, such evidence depends upon context and interpretation. This was acknowledged by Edgar Cayce, a self-styled clairvoyant and fundamentalist Christian, who died in 1945. Cayce noted that one could read reincarnation into the Bible or not do it depending on their prior views. Many scholars, however, believe that several biblical passages only make sense if they are interpreted in the context of repeated lives on earth.

A few such biblical references include:

> "Behold, I will send you Elijah the prophet before the coming of the great and dreadful day of the Lord." (Malachi 4:5)

"Verily I say unto you, among them that are born of women there hath not risen a greater than John the Baptist; notwithstanding he that is least in the kingdom of heaven is greater than he.

"And from the days of John the Baptist until now the kingdom of heaven suffereth violence, and the violent take it by force.

"And for all the prophets and the law which was prophesied until John.

"And if ye will receive it, this is Elijah, which was for to come." (Matthew 11:11-14)

"But I say unto you, that Elijah is come already, and they knew him not, but have done unto him whatsoever they listed. Likewise shall also the Son of Man suffer of them.

"Then the disciples understood that he spake unto them of John the Baptist." (Matthew 17:12-13)

"Jesus said unto them, Verily, verily, I say unto you, before Abraham was, I am." (John 8:58)

"And Jesus went out, and his disciples, into the towns of Caesarea Philippi: and by the way, he asked his disciples, saying unto them, Whom do men say that I am?

"And they answered, John the Baptist: but some say, Elijah; and others, One of the Prophets.

"And he saith unto them, But whom say ye that I am? And Peter answereth and saith unto him, Thou art the Christ.

"And he charged them that they should tell no man of him." (Mark 8: 27-30)

"And as Jesus passed by, he saw a man which was blind from his birth.

"And his disciples asked him, saying, Master, who did sin, this man, or his parents, that he was born blind?

"Jesus answered, Neither hath this man sinned, nor his parents: but that the works of God should be made manifest in him." (John 9:1-3)

This last biblical quotation deserves some comment. In this regard we might turn to the Reverend L. Weatherhead, Methodist minister of the City Temple of London from 1936 to 1960, who noted that one must not take just Jesus' answer, but note that the idea of reincarnation was current at the time. Clearly, if the man was born blind as punishment for a sin committed, then the sin must have been perpetrated at a time prior to being born into the world, and potentially, in an earlier life. It is noteworthy that while Christ had never taught reincarnation directly, he sometimes referred to it as though it were part of the accepted ideas of his day. More importantly, Jesus never repudiated or denied reincarnation or taught that it was a false doctrine.

Chapter 3:

Karma

George Holt was a young man with immense potential. The captain of his football team, one of the most popular men in his senior class, valedictorian at a high school commencement, and possessing the highest credentials, George seemed to have everything going his way. He had received both athletic and academic scholarship offers from a dozen respected universities. His ambition to become a medical researcher at a major university hospital seemed almost a foregone conclusion. Until the fire.

It had begun in a small duplex. A gas-heated hot water tank had exploded, starting the fire in one of the duplex apartments. The family in the affected apartment had quickly run from the building, but they had failed to warn the young girl next door who was baby-sitting for a seven-month-old baby. When the girl finally realized the building was on fire, she had panicked and run from the building.

George was biking with his friends, just outside the duplex, when flames began to shatter the window glass on the second floor. The baby-sitter practically ran into his arms. When George tried to calm her down, she suddenly remembered the baby. George quickly realized what was happening, found out that the baby was sleeping in a second-floor bedroom, and sprinted for the building.

An exceptional athlete, he was in the building and up the stairs before most even realized what he was doing. He quickly found the baby girl, wrapped her in her blanket, and with fires beginning to engulf the building, turned and raced to the stairs. But just as he began his leaping descent, the upper portion of the stairs gave way. Both he and the baby fell into the mass of flames and burning debris. At virtually the same time, a heavy ceiling beam collapsed, crashing into his lower back. The impact threw him forward onto a protruding step where he took the blow immediately above his right eye.

Despite the immense pain in his back, with his jacket arm already on fire, his head and eye critically injured, George managed to stagger from the building with the baby still cradled in his arms. Reaching his friends, he suddenly lost feeling in his legs and collapsed in a heap. Even as he fell, he did his best to protect the baby from the fall.

Within a few days the baby was fully recovered from the ordeal. George was paralyzed from the waist down, his face and left arm badly burned, his right eye seriously scratched, and his mental capacities encumbered by a severe head injury. The prognoses for his paralysis and mental impairment were bitterly pessimistic. George's future potential was suddenly much less.

Cause and Effect

Where's the justice in a world where an innocent, heroic young man can lose so much? How can we rationalize the horror of seeing bad things happen to good people? If George had been a notoriously evil individual, perhaps we could accept his fate as just punishment for previous sins. But George seemed blameless.

In the world of reincarnation, however, one need not confine themselves to the deeds in a single lifetime. Perhaps George was actually receiving his just desserts for deeds committed in a lifetime prior to this one. Perhaps justice was indeed being served. Only in this case, it would more likely be referred to as "karma."

Karma, in its simplest form, is a belief in the law of cause and effect, i.e., the rebirth of a soul into a lifetime where the trials and tribulations or the joys and happiness encountered may be punishment or reward for deeds done in previous incarnations. In this simple form, karma is considered to be fundamental to the Hindu religion, where it is believed that a soul evolves by increasing purity achieved over successive existences, until that soul eventually reaches a state of nirvana. The state of nirvana is essentially a state of divine bliss.

In *Introduction to Yoga Principles and Practices*, Sachindra Kumar Majumdar describes karma as a doctrine regarding human bondage and freedom:

> The doctrine of karma offers a philosophical explanation of the life and experience of an individual in terms of a moral law operative in the universe and not as the working out of blind chance or fate or the fiat of a whimsical ruler of the world. The individual is the maker of his own destiny; he determines by his own actions his future life and experience, his happiness and misery, his success and failure.
>
> Karma views the present life not as an isolated incident but as an episode in the larger career of the soul. The life we live now is one link in a long chain; it is the result of our thoughts and actions in the previous existences. Although our present life is determined by the past, it is not an absolute determination, for we can alter its course within limits. We never lose our freedom completely, and there is always the possibility that we can attain complete freedom by discovering our true identity through knowledge.
>
> Our present life can be compared to a game of bridge. The cards have been dealt out; we cannot change them. But how we play our hand depends on us. We can play well or poorly; we can make the best use of our opportunities or miss them.

The tone of this description might give one the impression that karma is predominantly a product of Eastern philosophies. Such an impression would not be entirely correct. Consider, for example, a more Western viewpoint. In *Life Between Life*, Dr. Joel L. Whitton and Joe Fisher (both of whom happen to be Canadian), describe karma in much the same way, as carried from lifetime to lifetime and based on an individual's attitudes, behavior, and motivation. These authors dismiss the idea of pawns in a chess game and assume that all conditions are a result of past conduct–thus eliminating inequality, unfairness, and misfortune. Whitton and Fisher clearly advocate the concept of cause in one life affecting a subsequent life. These two authors also consider karma as intrinsically tied to justice and the need for rebirth, such that an individual will eventually experience the same emotions of joy or sorrow that they perpetrated on others.

A Christian View

Although karma is a Sanskrit word (loosely translated as "action" or "destiny") and intimately associated with Hinduism and Buddhism, the concept is also implied in biblical passages. For example, recall our quotation from the previous chapter:

> And as Jesus passed by, he saw a man which was blind from his birth.
> And his disciples asked him, saying, "Master, who did sin, this man, or his parents, that he was born blind?"
> Jesus answered, "Neither hath this man sinned, nor his parents: but that the works of God should be made manifest in him." (John 9:1-3)

Not only does the passage imply the ready acceptability by Jesus' disciples of the idea of reincarnation, but the context also implies their acceptance of something equivalent to karma. We can, for example, view the idea of a man being born blind as being punished by the blindness for sins committed in an earlier life before he was reincarnated in the world. Accordingly, we might suggest that a concept akin to karma, whereby sins in one incarnation are atoned for in a later one, were, to some degree, current and acceptable during the time of Christ.

The implication that early Christianity may have advocated its own form of karma suggests that the idea can not be limited to Eastern mysticism. Recall also our discussion of Plato's ideas on reincarnation in the previous chapter, where we found a clear indication of a belief that one's lot in this life was dependent upon a soul's degree of evolution. Ducasse, in paraphrasing Plato's ideas, states that lives are probationary, in which a righteous life improves and an unrighteous life deteriorates the progress of the soul. Plato apparently also believed that a human soul could move from man to beast and back, as part of a soul's improvement/deterioration.

Interpretations of Karma

Historically, the last three to four thousand years have seen significant modifications to our concepts of karma. In the ancient Egyptian text, *The Instruction of Ptahhotep* (dating back to 2600 B.C.), we find such concepts as your actions become your judgments. The Bible was even more specific in balancing a soul's moral accounts with retribution for past debts. The Old Testament's an "eye for an eye" is relatively clear in its intent, as is the New Testament's "He that leadeth into captivity shall go into captivity; he that killeth with the sword must be killed with the sword" (Revelations 13:10).

Subsequent interpretations by the Christian Gnostics and the Hebrew Kabbalists, however, involved a simpler and perhaps more sophisticated form of compensation. Instead of condemning a murderer to die in similar circumstances, the person's soul is allowed to make amends and balance the books in some other way–perhaps by caring for the dying or maimed in a future life.

This second view is certainly a bit more practical. The approach of "an eye for an eye" assumes that for any misdeed for which karma would be incurred there would be a compensating deed available in the future. This may not always be the case. For example, a Frenchman who created considerable karma by his acts of guillotining innocent victims might be hard pressed to find a guillotine in a future life over which he could lose his own head. Times change, and compensation in precise forms is not only unlikely, but it also may not be equal in any case.

Another problem with the strict an "eye for an eye" form of karmic justice is the potential for self-perpetuating problems. If Tom chooses to die by Dick's hand, in order to account for the fact that Tom killed Harry in a prior life, what about Dick's karma? Karmic tradition does not necessarily let Dick off the hook if he chooses to kill Tom. Where does it all end?

A third view is that karma may be the ultimate learning process, whereby knowledge and understanding are obtained through the age-old tradition of "trial and error." In this view, someone who has killed another may not necessarily be required to be a murderer's victim or to make restitution in some active way. Instead, the repercussions in a later life may be sufficient to settle the accounts if they instill in the past-life murderer an understanding of the self-destructive nature of his or her actions.

This latter view might be a bit too permissive, as it could be said to accept karma as cosmic justice, but one we can perhaps do without. Bad deeds in a prior life could be viewed as nothing more than motivation to do good deeds in the current life. The concept of justice would be more strained in this situation if the only real sense of karma was to allow the soul to evolve or graduate to the next step. Nevertheless, such a view is often accepted, and as such, deserves some consideration.

Karma as Learning

Past-life regressions have tended to illustrate all three forms of karma, with the more ruthless balancing of justice ("an eye for an eye") being more likely in the earlier stages of a soul's evolution. This may be a very important point, in that karma may very well be "in the mind of the beholder." If some feel that they must pay for murdering someone by being a victim, then so be it, but if they can find other means of compensation, that's okay as well. The implication (i.e., the "good news") is that each of us is our own judge. The bad news is that you are probably the toughest judge you will ever have to face.

Some subjects of past-life regressions consider karma as a development of the self, wherein the intent is to further the evolution of their own souls. In this case the belief is that certain experiences are necessarily encountered over and over again in order to learn the essential but difficult lessons of their existence. How often the same lessons are repeated is determined by how well subsequent experiences are handled.

Whitton and Fisher, utilizing the reports of Dr. Whitton's subjects regressed to the state between lives, note that the stricter definitions of karma are not necessarily applicable to every situation, and in fact things are not required to work that way. These reports suggest that the essential aspect of karma appears to be learning and ultimately the development of the soul. They also note that while learning is paramount, the actual manner of learning–through gentle acceptance or laborious and violent exchange–is relatively unimportant.

Whitton and Fisher state that contrary to Buddhist and Hindu beliefs of souls strapped to a wheel of rebirth, souls can design their own curriculum and determine their own methods of dealing with karma. For example, karma can be modified by reincarnating with those souls with which karma had previously been established and then taking this opportunity to repattern or improve the situation with specific, planned challenges. Apparently, however, it is necessary to return to the physical world.

Stewart C. Easton, in *Man and the World in the Light of Anthroposophy*, states:

> Whenever we bemoan our destiny on Earth and complain of our ill-fortune, we are railing against our own choice, not the choice of some arbitrary god or gods who have done us a bad turn. In consequence the one vice which no one with knowledge of karma should permit himself is envy, be it envy of anyone else's life situation, or of his talents, fortune, or friends. For we have what we have chosen and earned . . .

This may not sound like the best news that you've heard this week, but there is one possible saving grace. It is possible that some of the soul's choices for this life were not made in order to account for misdeeds in a past life, but as a means of preparing that soul for tasks and accomplishments in a future life. Karma does not have to be viewed simply as a means to force us into predictable behavior, but can be thought of as the means to allow for the soul's evolution. If motivation is the essence of karma, the exercise of free will is an inevitable aspect of it as well.

Perceptions

Whitton and Fisher also report (in considerable detail) the case history of a woman named Jenny. This particular lady had lost two children in successive past lives, and despite the fact that virtually any reasonable judgment authority would hold her blameless for their deaths, Jenny's perceptions of her behavior in both situations was distorted by guilt. Her karmic choice was then to atone for her children's deaths by events in her current life.

As Whitton and Fisher pointed out, whether incarnated or not, one's perception can be one's reality. This is an important point, for Jenny chose to return to earth as a victim of continual brutality and sexual abuse. Thus, not only must a soul strive in this lifetime to overcome the real karmic accumulation of previous lives, but the *perceived* karmic accumulation as well!

William J. Baldwin, Ph.D., of Carmel, California, has made a similar statement: "Our choices for a future life can be the result of misperceptions, misinterpretations, inappropriate decisions based on those mistaken thoughts, harsh self-judgments and self-imposed punishments."

According to these experts, it would appear that our self-judgments are more severe than the judgments of others.

Karmic Continuation

Assume for the moment that you have just completed a past-life regression (or a psychic reading or whatever), and have now become aware, much to your karmic horror, that you lived one life as a Portuguese priest during the Spanish Inquisition. At that time you were responsible for the torture, maiming, and death of a large number of innocent victims. Does this mean you have a very large karmic debt to work off during this lifetime?

Not necessarily. There is some evidence to suggest that karmic ties may be settled in succeeding lifetimes; that in fact a relatively swift form of justice may prevail. Dr. Whitton, for example, has noted that his subjects moved from incarnation to incarnation, continually interacting with the same entities in constantly changing relationships. While one's deeds in one life may determine the setting and challenges of the next or succeeding lives, there is no require-ment that karmic ties need be extended over centuries.

Manly P. Hall, writing in *Death to Rebirth*, notes that:

> The individual pays his karma very largely by the process that perpetuates an attitude existing at a particular time. If this attitude exists at the time of the previous death, it will go on to become the drive for the re-embodiment of the new personality.

In other words, there is a strong tendency to start balancing karma as soon as possible.

Mind you, karma has a much longer arm than any earthly law enforcement agency might have, and will happily wait for a millennium to be satisfied. But the relationships between many souls appear to resolve many of their karmic ties sooner than later–perhaps not in the very first incarnation immediately following the karma-incurring deed, but within a few lifetimes. Furthermore, this presupposes that it was the soul's choice prior to one of the succeeding incarnations to balance their karma. Assuming the continuing evolvement of the Portuguese priest's soul, there is some hope that he will be off the hook in the reasonably near future. Perhaps by the year 2250 A.D.?

On the other hand, if an attractive, sexy individual coyly suggests that you were the Roman soldier who threw him or her to the lions in ancient times, and that perhaps you might be looking to make up for this crass move by some thoughtful gesture in this incarnation, you might at least consider the possibilities.

A Contrary View

In distinct contrast to the reports of Dr. Whitton's thirty subjects, Dr. Ian Stevenson, whom we encountered in a previous chapter (and who is being reincarnated in this one?), found minimal evidence of an empirical basis for karma in his extensive investigations. Stevenson did not, apparently, encounter situations where differences in circumstances between personalities could be glibly accounted for by variations in evil or goodness. He also felt that Western observers who regard reincarnation and karma as inseparable are unaware that many groups who believe in reincarnation do not necessarily believe in the type of karma commonly associated with those originating in Southeast Asia. In other words, reincarnation does not necessarily imply that our present lives are dictated in some way by our previous lives.

One could make arguments against Dr. Stevenson's conclusions from several different positions. For example, the view of karma being more sophisticated than "an eye for an eye" makes simple correlations between lives risky at best. Additionally, actions in a current life with an eye toward the future also would escape anyone's ability to document. Karmic accumulation may also be a longer-term effect, in some cases evolving over a multitude of lives–a record that may not be readily apparent in even a lengthy investigative effort of someone's numerous past lives.

There is also the question of balancing bad deeds with good deeds during the same lifetime. In other words, there is no a priori reason to assume that karmic debts incurred in this life cannot be repaid immediately. Or, perhaps more significantly, the rewards for the good deeds of this life may very well be received in this lifetime and, hopefully, before one is too far gone to enjoy them. Many modern concepts of karma, in fact, have noted that the pace of karmic retributions seems to be increasing and that karmic-induced rewards and/or punishments are following closer and closer on the heels of their causes. Actress Shirley MacLaine has argued that justice will be done, not only in the long run, but often in the short run. She has claimed that her karma is registering back to her in exceedingly short periods of time (i.e. minutes as opposed to months).

Could it be that justice, unlike our court system, is becoming swifter?

Why Karma?

Instead of considering differing views of researchers and diverse religions, we might do better to ask questions about the basic viability of the idea of karma. For example, does karma make sense? Is there a clear reason to have karma in the first place?

Clearly one significant distinction of karma is the inherent fairness of the concept. We're talking Justice with a capital "J!" Nobody gets away with nothing, nohow! We can all rest assured that any and all misdeeds will invariably show up in indelible ink on the very complete account ledgers of every soul. Regardless of the number of past lives that pass between the misdeed and the current one, the karmic debt waits patiently (or perhaps impatiently) for the inevitable repayment.

From a profoundly philosophical point of view, it is perhaps comforting to know that the rat fink who sold you that lemon will sooner or later get his, even if it may not be in this lifetime!

We can also question whether karma is an essential attribute of reincarnation. Lytle Robinson, in his book, *Edgar Cayce's Story of the Origin and Destiny of Man*, notes that everyone is born with specific personalities, with a mixture of good and bad characteristics. From Mr. Robinson's viewpoint, if these characteristics are incurred entirely by heredity and environment (i.e. there is no carryover from a previous life), then how can one be held responsible for what is in effect God's creation? Mr. Robinson believes that karma is therefore meaningless from the viewpoint of only one life.

In other words, from Mr. Robinson's viewpoint, reincarnation is essential to karma. Saint Paul's advice to the Galatians: "Be not deceived; God is not mocked: for whatsoever a man soweth, that shall he also reap" (Galatians 6:7) can be interpreted as not being a true statement unless the time for reaping is spread out over a longer period of time than a single lifetime.

By the same token, there is the complementary view that good deeds performed now will provide for rewards in the future. With the potential for future lives, everyone can be confident of receiving their just desserts. Perhaps more importantly, everyone can assume that their free will is still intact and that they can by their own actions make things better in the future simply by taking appropriate steps now. Furthermore, everyone can reduce karma (theoretically) by doing good, as well as by enduring the current pain and suffering.

Justice

But is karma as essential to the theory of reincarnation as reincarnation is to the theory of karma? As Ian Stevenson has already pointed out, reincarnation can be perfectly true without karma. The evidence for karma must, therefore, not rely on the proof of reincarnation, but upon the concept of universal justice (assuming that such justice exists).

For example, the motivation to eliminate karma (i.e. reduce the misdeed debits on the account books to zero) is predicated on a belief in the existence of justice and a just result. We often think of our ability to enter heaven as being dependent upon our receiving a "passing grade" in the sum total of our life. But instead of allowing anyone to sneak in with a C- (while a D+ sends you in the other direction), karma implies that everyone has to eventually bring their grade-point average up to A+ (no matter how long it takes to get there)!

Reincarnation allows for the opportunity to retake the test again and again until you score one hundred percent, while karma ensures that only one hundred percent scores are acceptable for that all-important passing grade. Reincarnation allows for equal opportunity; karma ensures equal results.

Logically then, acceptance of karma implies a fundamental and profound assumption. The reality of karma assumes a just God (or gods) or, minimally, a God who desires justice. If god is not just, then karma may be nothing more than the figment of the imagination of someone suffering from injustice. But if God is just, karma is the philosophical personification of Saturday morning's Justice League–and just, perhaps, slower than a speeding bullet.

Summary

In summary, we might arrive at the following:

1. Karma implies the law of cause and effect.

2. Karma insists on the individual being responsible for his or her own deeds and misdeeds and that actions in a past or current life will give shape and substance to the individual evolution of a soul.

3. Karma is determined by each soul in its own self-judgment.

4. Karma implies the presence of motive, which in turn necessitates the exercise of free will.

5. Karma requires that karmic accumulation (the sum total of uncompensated misdeeds) must be reduced to zero over the course of however many incarnations are necessary before a soul can escape the "wheel of life." (A corollary is that karmic reduction may be done in part by others, such as Jesus Christ, who many believe died for other's sins [and thus helped to reduce their karma].)

6. Karma reduction requires physical existence.

7. Any reduction in karmic accumulation invariably involves interactions with other souls, as do karmic-related rewards.

8. Karma may be spread over several lifetimes and/or within a single lifetime.

Chapter 4:

Adding a
Few Spices

Imagine, if you will, Joe Cool, as he walks into a bar and spies a charming lady. What more direct approach could he use than asking (with appropriate emotion and apparently genuine awe), "Weren't we lovers in a past life? Soulmates from the time of kings? Passionately in love as never before and never since?"

Let's face it; it might work. If Joe Cool can convince the charming lady that they were passionate lovers before, who knows where it might lead–if only from the lady's natural curiosity.

This potentially clever tactic derives from an inherent aspect of reincarnation. It would appear inevitable that an individual soul having multiple lives would eventually meet someone known in another life. Obviously, if you can have multiple lives, it stands to reason that anyone else can as well. Over the course of numerous past lives and the inevitable multitude of relationships with others, it is only a matter of time until a soul finds itself with someone whom it has known before. If we include karma in the equation, the probability of meeting that someone again is even greater. So what happens then?

According to reincarnation (and karma) it depends on the extent of your involvement with the other person in a previous life. If the intensity of your relationship was quite significant, then it is likely that you will have to deal with emotions from this prior life in the current one. The indirect evidence surrounding reincarnation suggests very strongly that individual souls tend to return to earth in subsequent incarnations for the specific purpose of dealing with other souls (but normally in different relationships). The most striking example of this is soulmates.

Soulmates

Anyone already familiar with the concept of a soulmate is probably a bit of a romantic. The idea of a lover from a past life currently searching the world for you in order to be reunited in unremitting bliss is the stuff of romance novels and other works designed to appeal to anyone who is currently without that "one true love." In *The Bridge Across Forever*, Richard Bach describes the ideal as one with whom you can be totally and honestly yourself, someone with whom you feel safe enough to open yourself up to be loved for what you are (and not necessarily what you're pretending to be). Each soulmate subsequently unveils the best part of their partner, shares their goals and deepest longings, and provides in all circumstances a safe harbor. A soulmate literally makes one come to life!

Unfortunately, it might not be quite that wonderful and glorious.

Reincarnation recognizes three kinds of soulmates: karmic, companion, and twin flames. The three kinds of soulmates allow for a rather impressive range of possibilities when two people are meeting again in this life. Not all of them are that wonderfully expectant. For the romantically inclined, the search for the soulmate who will make the "perfect mate" may instead be a search for that soul's twin flame.

Twin Flames

In *Soulmates,* Jess Stern describes the idea of twin flames as the ultimate love, someone with precisely the right amount of spirit, gentleness, and kindness, beautiful in the eyes of the beholder, and always with just exactly the right thing to say. A soulmate would be the one who's slightest touch or smile could say it all, who would give for the joy of giving. Moreover, twin flames would have no barriers between them, no boundaries, no rules of love. Instead, they would be one in spirit, flowing together as if from the same fountain. Their inner ties would be deep, profound, and contain the same secret longings and aspirations. They would be spiritually and mentally tied on a dozen different levels at once.

Yes, that should do it. I mean, if you're looking for someone who will fill every conceivable need you might have, surely your twin flame will be able to handle the job. But is it really a necessary ingredient in the larger scheme of things? Is the idea of a twin flame some sort of romantic idealism with no basis in reality, or is there some basic reason to have it? Before we attempt to answer this question, let us consider the two other forms of soulmates.

Companion Soulmates

A companion soulmate is in essence a mate of the soul. It refers to a service or task that one is destined to perform with someone other than a twin flame–a complementary calling in life, an ideal partnership with similar likes and dislikes. Here we have mates who work well together, are project-oriented, well-mated, often have similar physical features, and who are extremely compatible. The latter aspect derives from the soulmates being at very nearly the same level in the development of their souls.

But the joining of companion soulmates, unlike the twin flames, does not necessarily signify a permanent relationship. In many cases, once a project is completed, there may be no further need for the relationship and the together-ness vanishes. Companion soulmates are not necessarily marriage partners. While it is true that the soulmate condition may have been established by shared physical experiences over a long period, the relationship is often more than just physical attraction. There exists the capacity to help each other at the mental as well as the physical level.

Karmic Soulmates

The third form of a soulmate is the karmic soulmate. Here we are dealing with someone to whom we are uneasily drawn in order to learn some hard lessons from prior lives together. It is a time for growth; there are often a great deal of growing pains in loving someone as you yourself would want to be loved. It's not all strawberries and cream.

Astrologically, the planet Saturn is usually associated with karmic soulmates. Theoretically, Saturn represents our karma, the carryover from our past lives, and the resultant conditions we put on ourselves and others in this life. It represents that portion of ourselves with which we must deal in working with others. As the karmic planet, it supposedly governs our aspects with those we love; for these are the people with whom we have the most karma–the most to work out from the past.

In Stern's view, Saturn was always strongly aspected (conjunction or op-position) in the composite chart of any two soulmates. This aspect provided stimulation and challenges, bringing out the best in each person. The incentive was to let go of bad habits and attitudes and allow one another to be them-selves. With multiple Saturn ties, people often married, only to wonder later why the relationship was so trying. Saturn effectively limited or placed stric-tures and conditions on the other person that then had to be resolved.

Clearly there are potentially many areas of karma, and it is likely that some can only be balanced through marriage. Once the karmic debt is re-solved, however, does that leave only divorce? It would appear that once a relationship is over, it is over for a reason–everything that could be derived from it already has been derived. In this case it may be more costly to remain together than to separate.

An Example?

Soulmates, in any of the three forms, have considerable latitude in the potential for happiness, longevity, and possible growth. It is possible to have more than one soulmate; equally obvious is the fact that soulmates can vary greatly in degree and quality. In effect, you never quite know just what to expect.

A classic example is the story of Liz and Sewell. These two charming people had been dating for a year, and while they were both enjoying each other's company, Liz was becoming a bit more serious than Sewell. Much to Liz's chagrin, the relationship was not taking the inevitable course she might have wanted. Then she heard about soulmates, and immediately sensed that this might be the answer to her dilemma. For if she could convince Sewell that the two of them had been lovers in a past life, romantic soulmates as it were, this fact just might be enough to move Sewell in the direction of a more permanent relationship.

Inspired by the idea, Liz quickly contacted a psychic in whom she knew Sewell had some faith, and posed the critical question. The psychic's reply was everything Liz had sought...and a bit more. "It was true," the psychic replied, "Both Liz and Sewell had had many previous lives together. The most notable one occurred many centuries ago when they were both healers and teachers in an ancient Greek temple." According to the psychic, the two had met and fallen deeply in love, despite the fact that Sewell was already married to another. They had become passionate lovers!

At this point things were looking pretty good for Liz. But then the psychic went on to point out that their beautiful but illicit love affair was eventually discovered by the temple's hierarchy, and in order to discourage such extracurricular activities, the local priests had Sewell beheaded!

Oops! Apparently Liz and Sewell's current mutual attraction may have been less the result of two reunited lovers and more that of karmic soulmates. Instead of the unification of twin flames, the result appeared to be more that of karmic debts owed and paid. Such is the way of karma; not to mention the way of soulmates.

Why Soulmates?

Lest we find the romantic notion of soulmates too attractive to do without, we should perhaps ask a few pertinent questions. For example, is there any reason to have soulmates? Is the concept of a soulmate an essential ingredient in reincarnation and/or karma? Is the idea just a romantic convenience, or is there something more?

It would appear that karmic soulmates have as much justification as any other karmic relationship. We certainly should not eliminate this form of relationship from consideration merely because love is involved. Soulmates may simply represent a more intense relationship, with an attendant increase in the karmic involvement's intensity.

Companion soulmates may appear to be less essential to the evolution of the soul, but it is certainly conceivable that there may be joint projects that can be more beneficial to everyone concerned if carried out by two people in very close cooperation. While this type of relationship may not be the norm, it at least makes sense to exist in principle. If we plan our lives in advance (see Chapter 8), clearly it is logical that two souls might make joint plans.

The reason for twin flames is less obvious. It may be that the concept of a twin flame can only be justified on the basis of an individual's own personal beliefs. Some believe, for example, that originally (around the time of creation) the soul divided so that one's twin flame became quite literally "one's other half." Others take the more generic view that love, after all, is a giving act, not just one of receiving. It is believed that the receipt of love is the inevitable result of giving love, provided that such a gift is an unconditional one. A twin flame is thus a giver and receiver of love.

One perspective on the viability of twin flames is given by Jess Stern. In *Soulmates*, he writes that the purpose of life is growth, and that having a soulmate does not solve all our problems. In fact, there could be no growth without challenges and obstacles to overcome.

Growth?

Growth appears to be an essential motivating force in any theory of reincarnation. If you're not here to grow, why are you here? You're taking up a lot of space; is there any reason for that? If the evolution of the soul is not the primary reason for existence, what else is there?

Richard Bach, in *The Bridge Across Forever*, tells the story of his own personal search for his soulmate. At one point in the story, his soulmate gives us an effective analysis of growth in a loving relationship by viewing it as a musical metaphor.[1] In doing so, she notes that the sonata form, the basis of almost all symphonies and concertos, consists of exposition, development, and recapitulation sections. The exposition was where the themes and ideas were first introduced. These themes were then explored to their fullest in the development section, with the music varying from happy to unhappy, from major to minor keys, with everything woven together in increasing complexity. Finally, in the recapitulation, one arrived at the glorious expression of the developed ideas, now grown to their full maturity.

Richard's soulmate goes on to note how easy it is to become stuck in the exposition, the part of the relationship when one is at their best and is putting their best foot forward. It is a time when they are the most interesting, as well as most interested. It is, in fact, a time of delight for both people, and it's no wonder that one enjoys the exposition so much that one often tries to make life a series of expositions.

But the real opportunity for growth is in the development stage, where the chance to explore all the ramifications of a love relationship resides. Constraint in the exposition stage can only result in repetition of the same old themes, no growth and, ultimately, sheer boredom.

Twin flames may be thought of as the final stages of the development section–and perhaps more gloriously–the full joy of the recapitulation, where the symphony is completed. Twin flames may then be looked at from the viewpoint of being more reward than challenge. It is perhaps the completion of plans and events established in prior lives, a little icing on the cake that has taken "so long to bake."

Stern makes a further argument for the existence, if not the need, for twin

---

[1] Metaphors be with you.

flames, by noting that growth comes not only out of an interaction of the two soulmates, but through their interaction as a unit with the creator. This correlates with Carl Jung's concept of synchronicity, in which events come together for a specific purpose. It is just so with soulmates, who come together for a combined soul development and by their very physical presence as soulmates emerge as a decisive force themselves.

The combining of two parts to make a sum greater than the parts may in fact justify the possible reality of twin flames. With karma and the conceivability of joint projects being real, soulmates may just have some actual basis in fact. In support of this point of view, we might note Edgar Cayce's comment that if one did not have a soulmate–whether twin soul, companion, or karmic–life would have no point.

Oh, yes, one final word. Just in case you're looking for a soulmate, there is one question that you need to ask: Would you be happy to meet you? A soulmate is a mirror and a mirror tends to reflect perfectly.

It might be wise to be sure you are happy with yourself before you meet your soulmate. Clean up your act before you have to deal with a mirror image. For what you create in yourself, you will likely find. You may not know yourself until you see the recognition of what you are in the eyes of the someone who will love you.

Chapter 5:

Plus a Few
Twists of Lime

Were you an animal? Not last weekend, but in a previous life? Many proponents of reincarnation assume that such is a logical progression. In fact, the so-called ancient wisdom of the East thinks in terms of a Great Chain of Being, wherein the soul incarnates first as a mineral, then a plant, then an animal, and finally as a man. In more poetic form, Jalalu' L-Din Rumi has written:

> A stone I died and rose again a plant,
> A plant I died and rose an animal;
> I died an animal and was born a man.
> Why should I fear? When was I less by dying?

In similar fashion the Barddas of Celtic antiquity thought of the soul passing through every phase of material embodiment before becoming human. The Rosicrucians, an ancient mystical order, maintain that every mineral contains a "jewel of light" or soul. Peter Tompkins and Christopher Bird, in their book *The Secret Life of Plants*, point to various experiments that they claim show that plants have all the attributes of a soul, as well as being living, breathing, communicating creatures who even are endowed with personalities. People who talk to their plants may agree. People whose plants talk back to them we may want to avoid.

Modern Considerations

It must be noted that modern proponents of such a scheme, such as Manly P. Hall, president-founder of the Philosophical Research Society of Los Angeles, point out that only the physical aspects of minerals, plants, and animals are individualized, their entity and mind are collective. In effect those species of subhuman types develop through group consciousness instead of the individualized progression of humans. In this way the sheer numbers problem of their being countless grains of sand as compared to the human population can be averted.

The evidence that might suggest such a genesis is minimal. Many aspects of society tend to be animalistic, however, and this might give some credence to the idea. For example, when we refer to "herd instinct" or accuse someone of "being an animal," one might begin to wonder. As one wit put it:

> We must realize that many souls that are currently sojourning on the planet are new souls; in other words, they were animals in the previous life. It is then clear why they are still behaving like animals; it's their first time as humans and they haven't quite gotten the hang of it yet.

While regressing patients into a variety of past lives, Dr. Helen Wambach has sometimes inadvertently found her subjects seeing themselves on four legs, whereupon they look down and see furry little paws. Dr. Morris Netherton says that his patients often report an animal wound or death when searching for the earliest source of a patient's particular problem. Netherton has found his patients to report previous lives as everything from rodents to insects to prehistoric creatures. Other therapists have found similar reports from their patients under regression analysis. Obviously, some of these patients need therapy!

Future Beasts?

An inescapable, logical product of this theory is the question of whether or not a human could become an animal in a future life. Here again, the ancients seem convinced, one way or the other (which is always the way).

Plato thought that a human soul might go from a beast to a man in a succeeding incarnation and vice versa. His perspective was that the evolution of birds and animals derived from the deterioration of human souls. As previously noted, Pythagoras admonished a man beating a puppy to stop, as the puppy was the soul of one of his friends.

The Neoplatonist Plotinus went so far as to specify:

> Those who have sought only to gratify their lust and appetite pass into the bodies of lascivious and gluttonous animals . . . Those who have degraded their senses by disuse are compelled to vegetate in the plants. Those who have loved music to excess and yet have lived pure lives go into the bodies of melodious birds. Those who have ruled tyranically become eagles. Those who have spoken lightly of heavenly things, keeping their eyes always turned toward heaven, are changed into birds which always fly toward the upper air. He who has acquired civic virtues becomes a man; if he has not these virtues he is transformed into a domestic animal, like a bee.
>
> The experience of evil produces a clearer knowledge of good, particularly in the lives of those who cannot without such experience comprehend what is best.

This view corresponds to Manu, a legendary Hindu legislator and saint who lived over two thousand years ago. In his Laws of Manu, he listed a multitude of crimes for which the punishment was inevitably a rebirth in an appropriate but disagreeable form. An unfaithful woman, for example, would be born in the womb of a jackal, a thief of meat would return as a vulture, a thief of grain as a rat, and so forth.

The ancient Brahmin priests found such laws to be a great convenience in enforcing caste practices, the threats of subhuman rebirth being a marvelous tool in encouraging strict obedience to any man-made law. Modern Hindus do not necessarily take the Laws of Manu quite so literally, and in many respects argue that neither plants nor animals are capable of degenerating into a lesser species and that humans can never be less than human.

Contrary Views

The fact that the Laws of Manu and Plotinus's views were, in some instances, used as a means of enforcing man-made laws might make us pause. A principal argument against Christianity's lack of support for reincarnation is that the Fifth Ecumenical Council of the Church in 553 A.D. denounced reincarnation as an anathema as a means of encouraging discipline among the masses. The self-reliance of those believing in reincarnation can in fact be a virtual thorn in the side of those authorities who seek greater control over the populace.

When the Laws of Manu are used as a similar means to control the masses of reincarnation believers, the same argument would strongly suggest that such strictures are no more reasonable than the 553 A.D. council's denouncement of reincarnation. If we are to use philosophy as a means of control or enforcing adherence to temporal law, the odds are very good that we are dealing with a lousy philosophy. The fact that such philosophies continue to be expounded today makes them no better.

In *The Theory of Eternal Life*, Rodney Collins goes to considerable effort in formulating a theory that equates hell with a rebirth or return to mineral form. At one point Collins makes the argument that the tortures of hell may be thought of not as punishment or retribution but as a means of breaking down an otherwise indestructible soul. In his view criminals and the like have become petrified or hardened to the point where they must in fact be consigned to the rock pile—only in this case, as the rocks and not the prisoners attempting to break up the rocks! In effect, these hardened criminals have loss the power to change or respond, and thus they are fossilized.

Collins not only consigns the "hardened criminal" to the rock pile, he also emphasizes the need for suffering. Collins goes on to argue that one can cheat nature and death by suffering and by demonstrating one's power in separating his or her will from the body. In so doing, one prepares for an independent existence in the afterlife.

The implication seems to be that suffering allows us to become immortal and thus escape the "rock pile," where we will pay for our transgressions. While this "solid" philosophy may be a bit extreme, the other schemes whereby the good ascend, the moderately good get another chance at being human, and the evil fall prey to an animal existence (or worse) do not seem a great deal better. For if we assume the possibility of human failures returning as animals, is it not logical that the soul newly arrived from the animal kingdom would be the most likely one to fail as a human and thus return to the animal kingdom? Is that fair? Is that just? Is that even relevant?

While it may be logical to assume a progression upward from mineral to plant to animal to human, there seems absolutely no justification for the view that the evolution of our souls may occasionally require disciplinary sojourns as lesser beings. On the other hand, and despite the fact that only God can make a tree, maybe you'd like to be a giant redwood next time.[1]

Reflecting on Past Lives

Many people may find highly objectionable the idea that they perhaps once lived a life as an animal. The corollary that they may revert to an animal in a future life is perhaps even more disquieting. But we should ask if it really makes that much difference. Is the question of possible transmigration among species all that important?

Perhaps not. It is not necessary to dwell on, or for that matter, even to be concerned with one's past lives. Rather, the ideal should be to live this life in the best way possible. We should be aware that emotions and attitudes from a past life may very well influence this life, and therefore we may wish to learn of our past lives in order to better understand and live the current life. A knowledge of past lives should not be used in order to provide us with excuses for our current situation, but should be used rather as a means of coping and growing. Concentrating on past lives as a crutch for today's problems does not help anyone, especially oneself.

Accordingly, it may not be all that relevant whether or not one has lived as a mineral, plant, and/or animal. Instead, more significance should perhaps be placed on not living this life as a mineral, plant, and/or animal. Of course, if you think that your deceased grandmother may have become a cow, this may effect your dietary habits (which is a sneaky way of arriving at our next subject).

Vegetarianism

Vegetarianism is in part a belief that living creatures are infused with a soul and therefore should not be consumed by human beings. The classic example of this is the refusal of Hindus to slaughter their cattle for fear the animals might be the reincarnation of their ancestors. This view of possibly looking out for Grandma has been taken to extremes by the Jain monks of India, who wear masks to prevent the accidental inhalation of living creatures and carefully whisk away all insects from their path lest they be squashed inadvertently.

---

[1] A potential flaw of this goal is that choosing to be a giant redwood is a very long commitment.

Burmese fishermen, whose livelihood runs contrary to their nation's religious beliefs, do not kill their fish (and thus risk the wrath of a retributive rebirth), but instead place the fish on the riverbanks in order to dry. They are, of course, grieved to find that all too often the poor creatures die for lack of water. However, these unfortunate deaths are *not* done by the fisherman's hand.

Modern proponents of vegetarianism, with supposedly greater sophistication, take a different tact: Instead of the more extreme positions of the Jains and Burmese, modern vegetarians believe you are what you eat. Such a view is perhaps a bit more defensible.

The most noteworthy prohibition of vegetarianism is the refusal to eat red meat. Others draw the prohibition line to include meat of fowl, and in some other cases, fish. Others may include eggs, based on the idea that an egg is a future fowl.

A reasonable (if not esoteric) view is that the prohibition against eating red meat is predicated on the alleged adverse effect of the digested food on the physical, mental, and emotional well-being of the consumer. Red meat is said by some to carry "bad vibes" or the seeds of fear. The animal's death may presumably raise a strong fear response that then can be transmitted to the consumer by a chemical change in the meat at the time of death. It is on this basis that some vegetarians, in their efforts to avoid the chemical constituents of fear, avoid such meat.

If this latter observation has some basis, then the slaughtering of cattle (and other animals) using some form of euthanasia might noticeably improve the local butcher's product. While such an idea may have little or no appeal to our average vegetarian, it might also be worth noting the argument that this form of vegetarianism could be an illusion, if only because the "death screams" of a carrot are simply much too soft to be heard.

All kidding aside, there are some definite arguments on both sides of the question. Unfortunately, they tend to deteriorate to the point where many nutritionists argue that red meat protein is essential for proper development of the physical and mental abilities, while vegetarians insist that they feel fine and are as smart as ever.

Ultimately, however, there appears to be no reason for a belief in reincarnation to imply the necessity to being a vegetarian. There may be many valid reasons to restrict oneself to meatless (or selected meats only) diets, but being a vegetarian purely in order to avoid eating an ancestor or deceased brethren does not appear to carry much weight.

Pardon the pun.

Chapter 6:

Birth

Experiences

They all arrived at once; two sets of beaming grandparents, a shell-shocked father, and a four-year-old sister. The father held his daughter in his arms to allow her to see her new brother through the nursery window, while the newborn baby, on the other hand, appeared to be content to ignore his relatives and their gushing. Instead, the first son of the young family was more intent on coping with the new world and doing everything possible to sleep through it.

It was the maternal grandmother who first brought up the question foremost in the adult's minds. Surely, naming the baby after her own father was the best idea. Just as surely, the two votes against such an idea came from the father's parents. Each of the grandparents was very cordial but casually insistent concerning their own views, while the father merely smiled and tried to be as diplomatic as possible. Everyone, it seemed, had now lost interest in the appearance of the baby and was instead intent upon his future nomenclature–except, of course, for the baby's sister. To her it was her baby brother's moment. In a child's typical, direct fashion, she asked her new brother, "Did you enjoy being born, little baby?"

Cute. Just like a little girl to ask such a question. We adults, of course, all know that the baby is very unlikely to answer. But perhaps we should recall the old wisdom, "Out of the mouths of babes...." For it really is a rather good question. How did the baby feel about being born? Was he pleased? Disappointed? A little shell-shocked himself? What was the baby's view? Wouldn't it be interesting to know?

Naturally, it would be pointless to ask at this early time; the baby would have obvious difficulties in answering. But why not ask later, when the boy had grown into a man and could then answer? Consciously he is unlikely to remember, just as few people recall their past lives. But under hypnotic regression, could he be taken back to the time of his birth, relive the birth experience, and then relate his newly discovered memories?

Another Source of Information

A nice feature of this idea is that we can tap into a whole new source of information concerning what happens before and during the time of birth. If the boy, whose name is yet to be determined, is reincarnated from a previous existence, why not investigate the circumstances of his entry into the world? By doing this we can compare our results with the so-called wisdom being handed down to us in the form of quotable quotes and long, rambling descriptions.

Earlier in this book we determined to treat, at least for the moment, the ancients as reasonably intelligent human beings. But lest we overshoot the mark and give them too much credit for figuring out the status of the universe, let us gather a little skepticism and avoid buying wholesale everything that has been written by our distant ancestors. We are, after all, reasonably intelligent ourselves. Well, some of us anyway! On the basis of investigations and what we are able to learn today, we should be able to substantiate or formulate theories of reincarnation and psychic phenomena.

We do have, for example, many sources of information from literally thousands of individuals, which can enable us to develop an up-to-date theory. Through hypnotic regressions into past lives and other important periods in a soul's evolution, we can gain insights into what came before, what will come after, and what seems to happen in the meantime between lives.

A logical first step in discovering our origins would be to extend just a bit further the modern therapeutic technique of hypnotically regressing an individual into childhood. Instead of searching for a specific cause that may be causing current-day problems, the purpose would be to inquire directly about the birth experience. In fact, we could inquire about what has happened from the time of conception until the moment of birth (and in some cases, shortly thereafter).

Validity of Data

The potential flaw in this method is the mind's ability to imagine whatever the therapist requests, particularly under a hypnotic suggestion. If, for example, a therapist asks a person what he or she is experiencing in the womb, the hypnotized person may attempt to respond to the therapist's "demand" and imagine some sort of experience, despite the fact that the individual has no memory of this period in his or her life. On the other hand, if a thousand or more subjects independently describe very similar experiences, then the credibility of the method would be considerably more valid.

Regressions to the birth experience have been done and reported in several excellent texts. In *Rebirthing in the New Age*, authors Leonard Orr and Sondra Ray describe their experiences in taking subjects beyond hyperventilation into altered states of consciousness, where they are able to recall and relive the birth experience. Thomas Verney's *The Secret Life of the Unborn Child* provides for an exploration of the reported memories from the last trimester in utero and the effects of these memories on the adult. In *Life Before Life*, psychologist Dr. Helen Wambach reports on her success in regressing 750 subjects to their birth experiences. Dr. Wambach not only details many of the individual and specific birth experiences of her subjects, but also provides a wide range of intriguing statistics.

The data from these reported investigations is validated in part by the sheer number of reported cases, including those that were unsuccessful. In Dr. Wambach's *Life Before Life*, nearly forty percent of her subjects did not recall anything from the time she began the regression. Slightly more than ten percent had no answers to her questions (even though they were quite relaxed) or they were simply not hypnotized. In spite of the fact that Dr. Wambach received detailed answers from 750 subjects (nearly fifty percent of those attempted), the null reports are significant in the evaluation of the data.

It is noteworthy that nearly ninety percent of Dr. Wambach's subjects managed to recall past lives, but only fifty percent recalled the birth experience. In attempting to explain this statistic, Dr. Wambach noticed that the people giving answers regarding their birth experiences were usually better versed in spiritual matters, had attended several transcendental meditation classes, or had done meditation on their own. According to Dr. Wambach, the people who received answers on the birth regressions were those people already into the consciousness movement.

This portends the possibility of a significant flaw in the findings, and Dr. Wambach was well aware of this problem. While she could not rule out the possibility of her subjects simply responding to a common set of conscious beliefs, she did note several important factors. For example, her discussions with subjects indicated that their conscious beliefs were much more diverse than the responses obtained under hypnosis. Also, many subjects were quite surprised by their own responses and typically felt themselves to be out in left field. Finally, Dr. Wambach felt that the depth of emotion expressed during the birth experience also argued for the credibility of the results.

Nevertheless, the possibility persists that her subjects are unknowingly reporting from the basis of common beliefs. This point is not easily decided one way or the other. But it is worth keeping it in mind as we discuss Dr. Wambach's and other's results in the following pages. The results do tend to be consistent with other sources of information and internally consistent with reincarnation theory, but some skepticism on specific data points may still be in order.

Choosing Birth

According to Dr. Wambach's research, of the 750 subjects who did report recalling the birth experience, eighty-one percent said they chose to be born, and that it was their choice to make. While a majority made the choice, many did so reluctantly and only after consultations and encouragement by others.

The subjects indicated that they had the right to refuse to be reborn into another lifetime, but that they normally felt a duty to do so. It was, apparently, the correct thing to do, but the majority were not eager to undertake the task.

Of those subjects who were aware of the choice, virtually all agreed that others helped them in their decision. Forty-one percent of the subjects, however, reported an inability to identify their advisors or counselors. They were just aware of instructions and counseling and that they would receive guidance and advice once they were alive in the body chosen by them. Conversely, nineteen percent reported that they were either unaware of the choice or received no clear answer to the question.

Only 0.1 percent of the subjects felt that God or some other deity was the force that led them into birth. On the other hand, ten percent of those counseled before birth indicated that their advisors or counselors were people in the lifetime in which they were about to be born! Fifty-nine percent of all of the subjects mentioned more than one counselor.

These counselors or advisors seem to be a consistent theme through a variety of techniques to discover what lies before, after, and between lives. Because these other entities often offer guidance and advice during a soul's sojourn in a lifetime, they are typically referred to as "guides." We will hear more about these guides in later chapters.

The seeming reluctance to be born is exemplified by the statistic that only twenty-eight percent of the subjects felt enthusiastic about being alive again, felt that they had planned carefully, and were ready for rebirth. On the other hand, sixty-eight percent felt reluctant, anxious, or resigned to the prospect of living another lifetime. Even more noteworthy was the fact that death was experienced as pleasant by ninety percent of Wambach's subjects, but that being born and living another lifetime was unhappy and frightening to the clear majority.

So why did they choose to make the trip again? If karma is playing a role, were the choices made to settle karmic debts? Was the rebirth intentional in order to undergo some experience that the soul felt was important for further development? Helen Wambach's subjects provided a wealth of information.

The Twentieth Century

Fifty-one percent chose to be born in the twentieth century because of the great potential of this time for spiritual growth. Forty-one percent, on the other hand, had no response or reported "no." This latter fact may be related to the concept of time in unearthly existences (see Chapter 12), or may be, as one person reported, because she felt it was time to return since recess was over.

The subjects interest in the twentieth century seemed to tie in with his or her purposes for being reborn. Dr. Wambach has suggested that it is the emotional aspects, the learning of the heart, that is the most important. Over seventy percent of her subjects indicated that the last half of the twentieth century would be characterized by a new development of spiritual awareness. At least one subject chose the period because of the historical transitions of a religious age to a scientific one to a time of spiritual awakening.

Before we make too much of the importance of our present-day lives, it is perhaps instructive to note that people virtually always think of their age as an important, if not a critical, one. Ages and localities can be just as ego-oriented as individuals, and it is all too common for people to embellish their own worth by ascribing great value to the time (and/or the place) of their lives. Even though the subjects' statistics argue for the latter part of the twentieth century being of great significance, the common bond of ego may be misleading.

There is undeniably a feeling among members of the New Age that things are not only happening, but also accelerating, in their haste to bring about change. At this point in our narrative, however, the evidence is circumstantial and slim. We will find other indicators of imminent momentous events in the latter portion of this book, but the tendency of people to add significance to their lives by adding significance to their age cannot be ignored.

Selections

Now for a subject you've all been waiting for: sex. Do we, for example, choose our sex in different lives? From Dr. Helen Wambach's subjects, we find that twenty-four percent felt they had *not* chosen their sex, or that the sex in the coming lifetime was not of importance. Alternatively, forty-eight percent had chosen to be female in their current lifetimes. Nearly a third of these indicated that the reason for their choice was to have children. Others chose their sex in order to be with known others in opposite sexual roles. In one case, the female chose to be a woman because her mate wanted them to be the same sexes they were in 1503.[1]

Interestingly enough, our sexuality appears to be more of a left-brain, superficial aspect of our being. While most people feel that sex is a deeply innate part of our personality, the right brain seems to be taking a different view. Dr. Wambach concluded that of 750 subjects, none felt themselves to be, in their true, inner self, either male or female; and that the process of gathering experiences over many lifetimes was above sexual distinctions. Apparently the need was to develop both aspects–yin and yang–to reach deeper understanding.

Sexual relationships do appear, however, to determine our selection of parents and other people who will be important in our forthcoming lives. Husbands and wives in this lifetime often appear to have had ties of a sexual nature in prior lives, indicating a trend for people to work out sexual relationships by assuming the same sex roles in several lifetimes. Such a trend may, in part, be explained by karmic ties or just the need for completion of unfinished

---

[1] Imagine, if you will, a soul hovering about her future parents, and exhorting, at the moment of conception: "Swim, you guys! I wanna be a girl!"

relationships.

An additional, rather curious observation by Dr. Wambach is that the birth of boys increases during times of war! Think about that one for a moment.

Relationships

Dr. Wambach's subjects reported an astonishing variety of relationships between souls over the course of many lifetimes. Fathers in this lifetime may have been brothers, sisters, lovers, mothers, or friends in past lives. There was no consistency to the changing combinations, and there was no evidence to suggest Freudian theories of fathers and daughters wishing to be lovers or otherwise.

Fully eighty-seven percent of the subjects reported that people important in this lifetime were well known to the subjects in past lives. Even more noteworthy was the fact that some of the relationships were from the state between lives and not just from past lives. The essential result appeared to be that we continually interact with those we love (and those we hate) in a continuing series of different relationships, and that only when we have resolved our issues with one another (i.e., feel only compassion and affection) are we granted a reprieve from living over and over with the same souls (who have, of course, been forced to live with us!).

Dr. Wambach also notes that these relationships are not necessarily based on blood ties. In fact, in many cases, friends were known more intimately in past lives than were brothers and sisters or parents. Dr. Wambach concluded that past-life ties seemed to be more important than blood ties in this life.

Such repetitions of relationships have been observed by many psychologists in terms of a single life. Past-life influences on parental and other selections may be mirrored by what is viewed as the forces creating patterns in love and marriage in today's world. This tendency for people to replicate the themes of early life or of previous generations in the context of later, intimate relationships has long been commented upon by many theorists and therapists. As social worker Lily Pincus, founder of the Tavistock Institute for Marital Studies, and therapist Dr. Christopher Dale have observed, there is a tendency for people to develop repetitive patterns of relationships in order to satisfy certain needs. Examples include the woman who had an alcoholic father marrying a man who becomes an alcoholic himself. Even after divorcing the man, the same woman may marry yet another alcoholic! Alternatively, a man may continually find himself becoming involved with women with congenital heart trouble.

This is not to imply that these psychologists in any way are addressing the question of reincarnation, but to show that the same tendency to replicate certain patterns may well be extrapolated to include the effects of multiple lives. Additionally, a life's plan might include the necessity of experiencing a certain type of relationship (such as an alcoholic family member), and the repetition in this life is accomplished in order to fully exhaust the possibilities of this type of relationship. Or it may be akin to the situation typified by the elementary school teacher who tells her lover: "If you don't get it right the first time, you're going to have to do it over and over again until you do get it right!"

Other Selections

In addition to the selection of parents, there were also reports that some subjects knew, before they were born, of their relationship with adoptive parents. These subjects chose not to come to them as their own genetic children, but rather chose adoption as a means to reach their parents. In one case a subject reported that she had chosen one set of parents for genetics and another for environment.

One other connection is that of twins. If, according to one theory of reincarnation, the DNA molecules that carry the basic blueprints of our mind and body also carry the memories of past lives, then identical twins may be able to remember the same past lives. Unfortunately for the statistics, Dr. Wambach only had one pair of twins regressed. Ten others were twins whose twin was not present at any regression.

The results were nonetheless consistent. Twins invariably reported having known each other intimately in past lives and in the period between lives. Their relationships were extremely close, but not because they were twins. Instead, they had decided to enter this life as twins *because* they were close.

The prospect of spending another lifetime with an ex-mate or spurned lover might not be the best news you've heard so far. But the apparent existence of karmic ties in Dr. Wambach's results does give one pause. One implication might very well be that it is advisable to work out the problem in this lifetime and thus find relief in a future life. After all, surely there are better things to do in that future life than rehash the unresolved problems from this one.

Twenty-five percent of Dr. Wambach's subjects reported that the purpose of their living their current lifetime was to gain additional experience. In fact, this experience was often personified in the need to learn and relate to others, as well as love without being demanding or possessive. Twenty-eight percent also felt the need to act as a teacher in helping others to understand the basic unity of mankind and to develop a higher consciousness for mankind as a whole.

There was little or no evidence to suggest that wealth, status, power, or the development of talents was the motivating force for rebirth into another lifetime. Furthermore, the Golden Rule appeared subconsciously as the basic law of the universe. In many respects reincarnation and karma enforce this rule by insisting that we will, in fact, be treated as we have treated others.

Astrological Choices

If the thought that we actually chose our parents, our sex, and our potential for a return date with an ex-mate tends to cast a chill over your demeanor, then consider the logical extrapolation of that train of thought: We probably chose our basic personalities as well.

How might this be accomplished? One answer lies within the purview of astrology. A basic precept of astrology is that the time and place of our birth determines our basic personality. If this is true, then the relatively simple selection of conception and then the time and place of birth would allow for a rather precise determination of a person's personality in the coming life.

While most people are aware of the importance to astrology of our time of birth, the significance of the birthplace is less obvious. Astrology, however, maintains that the position of the sun and planets (but not necessarily the stars) in the overhead sky at the time of our birth is the main determinate, and because these planetary and solar positions are determined at any specific moment by our location on the planet's surface, the birthplace is important to any in-depth review of our astrological charts.

In Chinese astrology the year of one's birth ranks first in importance, followed by the hour and then the month. The extent of the belief in astrology by the Chinese is best exemplified by the fact that abortions in certain years are at an all-time high because such birth years are considered extremely undesirable. On the other side of the coin, the Chinese believe their leaders must be born in the Year of the Dragon (or at the very least, the Year of the Tiger) in order to be effective as leaders.

Astrology, as viewed by the Westerner, tends to place the emphasis on the time of birth in terms of the astrological month. These times extend from Aries (beginning March 20) through Pisces and represent, according to astrology, the evolution from the infant (Aries) to maturity (Pisces). These "Sun Signs" represent the position of the Sun with respect to our month of birth and supposedly have the greatest effect on our personalities.

Also important to the Western astrologer are the exact positions of the planets in our astrological natal charts. The planetary positions provide for a much greater diversity in personalities and allow for subtle (and not so subtle) variations in the overall effect of whatever our Sun Sign is.

The applicability of astrology to reincarnation would appear to be related primarily to our selection of the environment and our personality in a forthcoming life. Our apparent choices of parents, sex, birth dates, and so forth during our time between lives may be a means to further set the stage for our next life. Such a concept might imply the desirability of natural childbirth. Premature or induced-labor babies may be arriving prior to their planned entrance and may be having their predetermined or planned personalities altered. If the early arrival is over a period of days, there is the potential for major differences. For example, the distinction between a Pisces and an Aries personality is quite substantial, but is separated in time by less than a day. In some views the separation is as little as four minutes either way. Whether or not such contingencies for premature arrivals are being considered in our prebirth choices and deliberations has not yet been addressed in the statistical research thus far conducted.

Abortion

Another important result of Dr. Wambach's research was that all of her 750 subjects were unanimous in their feelings that the fetus was not truly part of their consciousness and that the existence of a fully conscious entity was quite apart from the fetus. Furthermore, eighty-nine percent of the subjects did not become a part of or otherwise involved with the fetus until the last trimester of the pregnancy (or after six months of gestation). Fully thirty-three percent of the reports said that they did not join the fetus, or experience inside the fetus, until just before or during the birth process.

Such results may be of significance with respect to abortion. Only eleven percent indicated any awareness of being inside the fetus at any time between conception and the first six months of gestation, while twelve percent reported being in the fetus after the first six months. Nineteen percent described themselves as being in and out of the fetus during the period before birth. Yet virtually all of the subjects reported being aware of the "first kick" (which typically occurs during the fourth or fifth month of pregnancy), even if only eleven percent perceived themselves as inside the fetus at this time. This latter group's description indicated that they might also have been experiencing being in and out of the fetus.

Also relevant to the subject of abortion are the subjects' prebirth awareness of mothers' feelings, emotions and, in some cases, the mothers' thoughts before their children were born. Fully eighty-six percent of the subjects reported this phenomenon and indicated that their awareness was because they weren't fixed into the fetus but were able to hover around it. Many of these subjects were quite surprised at becoming aware of their mothers' feelings under the hypnotic state. Those not obtaining any impressions of their mothers' feelings felt that they may have blocked it out of their minds because of their general resistance to being born.

It is difficult to draw conclusions in regard to abortion from these statistics. The tendency is to latch on to those points that seem to be most supportive of one's preconceived opinion. It is noteworthy that one subject reported hearing people discuss an abortion or trying to talk her mother into an abortion. The subject, however, felt quite determined to be born. Apparently, she was successful.

Dr. Wambach's observation was that birth and the onset of living another lifetime was thought of as a duty, and that if one fetus was aborted, it was apparently possible to choose another lifetime. Dr. Wambach also felt that the incoming soul could influence the mother and her decision regarding abortion. Furthermore, Dr. Wambach also speculated that sudden infant death syndrome might actually be caused by a soul's decision not to go ahead with a life plan.

Moment of Birth

The birth experience itself, as investigated by Dr. Wambach, was less open to statistical analysis. Apparently the moment of birth caused disturbing and unpleasant sensations as the soul left a quite different environment and was immediately besieged by the physical senses. Ten percent reported they were sad or actually cried at this point. Many felt cut off or diminished or "drowned" in light, cold air, and sounds. In their new body they felt alone and unconnected. According to Dr. Wambach, no matter how enthusiastically they chose to enter the world, most of her subjects found the actual experience to be one of loneliness and alienation from the heavenlike light that they lost upon entering the physical world.

Loss of Memories

Another aspect of the birth experience is the fact that a soul apparently goes from a state of knowing its life plan and all of the events leading to its decision to be reborn and then shortly after birth having these memories fade away. These "fade outs," as they have been called, deserve some comment.

Various traditions describe the return to earth in physical form as passing through a veil or etheric barrier that erases the memories of past lives and the events between lives. This "River of Forgetfulness" serves to block the memories of the prebirth time and space and its inherent appeal.

Dr. Ian Stevenson has reported on subjects in Thailand who had maintained their past-life and birth memories. The subjects told of being offered, in the space between lives, the "fruit of forgetfulness" before rebirth. But they avoided this erasure of their past-life memories by avoiding the tempting offer. Such reports seem rare, however.

We may in fact need the "fade outs," if only to reduce the number of memories that we carry from life to life. After all, a confusion or proliferation of memories could be distracting, to say the least. In some cases of children remembering past lives in considerable detail, the children soon discovered that it was best to let sleeping dogs lie in order to be able to live their current lives.

There is also the possibility that the before-life state is significantly better than life itself, and a remembrance of it might lead only to regrets. Perhaps the happiness of death is concealed from us so that we can endure life.

In *Life Between Life*, Joe Fisher and Joel Whitton point out that not only is amnesia of past lives beneficial in preventing homesickness for the grandeur left behind, but it also allows a new life unimpeded by past deeds and misdeeds. In addition, knowledge of the future of one's life would also have to be subjugated in order to obtain maximum benefits from the challenges and opportunities planned for this life.

Dr. Whitton, for example, noted that several of his subjects reported their concern that conscious knowledge of approaching events might impair their karmic unfoldment. In one case, the subject asked Dr. Whitton to erase a particular memory inasmuch as the subject might be tempted to tamper with his karma. Dr. Whitton also noted that some of his subjects could censor their recall by withholding information (despite the fact they could not lie).

Mohandas K. Gandhi once remarked, "It is nature's kindness that we do not remember past births. Life would be a burden if we carried such a tremendous load of memories." This idea of too many memories being more a burden than a benefit also has arisen in connection with a human's potential creativity. The concept has been neatly described in Jean Auel's *The Clan of the Cave Bear*. Ms. Auel's novel describes members of the Neanderthal species as having prodigious memories, generated over countless lives and passed along from generation to generation. The problem that arose was that the inclusion of this vast array of memories required an ever-larger brain, until the skull had grown so large as to defy passage through the birth canal. Conversely, Ms. Auel's Cro-Magnon man did not have past-life memories but made up for this handicap with his creativity. The result was the demise of Neanderthal man and the rise of Cro-Magnon man. Such a theory might offer an additional explanation for the need of fade outs at birth.

Many proponents of reincarnation and its related theories also point out the ready accessibility of our guides for help and advice should the need arise. Admittedly, the accessibility is not so apparent to many, but the combination of guides and creativity would seem to imply a better learning situation than a mass of past memories.

Summary

Nothing in Dr. Wambach's findings, or those of other investigators into the birth experience, contradicts any aspect of reincarnation. Instead, the regressions to the birth experience support the concept of reincarnation and provide many answers to questions of detail in reincarnation theory. Dr. Wambach's findings also support in general terms the concept of karma and, more specifically, directly support the concept of soulmates. Finally, it is noteworthy that Dr. Wambach's findings are consistent with much of the ancient wisdom as contained in the Bible and other historical and/or religious documents.

Chapter 7:

Beyond

Death

George Richie died in 1943. He had just completed his army basic training in Texas and was scheduled to be shipped to Richmond, Virginia. His plans were waylaid when he checked into a hospital with a chest cold and collapsed while in the X-ray room. The diagnosis, of which he was unaware until later, was double lobar pneumonia.

When Richie awoke in an unfamiliar hospital room, his first thought was that it was time to leave for Richmond. But when he climbed out of bed, he noticed that someone was still lying there. Feeling himself completely recovered, he began to look closer at his hospital room companion–to all extents the man appeared to be dead. As Richie looked more closely, he saw familiar features. Astounded and appalled, Richie recognized the man in the bed as himself.

Richie ran from the room and passed *through* an orderly in the outside corridor. He quickly left the hospital, hurtling through the air at tremendous speed. Seeing a town below, he swooped down beside a telephone pole, which despite his efforts, he was unable to grasp.

Dr. Donald Francy, meanwhile, was examining his patient for life. Finding no trace of respiration or heartbeat, he ordered an attendant to cover the body with a sheet. At about the same time, apparently, Richie remembered the body on the bed. At the instant of his decision to return, he found himself back at the hospital searching for his room. When he thought he had found it, he attempted to remove the sheet that covered the body in the bed. But his hand passed through the fabric and, at that moment, Richie realized that he could not get back into his body and that he was, in fact, dead.

With that thought, Richie suddenly found himself in a room filled with brilliant light. A sense of compassion and comfort instantly swept over him, and he found himself exuberantly happy. With incredible speed but enormous clarity, he was able to review his life. Every event and thought and conversation flashed by in separate pictures and, from some unknown source, he sensed a gentle questioning of his life on earth.

Abruptly he left the hospital room and found himself in another realm. There he saw a city constructed entirely of light. He had never read the Book of Revelations or even anything on the subject of death. But he now found himself in a place where walls, houses, and even streets seemed to give off light. The inhabitants were beings of blindingly bright light, including one standing directly before him. Then, just as abruptly, the dazzling light faded, the walls of the hospital returned, and he seemed to fall asleep.

When he awoke he was back in his body. This was not good news to Richie–he wished he was back in the city of light. Richie was alive and well despite the fact that his medical chart, signed by his physician, showed that he had died of double lobar pneumonia on December 20, 1943. He had been dead for nine minutes when an attendant had noticed a movement under the sheet. Immediately summoned, the doctor had jolted Richie back to life with a shot of adrenalin. Despite the expected oxygen deprivation, Richie had suffered no brain damage.

A reader's first reaction to this story might be that Richie *did* suffer brain damage, evidenced by the contents of his story. When anyone continually tells wild and incredible stories and tells, on one occasion, that when he was a child he was kicked in the head by a horse, there is a tendency to totally believe the horse story. Can we apply the same reasoning to George's "horse story"?

Near-Death Experiences

If Richie's story was an isolated example, there are a host of explanations for this incredible tale. The mind's ability to create, imagine, or fabricate stories, and the wide variety of motivations to do so, is well recognized by modern-day psychologists and psychiatrists. It is noteworthy that in this example Richie did not come into knowledge or information that was verifiable by other means.

But this "near-death experience" is not an isolated example. There are literally thousands of documented cases of people who have had a near-death experience. Well-established medical doctors, psychologists, theologians, cardiologists, and social scientists of various kinds have done extensive research and study of the phenomenon. Researchers such as Cobb, Crookall, Savage, Hyslop, Richet, and many others have accumulated data from subjects over the last hundred years. More recently, books by Doctors Moody, Kübler-Ross, Sabom, Lundahl, Gabbard, Twenlow, and others have been added to an extensive and varied library of professional journal articles and previous research papers.

If there were any questions about the pervasiveness of the near-death experience, George Gallup, Jr., of Gallup poll fame, has laid them to rest. In *Adventures in Immortality*, Mr. Gallup reports that five percent of the U.S. adult population have had near-death experiences. This percentage means that about 8,000,000 people who have had such an experience. If nothing else,

Gallup's statistics speak well for the medical emergency technology that was able to resuscitate clinically dead or near-dead patients.

But the pervasiveness of the phenomena has not always been convincing in itself. When one of the first widely disseminated books on the subject, Dr. Raymond Moody's *Life After Life*, was first published, Dr. Moody's descriptions and conclusions were often viewed with considerable skepticism or simply dismissed out of hand by members of the medical and scientific community.

Sociologist Dr. Harold Widdison, for example, has noted a significant emotional reaction by scientists to Moody's book. Dr. Widdison compared it to the classic struggles of a fledgling science against a dominating religion, particularly as seen in such individuals as Galileo and Michelangelo. Dr. Widdison believed that the labeling of near-death experiences as "religious" is erroneous and is often used as an excuse to avoid scientific research into the subject, much to the detriment of science.

Dr. Michael Sabom, a cardiologist, reports that he was initially highly skeptical of Moody's work, but after conducting a survey of hospitalized patients, he, along with colleague Sarah Kreutziger, concluded that near-death experiences were a real and consistent event for many patients who were unconscious and near death. Dr. Sabom also noted that most patients were reluctant to discuss their experience for fear of ridicule. The two researchers found that the elements of the experiences of their patients were identical to those reported by Moody. They further noted that sociological and demographic factors did not account for the occurrence of the near-death experiences.

Writing in the *New England Journal of Medicine* in June 1977, Dr. Lewis Thomas, president of the Sloan-Kettering Cancer Institute, found that research into dying was not correlating with the idea of agony at the end, and that instead people experiencing near death invariably described the moment in terms of tranquility and peace. These same people did not mention pain or anguish. Dr. Thomas has come to the conclusion that there is something going on that we don't really know about, something quite different from what we might expect, and something we might want to look into!

There is nothing like the *New England Journal of Medicine* for massive understatement.

Characteristics of Near-Death Experiences

Perhaps the most remarkable aspect of near-death experiences (NDE) is the consistency of the descriptions. The consistency occurs in spite of the fact that the persons involved uniformly characterize their NDE as inexpressible or ineffable. The difficulty people have in describing their near-death experiences appears to be due to the fact that our language is symbolic–words are only names for our experiences. Inasmuch as NDEs fall outside our common experience, adjectives and superlatives may be inadequate to describe the events that occur during an NDE.

Descriptions of near-death experiences include a variety of common characteristics. Subjects often report hearing their doctor or other attendant pronounce them dead. Some subjects describe an intense feeling of peace and quiet, while in other cases various unusual auditory sensations are reported for short periods of time. These "noises" range from pleasant music to annoying sensations of hearing buzzing, loud clicks, ringing, roaring, or banging.

Subjects often report being pulled very rapidly through a dark space. This space may be described as a tunnel, funnel, cylinder, sewer, trough, cave, well, enclosure, vacuum, void, or valley. The last descriptive term brings to mind "Yea, though I walk through the valley of the shadow of death . . ."

Many subjects report leaving their physical bodies and/or viewing it from a vantage point outside of their bodies. Often this vantage point is located on the ceiling or in a corner of the room in which their physical body remains. The emotional reaction of subjects seeing their body from a spectator's viewpoint is often one of panic and a desperate desire to reenter their physical body. Invariably they have no idea of how to do so.

In their out-of-body state, subjects may become aware that their spiritual body lacks solidity, that physical objects appear to move through it with ease, and that they are unable to grasp any object or person that they try to touch. The spiritual body is reported as weightless, while the person describes sensations of floating or drifting. Almost everyone remarks upon the timelessness of the out-of-body state.

While the characteristics of the spiritual body may seem at first to be limitations, some subjects begin to appreciate them as an absence of limitations. If they cannot grasp a doorknob, they realize they can simply go through the door. Travel becomes exceptionally easy, physical objects represent no barriers, and movement can be virtually instantaneous. Such capabilities become even more significant when one considers the possibility of people being able to achieve such an out-of-body state voluntarily and at will (See Chapter 9).

Some subjects have reported that in the out-of-body state they begin to think more lucidly and rapidly. Their physical senses of vision and hearing seem heightened and improved from what they had known in their physical bodies. Often subjects feel a comfortable "warmth," although in some cases there is no sensation of temperature at all. But apparently no one reports either odors or tastes while in the out-of-body state.

Subjects often report being surrounded by a brilliant, guiding light. The light is invariably sensed as being quite bright, but never to the point of being uncomfortable for viewing. Once in the presence of the light, the feelings of loneliness are often replaced by a remarkable feeling of peace, tranquility, and intense happiness. Many subjects sense the presence of a close friend or relative, or in some cases a religious figure of importance to the subject. The relatives or friends, surrounded by brilliant light, seem to be beckoning to the subjects or in some cases merely smiling and radiating a kind of constructive, loving energy toward the person who has temporarily died.

Communication between the subjects and the beings in the light, in those cases in which it occurs, is reported to be a direct, unimpeded transfer of thoughts. Subjects claim that there is no possibility of misunderstanding or lying. There is no apparent use of language, yet understanding and awareness are complete and instantaneous.

Many see flashbacks of their immediate past life, often in the form of a cinematic, instantaneous review of their entire life. They seem to be in a situation that makes it very clear to them what is of value and what isn't. The flashbacks are often initiated by a brilliant presence asking the dying person to review his life. One of Moody's subjects recalled that as a light appeared, the question foremost in his mind concerned what the subject had to show for having lived his life. This question then apparently triggered the flashbacks.

The intent of this life review is sensed by the subjects as being primarily for reflection. There is no sense of judgment or condemnation. The review is extraordinarily rapid, incredibly vivid and real, and the emotions and feelings associated with each memory or image may be reexperienced. Some subjects, even for a period of time following their NDE experience, are able to continue to recall the events of their lives in incredible detail.

Subjects encountering the life review have sensed a lack of judgment and have felt unconditional love directed to them for their past actions, whatever these actions might have been. This feature of the NDE has led many subjects to abandon and disavow the reward-punishment model of the afterlife, even in those cases where the subjects had been accustomed to thinking in such terms. It came as a major surprise to many of the subjects that even some of the most apparently awful and sinful deeds elicited responses from the beings of light of understanding and humor rather than anger or disappointment. One subject described the being of light as a fun person with a definite sense of humor. (Considering the conduct of many of our lives, a sense of humor of beings on the other side would seem essential.)

Some subjects reported approaching a limit or border of some kind. Many of these people sensed that they had reached some sort of dividing line between their current condition and a more permanent death. The border often represented a barrier and a point of no return. In some cases the subjects reported that they did not know how or why they returned, while others either made conscious decisions to return (for the sake of children or loved ones, for example) or were told to return.

In *Return from Death*, Margot Grey characterized the decision to return as invariably associated with a consideration for the suffering of those left behind, the difficulties that would be experienced as a result of the subject's death, or simply a sense that one had not yet fulfilled his or her destiny. Nevertheless, according to Dr. Grey, the choice to return was an individual one, and the motivation for the decision to return was often an altruistic one of service and mission to others and God, essentially a selfless love.

It is noteworthy that most subjects were neither eager to return nor concerned about their physical body. Many reported their sense of amazement at seeing others struggling so hard to revive the body. The subjects often wondered during their observations why there was so much effort being expended. They seemed to feel that "Gosh, it's so peaceful here, why should I want to go back? I think I'll stay; it's neat here!" Then all of the sudden, zap! They were back in their bodies again and going through all the pain and agony as before.

Dr. Raymond Moody has analyzed the near-death experiences of his subjects and has delineated fifteen separate elements that recur again and again. On the basis of similarities between NDEs, he has constructed a theoretical "core" experience that he describes in *Life After Life*. This core experience essentially consists of the experiences described previously.

However, Dr. Moody goes on to point out several critical factors with regard to the "core experience."

1. No two accounts are precisely identical, despite many striking similarities.

2. No one subject has reported every single component of the core experience.

3. There is no single component of the core experience that every subject has reported, even though a few of the elements come fairly close to being universal.

4. No single component has been reported by only one subject.

5. The order of the individual elements in the core experience varies, but not widely.

6. Subjects who were "dead" generally report more components of the core experience than those subjects who only came close to death, and those "dead" for a longer period of time report a more complete core experience.

7. Some subjects who were pronounced dead were then resuscitated, and came back remembering nothing at all.

8. There are a few cases in which death was imminent, but no actual injuries took place.

9. The NDEs result in no apparent brain damage, even after several hours of apparent death.

Margot Grey has encountered similar results and has further noted that illness was more likely to include more of the features of the core experience, but that the later stages were less likely in accidents. The later stages, however, were entirely absent in cases of suicide attempts, (i.e. the relief of bodily attachment occurred, but the near-death experience tended to end up as a confused drifting in some sort of "twilight zone"). Dr. Grey emphasized that suicide-related near-death experiences did not include any transcendent experiences, but rather tended to fade out prior to such occurrences.

Suicide-induced near-death experiences will be discussed in more detail below.

The Bad News

Not all reports from near-death experiences paint such a rosy picture of peace and love. For example, the May/June 1979 issue of *Parapsychology Review* reports:

> A heart specialist from Chattanooga, Tennessee, has just finished a study of more than 100 patients brought back to life after being clinically dead. "The Good News," he said, "is that some of them had a blissful encounter with a being of light. The bad news, however, is that over half of the patients had a perfectly appalling time," walking through dimly lit caverns and seeing fiendish figures brandishing pitchforks beside a smoking, sulphurous lake surrounded by moaning bodies." The doctor now firmly believes hell exists. "Reluctantly," he said, "I have come to the conclusion it may not be safe to die."

It is comforting to know that with regard to understatement, *Parapsychology Review* is keeping up with the *New England Journal of Medicine*.

The evidence for unpleasant or terrifying near-death experiences is sufficient to cause significant concern. Many researchers, however, have found no evidence of cases that are suggestive of a "hellish experience." These latter researchers include medical professionals such as cardiologists, who have access to patients at the moment of resuscitation and who therefore supposedly have the opportunity to talk to the patient before the patient is able to reflect on the experience and possibly bury the memory deep within his or her own psyche. It seems likely that anyone undergoing a hell-like experience would be reluctant to discuss the subject at a later time, as they might be ashamed to admit to what had apparently happened to them.

On the other hand, negative encounters have been reported by Maurice Rawlings, whose research into negative near-death episodes was one of the first major studies that contended hellish encounters exist. George Gallup has also reported on negative NDEs, as has Margot Grey. Out of forty-one case studies, for example, Ms. Grey found five terrifying experiences. In one of her cases a subject had a hell-like experience on one near-death occasion, and a positive core experience on a subsequent one. Ms. Grey's results seem to correspond to both the reports of Rawlings and Gallup, but have no counterpart in the investigations by many other researchers.

According to Ms. Grey, a "negative" experience is associated with fear or panic, emotional or mental anguish, or utter desperation. Her subjects have reported being lost and helpless, extremely lonely, and experiencing an enormous sense of desolation. The negative environment was thought of as dark, gloomy, barren and/or hostile, sometimes the edge of a pit or abyss. All of the subject's inner resources were required to prevent them from going over the edge. In some cases, it seemed a matter of wits in order to avoid being tricked into death.

Dr. Grey's "hell-like" experience includes all the aspects of the negative phase, but with feelings of much greater intensity. In many cases the subjects sensed an evil force, occasionally identified as the power of darkness, dragging them down. Wrathful or demonic creatures often were envisioned, taunting or threatening the individual, while some subjects recounted attacks by unseen beings that might be hooded or faceless. The hell-like environment was either intensely cold or unbearably hot. Wailing of souls in torment was sometimes heard, or noises of maddened wild beasts snarling and crashing about. In some cases, an archetypal hell with fire, brimstone, and the devil himself were encountered.

The variation of the negative or hell-like near-death experiences from that of the core experience of very positive conditions is not fully understood. It has been suggested that negative NDEs are not true NDEs, but in fact have their origin in psychological factors, while most positive NDEs are "true NDEs" that cannot be adequately explained by the same factors. Alternatively, such an argument may be nothing more than wishful thinking.

Suicides

In the initial studies of suicide-induced NDEs, no evidence was found to suggest any distinction between this form of near-death experience and those caused by illness or accident. In a 1981 study by Kenneth Ring and Stephen Franklin, for example, these two experienced researchers came to the conclusion that there was nothing unique about NDEs triggered by suicide attempts. Furthermore, the reports of suicide survivors was not significantly different from illness- or accident-induced NDEs, all subjects reporting essentially the same positive feelings, although to different degrees. Moreover, none of the subjects felt judged or condemned by any force outside of themselves for their suicide attempt.

Ring and Franklin go on to report, however, a decrease in suicidal intent following a suicide-induced NDE. Furthermore, the two researchers concluded that the recollections of suicide survivors and other NDEs promoted the cause of life, not death, and in particular not death via suicide.

Ring and Franklin also pointed out in this early report that their respondents should not be considered representative and that their conclusions should be viewed as preliminary. This disclaimer has turned out to be quite fortunate, because further study has begun to suggest a different story.

In Margot Grey's 1985 book *Return from Death*, she reports that Professor Ring had subsequently found that attempted suicide NDEs were less likely to have a full core experience, and that the missing elements appeared to be the transcendental aspects of seeing a brilliant but comforting light and the encountering of a presence. It also was noted that while the sense of bodily detachment existed to the same degree as other categories, the experience tended to end with the same feeling of drifting about in a murky twilight zone, which promptly faded out before any "transcendent elements" of the experience had an opportunity to make their appearance. While the results were still considered inconclusive, Ring did suggest a possible modification of his original hypothesis, as the suicide-induced NDEs had the appearance of being aborted or truncated.

This revised view has been supported in part by Dr. Raymond Moody is his sequel volume, *Reflections on Life After Life*. Dr. Moody had only a few cases of suicide-induced NDEs, but in each case the NDE was characterized as being unpleasant. Dr. Moody went on to note that subjects experiencing NDEs that were caused by illness or accident returned to report that suicide was a very undesirable act that might incur a penalty. This "penalty" for an act of suicide might include witnessing the suffering on the part of others that this act would cause. In addition, those subjects whose NDE was caused by a suicide attempt agreed that their suicidal attempts solved nothing, and strongly disavowed suicide as a means of returning to the afterlife state. All noted after their experiences that they would not consider suicide again.

The existence of some sort of "limbo" state is described by several people who had attempted suicide. The penalty for such an act appeared to be that the victim would be in a dark, dreary limbo state for a very long time. Annabel Chaplin, writing in *The Bright Light of Death,* describes this "Land of Despair" in some detail. While Ms. Chaplin gathered her information in the "midst of a session of mental imagery," her description nevertheless closely dovetails with descriptions from NDE subjects who had attempted suicide.

According to Ms. Chaplin, the next stop for suicides is an alien and strange place enveloped by a dull, heavy foreboding. Victims resided in the still air, completely bent over with their heads buried in mud and covered with dark shrouds. There was no communication with the victims immersed in their own bleak world of gloom who were unaware of anything but their self-imposed misery. New arrivals were powerless to reverse their descent to the awful place even as they recognized their fate and struggled against it. Ms. Chaplin's only cause for hope was that the souls who had repented "long enough" would fulfill their need for self-punishment and could eventually find their way back to the light.

Suicide is condemned by most philosophies. The act is invariably viewed as the worst of crimes with the severest of penalties. Tales of special places in purgatory for suicides have ranged from Dante's *Inferno* to modern science fiction by writer Larry Niven. Richard Bach, in *The Bridge Across Forever*, gives the contemporary view that suicide is simply uncreative and that anyone desperate enough to attempt suicide should be desperate enough to go to some rather creative extremes to solve their problems.

The alleged penalty for suicide raises a host of questions. What happens, for example, to Japanese samurai who commit hara-kiri? Viewed as a matter of honor instead of an attempt to escape hardship, hara-kiri appears less objectionable. But what of Western man who smokes, overindulges in alcohol (and/ or drugs), or even eats and drinks foods with high levels of caffeine? Knowing that such things are deadly or at least unhealthy, is the Westerner any less suicidal? Are "heroic" deaths or accident-prone individuals with a subconscious wish to kill themselves exempt from suicide-related penalties? What about attention-grabbing "mock suicides" that go too far?

The question of suicide resulting in penalties (imposed by the self or others) is unanswerable. Clearly, there is a deep-seated aversion to it from virtually all philosophies, but this does not, in and of itself, guarantee that a penalty will result from an act of suicide. On the other hand, there seems to be little or no justification or motivation to commit suicide. From the viewpoint of reincarnation and karma, one would simply have to return and get it right on the next try. At the same time, perhaps, it might also be necessary to reduce any karma resulting from the suicide itself.

In summary, suicide appears to have no advantages and, potentially, some rather severe disadvantages. It can never be recommended.

After the NDE

The aftereffects on those who experienced near-death experiences were invariably profound. Frequently subjects felt a deep shift toward experiencing life in a more positive way, especially with regard to people and nature. Returnees reported a greater sense of love, an increased thirst for knowledge, and an enhanced need to adequately develop their gifts and talents. Invariably they had lost all fear of death, a condition that continued throughout their lives.

Subjects became convinced of life after death, including a belief in both heaven and hell. Belief in God, or some supreme power for good, as well as a conviction that some force for evil also exists, was also increased. Interestingly, many reported that they did not believe in God as taught by the traditional, Western religions any longer, and many now believe in reincarnation. Researchers have noted a significant shift away from the theological doctrines of established religions to a more spiritual ideology in NDE returnees. Subjects often tended to become less dependent on the religious interpretations of the church and more contemplative and private in their beliefs. At the same time the subjects became more tolerant of existing religions.

Almost without exception, the person undergoing the near-death experience is a completely changed person afterward. All of the day-to-day worries and concerns they had been living with suddenly seemed relatively unimportant. There is a sense of more importance being ascribed to getting along with people, helping others, and being a loving kind of person. Suddenly the Golden Rule seems quite appropriate to their lives.

The aftereffects of negative near-death experiences are not noticeably different from positive NDEs. Subjects often feel as if they have been given a second chance to "change their ways." People attempting suicide all agreed on one point: They felt their suicidal attempts solved nothing. The implication was that "If you leave here a tormented soul, you will be a tormented soul over there, too." Not only did the problems that predicated the suicide attempt persist, but once in the disembodied state, the subjects were unable to do anything about it.

Paranormal Aftereffects

One of the more striking and controversial aftereffects of near-death experiences is the apparent endowment of the NDE returnee with certain inexplicable talents. These talents include alleged extrasensory perception and healing capabilities the individuals were not aware of possessing prior to the NDE.

The ESP capability appears to manifest itself in one of two ways. In the first type, the information gleaned from the life review sometimes includes images or visions of the future, and thus allows the recipient to have knowledge of future events. In the second type, the NDE itself appears to be the incident responsible for triggering some mechanism whereby the subject begins to experience ESP capabilities. These latter capabilities include telepathy, precognition, telekinesis, and such ancillary talents as automatic writing. The significance of these aftereffects are not easily dismissed.

Are They Crazy?

Is it possible to dismiss the reports of NDEs as the ravings of a bunch of lunatics? There is a certain amount of appeal to this point of view, but the more likely answer is no. Gabbard and Twemlow, in their book *With the Eyes of the Mind, An Empirical Analysis of Out-of-Body States*, have investigated the possibility using a PAL test. Their results do not allow an easy out.

Gabbard and Twemlow's testing method, the PAL, refers to a psychological questionnaire termed "Profiles of Adaptation to Life." The PAL is designed to assess the mental health of populations who are not necessarily identified as patients and who have not had circumscribed treatment experiences. Using the PAL as a measure, Gabbard and Twemlow found that as a group, the NDE subjects were significantly healthier than psychiatric inpatients and/or outpatients and somewhat healthier than college students. Overall, the NDE group represented a very close approximation of the "average healthy American," with few significant differences between the NDE group and two groups of medical professionals. (Of course, saying that the NDE group was no crazier than a group of psychiatrists is not necessarily a positive indicator of mental health.)

Corroboration

Many subjects see nurses, doctors, and sometimes relatives or friends frantically working over the body in an effort to "save the life," and often from the perspective of above and detached from the body. In a woman's case reported by Moody, the woman saw the back of the nurse's head, and even went so far as to comment on the nurse's hairdo. Often the subjects are all too aware of all the happenings in the room and can describe them in detail after their revival.

Moody has pointed out that subject's description of events from their out-of-body perspective tended to agree with actual events. Several doctors have indicated that they were utterly baffled at the detail and accuracy that patients with no prior medical knowledge were able to provide about their own resuscitation attempts–attempts made when the doctors believed the patient to be dead. Dr. Michael Sabom, in researching the evidence for *Recollections of Death*, took special care to examine independent corroborative evidence for the visual and auditory perceptions reported by near-death survivors when allegedly out of their bodies. His research data strongly supports the claims made by his subjects!

Another form of corroboration is the fact that the NDEs and their descriptions of the afterlife have numerous parallels in ancient writings from diverse civilizations, cultures, and eras. These parallels include biblical passages as well as statements by Plato and others. Swedish-born Emanuel Swedenborg was giving vivid descriptions of the afterlife in the early 1700s.

Of particular interest in this regard is *The Tibetan Book of the Dead*. This work was compiled from master teachings over many centuries in prehistoric Tibet, passed down orally through many generations, and finally written down around the eighth century A.D. The book is essentially a guide for the dying and was read or related to a dying person as a means of telling them what to expect in death and what might be expected of them. As such it has detailed descriptions of the various stages of what would now be called the near-death experience. Dr. Raymond Moody, for one, found the correlations between the early stages described in *The Tibetan Book of the Dead* and the reports of his NDE subjects as nothing less than fantastic.

Wishful Thinking?

Naturally, religious beliefs or a desire to find heaven may be the cause of such heartening, light-filled visions, but not all experience the same envelopment of love and light. Many survivors have found themselves to be mostly bewildered, with no sense of what to do next. Many sense the brilliant white light only at the end of a long tunnel, and may be hesitant to venture into the tunnel. Yet if there is any advice to be given to the dying based on the mass of data accumulated so far, it would be: *Go to the white light!*

Perhaps these experiences are nothing more than an example of what Dr. Jan Ehrenwald refers to as "man's quest for immortality." This is a possibility, but can such a relatively simple explanation account for:

1. The sense of the soul leaving the body and floating up and viewing everything from a vantage point;

2. The awareness while "clinically dead" of all the events surrounding the body;

3. The consistency of stories of the souls' ability to move through objects, and the ability to immediately do whatever is thought;

4. The feelings of peace and light;

5. The unconcern for the dying body, and the sense of objectivity when they ask, "Why are they are trying so hard to revive it?";

6. The instant replay of the past life;

7. The abrupt returns to the body, when the "crisis" is apparently over;

8. The reluctance to return to earth; and

9. The after effects, when the subjects realize their immortality, lose their fear of death, find their subsequent lives changed toward love and peace, and when suddenly they begin to wonder about the ancient wisdom of celebrating death and mourning birth?

Probably not.

Medical Explanations

Many subjects have a sense of relief, a sense of complete love and joy, and a feeling of contentment the intensity of which they have never before experienced. Many times these people who have a near-death experience are in enormous pain before they pull out of their body. The relief from the pain and agony is often one of the first things the subjects sense.

It is this sense of relief from pain that many doubters of these stories point out when questioning the reality of these experiences. Could this not be a trick of the brain to shut out the pain? Certainly there is considerable evidence to show that the brain is capable of just such feats.

Several knowledgeable investigators have considered the many alternative explanations for the elements of an NDE. Virtually without exception, those researchers who have considered a broad spectrum of alternatives to the reality of NDEs have concluded that current attempts at explaining an NDE by psychological, pharmacological, physiological, paranormal, or other possible explanations are doomed to failure.

This failure to arrive at a more "traditional" explanation of NDEs may be, in part, due to the difficulty of the problem. Michael Grosso, in his article "Toward an Explanation of Near-Death Phenomena," notes that three aspects of NDEs require explanation: (1) the consistency and universality of the reported experiences, (2) the paranormal effects, and (3) the resulting changes in attitudes and behavior. From Dr. Grosso's viewpoint it is the paranormal component that eliminates the idea of the NDE being merely an illusion. Moreover, as paranormal phenomena become more explainable, NDEs and the survival hypothesis becomes more intrinsically plausible.

Dr. Grosso goes on to point out that because NDEs are not publicly verifiable, science cannot consider them as direct evidence for the survival hypothesis. Nevertheless, there must be a critical point when the mass of accumulated and noncontradictory data must form a special consensus. Dr. Grosso goes on to suggest that it is possible that those people experiencing death may, in fact, know more about the subject than all the researchers combined!

The possibility that a patient knows considerably more about his experiences than his doctor could be thought of as a rather radical suggestion. But many knowledgeable people are beginning to suspect that patients may, in fact, have better answers than the medical professionals to whom they are paying so much. If this is true, then it would appear that the massive volume of data concerning NDEs may have reached the "critical point." The reality of the core experience must now be considered, at the very least, as the more reasonable and probable hypothesis.

Deathbed Experiences

In addition to near-death experiences, there is also mounting evidence of an afterlife and other extraordinary events, from what is termed "deathbed experiences." NDEs are reports by those persons who have, through illness or accident, nearly died or who clinically died and were revived, while deathbed experiences are reports and observations by medical people and others of what a dying person reports in the moments before the final death of the physical body. Often these latter reports include visions by the dying of deceased loved ones, religious figures, and afterlife scenes.

In 1961, Dr. Karlis Osis published a lengthy monograph entitled *Deathbed Observations by Physicians and Nurses*. The book was based on his request for the experiences of 10,000 American physicians and nurses. In analyzing the detailed reports of 640 cases, in which many of these professionals had witnessed their patients' reactions to and reports of unseen deathbed visitors, Dr. Osis drew these major conclusions:

1. The dying often go into inexplicable exaltation before death.

2. The dying see visions or apparitions to a much greater extent than people who are not approaching death.

3. Apparitions are usually of deceased persons, or in relatively fewer cases, of living or religious persons.

4. Drugs or other aspects of illnesses seemingly do not account for the visions.

5. Many of the dying intuitively realize that the apparition is coming to take them into death and on to a continued existence.

In 1977, Dr. Osis and a colleague, Dr. Erlendur Heraldsson, published *At the Hour of Death*, a book extending the original work by Dr. Osis to include another thousand experiences. This work included experiences of people dying in India as well as the United States. The deathbed visions were nevertheless similar despite the significant racial, cultural, and religious differences between the two countries. Both reports of Dr. Osis' work have been found to correlate with pioneering work done over a period of thirty years and reported in several publications by Dr. Robert Crookall of England.

Dying

The Tibetan Book of the Dead teaches, among other things, the art of dying. According to this ancient and revered book, the dying should approach death with a calm, clear-minded, even heroic attitude, and with a rightly trained and directed intellect, mentally transcending, as necessary, bodily suffering and problems. Many people now believe the modern-day practices in the U.S. involving extraordinary efforts to keep someone alive *unnecessarily and detrimentally interfere with the death process!* Dr. Elizabeth Kübler-Ross has suggested that with all of our knowledge of science and our emancipation, we should have available better means to prepare people and their families for the inevitable. She feels that it would once again be appropriate for a person to die in the peace and dignity of their own home.

In Margot Grey's view, dying has become more gruesome simply because it has become more mechanical. W. Y. Evans-Wentz, in his work *The Tibetan Book of the Dead*, argues that dying in a hospital, often under the mind-numbing influence of some tranquilizer or controlled by the stimulation caused by some life-prolonging drug, cannot yield a very undesirable death. He considers such cases as hardly better than a shell-shocked soldier dying on a battlefield.

Lest, however, we think to lay blame on the doorstep of the medical community for an "undesirable death," we should consider one other aspect of the deathbed experience that also ties in with the near-death experience. The reason a soul may return from the afterlife (a reason that is based more on a belief structure than on documentable facts) is that other people on earth are pleading for their return. The prayers, energy, and sorrow of the people urging their revival is thought by many to be a powerful force that can pull the dying back from the brink.

Dr. Moody, in *Life After Life*, has reported on one case history wherein a family was praying for an elderly aunt to regain her health. The aunt stopped breathing several times, but in each case the medical teams were able to bring her back. Then, on one fateful day, the aunt turned to her niece and explained that she had been to the afterlife, found it beautiful and joyous, and wanted to stay. But she couldn't stay as long as her family kept praying for her to stay with them. From the aunt's viewpoint, the prayers were keeping her alive. She then asked that everyone quit praying for her. When they stopped, the aunt died shortly thereafter.

One might begin to wonder if the prayers and hopes for life are always in the dying person's best interests.

Summary

The evidence for the reality of near-death experiences makes them one of the most documented and substantiated phenomena in reincarnation theory. The breath and depth of the research allows us a reasonable confidence that NDEs are a common, if not fundamental, aspect of reality. The general inability of other hypotheses to adequately explain the voluminous data on NDEs tends to place the burden of proof on those who find it difficult to accept at face value the reports by near-death survivors.

Clearly the near-death experiences provide a strong argument for life after death. Deathbed experiences add additional fuel to the fire (so to speak), and the birth experiences discussed in the previous chapter provide an indirect confirmation of NDEs' description of the afterlife. By the same token, nothing in the descriptions of birth experiences in any way contradicts the reports of near-death and deathbed experiences. Together, all three forms of "data collection" agree with one another and provide us with a better understanding of what might be occurring on the other side.

There are obviously some holes or spaces in our description of the afterlife. The near-death experiences take us into the beyond from one direction, while the descriptions of birth experiences allow us to glimpse the afterlife from the other end. An important question is what happens between the time of dying and the subsequent(?) process of being born. This subject will be discussed in Chapter 8. At this point in the narrative, we need only consider the effect of the death-related experiences on our developing theory of reincarnation.

Reincarnation and Karma

With regard to basic reincarnation theory, NDEs and deathbed experiences serve mainly to provide details of the dying process. These death-related experiences do not provide a great deal of evidence of reincarnation. They merely imply a life after death (as reincarnation does) but only marginally hint at the possibility of a return. While some subjects returned from a near-death experience with a newfound belief in reincarnation, there is otherwise no real evidence or descriptions of the process of reincarnation in all of the reports from people near death.

The instantaneous life review encountered in the near-death experience appears to correlate with one aspect of karma in that one is at least called to answer for their actions in their past life. However, with the possible exception of suicide and negative NDEs, there is no implication of punishment or a need to somehow make up for past misdeeds. Karma appears rather ineffectual in the afterlife if we are limited to a life review and nothing else. For karma to be a reality, it continues to require new and different incarnations.

The possible penalties for suicide and the possibility of hellish or near-hellish accommodations in the afterlife for a few members of the dying corps have less to do with traditional views of karma and correspond more closely to traditional Western views of reward and punishment for a single life. Negative NDEs tend to negate reincarnation unless one believes that all hell and purgatory descriptions are of a temporary nature. If these bad experiences are viewed as simply an additional learning time for souls having trouble with life on earth, then reincarnation continues unscathed. But if the suicide victims and those who would have had a negative NDE if they had survived find themselves trapped in hellish or near-hellish environments for essentially all time, then reincarnation would appear to have an important exception. However, the evidence for either of these two possibilities does not now seem to exist.

In other words, you may be wise to begin understanding the art of dying, but you don't necessarily have to concern yourself with the possibility of returning and having to be a teenager all over again.

Chapter 8:

Activities on the

Other Side

Mike was, for the most part, a nice fellow. As a teenager he had had a pronounced tendency to drive his small pickup truck a lot faster than the police department liked, he had broken more than one young lady's heart, and he had gotten into more than a few scrapes. Still, he was not a bad kid. No one had ever urged his arrest, and he had never broken a law–at least not one that was serious enough for anyone to get excited about.

Mike had struggled through four-and-a-half years of college, whereupon he ended up with a bachelor's degree, a C-plus average, and a look of complete relief from his now-destitute parents. Within a few years he married a college sweetheart and promptly began working on a small family. Then, after twelve years of marriage, Mike met someone very special, someone he doubted he could live without. Before very long, he had decided not to tempt fate, divorced his first wife, and quickly married his new, very special love.

Mike tried to continue to be a good father to his two children who were still living with his ex-wife, but it was difficult. She was anything but sympathetic, and after a few years of periodic fatherhood, Mike had just about given up. Then his life became suddenly less complicated–Mike died.

The accident had not been his fault, at least from a legal point of view. One could point out that had he not had those beers the night before, his alertness at the time of the accident might have been sufficient to avert the disaster. However, his reflexes had been just a trifle slow, and the resulting collision turned out to be his last.

When his sports car crashed into the side of the van, Mike felt, in short sequence, panic, pain, and then tranquility and peace. From just above the wreckage of his automobile, he viewed with total detachment his bloodied physical body. He wondered briefly why everyone seemed to be so disturbed as they ran to help free his body from the wreckage–Mike felt just fine.

Then Mike sensed something very strange. Drifting easily above the collision, Mike became aware of a brilliant light. He gazed at its dazzling intensity without any discomfort. Then he began to move rapidly toward the light. His movement was only vaguely voluntary, but the goal seemed more than appropriate and he had no hesitation.

As the light grew brighter, Mike became aware of someone else. Just as his mind briefly inquired of the new arrival, he immediately sensed that it was his grandfather. As a boy, Mike had dearly loved his grandfather. The older man had died of cancer just five years before Mike's own death. A strong sense of loving welcome encircled Mike as he felt his grandfather's influence.

The light began to envelop both of them in brilliance and warmth. An unearthly bliss combined with a sense of permeating love as Mike began to sense a cosmic awareness of his place in the universe. Awareness of other planes of existence, of evolved entities, and a dynamic universe came easily to him. Questions were answered as quickly as they entered his mind. Mike had always wondered about the ethics of abortion–suddenly he understood completely.

Around him Mike sensed a beautifully green countryside full of colorful flowers and vibrant if not stately oak trees. It was everything Mike had ever associated with peace and tranquility. Even the sound of a bubbling brook contributed to the idyllic setting. Mike felt that he had at last returned home.

Then Mike felt the presence of other beings, beings that fairly radiated love and understanding. One of them, gently and with reassurance and encouragement, asked, "So tell us Mike, what all did you accomplish this time?" Instantly, all the myriad events of his life began to flash through Mike's mind. The paranoramic review brought him a vision of every significant detail of his life along with the emotions and feelings associated with each step. He briefly felt the worry of his parents about his fast driving. He felt their concerns as they struggled to pay his tuition year after year.

Mike felt the happiness of his ex-wife as they married in complete detail. He also experienced her bitterness when she realized the determination in his decision to leave her. The hurt increased as Mike sensed his children's self-adjudged guilt at what they perceived as their fault in causing their father to leave their mother. Mike was ruthless in his own self-judgment of his faults and failures and his lack of making a few more efforts to help his children understand. Mike even sensed in intimate detail his ex-wife's difficulties as a single parent, and then he accused himself of the cause.

Even as he judged himself, Mike sensed a loving forgiveness from the beings around him. They seemed to understand every aspect of his life and, with gentle probing questions, gave Mike a better understanding of the ramifications of each separate event. Overall, his life had not been unsuccessful. There had been times of charity and love as well as their lack and, briefly, he sensed each of them. His faults and good deeds all joined to allow him to see that on balance it had been a good life.

Mike also remembered that it had been the decision of his children, prior to their births, to be born of his seed and then to possibly lose their father first from divorce and then from death. Mike recalled as well his own planning and remembered that one of his challenges in his most recent past life had been to resolve a longstanding problem with his ex-wife–a challenge that he had not managed to meet. Mike also knew that his new love had chosen her possible fates as well.

With the beings as his guides, Mike began to plan for yet another life. He consulted "temples of wisdom," communicated with his guides as to their suggestions and offered directions, thought of others who might incur vested interests in his next incarnation, and when his ex-wife had likewise joined him in his afterlife state, planned with her yet another life where they would both try once again to resolve their earthly differences. Eventually even his children and grandfather joined with him to plan another time when they could live together in new relationships.

The time and place of their next incarnation would be a very different one from the one before, but all of them looked forward to the new challenges. Throughout the planning, each of their souls comprehended their place, their goals, and their future growth. With their combined plans laid in general outline, Mike once again partook of a memory-erasing nourishment and entered into the fetus of a woman Mike had known before in many lifetimes. When he was born, his new mother named him Chang.

The general ingredients of this fictional account, particularly those between Mike's death and his reincarnation as Chang, coincide with ancient and current beliefs concerning the space between lives. Some of these ingredients we have already encountered in birth experiences, while other aspects have been suggested by near-death experiences. Other elements of the story derive their genesis from ancient writings and modern-day hypnotic regressions. It is the purpose of this chapter to discuss these latter sources and to describe what might be termed "the activities on the other side" (but not necessarily those activities on the other side of the tracks–those we already know about!).

Ancient Beliefs

An intriguing aspect of research into both birth and near-death experiences is the consistency between these reports and ancient beliefs. The ancient Egyptians, for example, conceived of *amenthe,* a place where souls lived in pleasure while they awaited their next incarnation. Confident of their beliefs, the Egyptians built lavish tombs while living in relatively meager houses. For their use in *amenthe*, they took with them to the grave clothing, weapons, cooking utensils, and other treasures for which they might have retained a craving during their earthly life. The logic of these people is apparent when one considers the length of time on earth and the anticipated time in the hereafter.

The Egyptian Book of the Dead, correctly entitled, is "the coming forth from day" and refers to the sacred Egyptian art of proceeding from this life into another life. The book inculcates an art of dying and coming forth into a new life in a symbolic and esoterically profound manner.

Predating the ancient Egyptians, the Sumerians, who built the world's first historical civilization in the Tigris-Euphrates valley, went so far as to kill (usually by poison) and bury the deceased master's household in the master's grave. It was intended that servants and family members be available in the event the master needed them in the life after death. However, in the case of royalty and other high-ranking officials, look-alike proxies might go to the grave in lieu of children and wives. Apparently "rank has its privileges" had meaning even in that early time.

Australian Aborigines believed that souls resided in Anjea between incarnations. Okinawans conceived of *gusho*, while the ancient Hebrews told of *pardish*, where they awaited the next life before they returned. According to the Hebrews' *Zohar*, these souls returned to earth "sorrowing in exile; to a place where there is no true happiness." To these ancient people the earth was exile, while *pardish* was the true home of man.

The Bardo

In *The Tibetan Book of the Dead*, the *Bardo Thodol*, we have an eighth-century description of the space between lives. "Bardo," literally translated, refers to a space that separates islands. In *The Tibetan Book of the Dead*, it is thought of as the state of existence between incarnations. Furthermore, the Tibetans believe that by reciting the book to the dying and the deceased, there was hope that the soul could find its way in the Bardo and in some cases avoid the necessity of rebirth.

It is in this Bardo where the soul of the deceased is believed to spend a symbolic forty-nine days enveloped in a brilliant "clear light," and during which the soul experiences an intense review of its past life. It is in this review that the soul sees every effect of its good and evil acts on the soul's karma. The *Bardo Thodol* also points out that in the life between incarnations, since you no longer have a physical body, no sounds, colors, and other occuring events can harm you (i.e. you cannot die). This constitutes the Bardo state.

The text of *The Tibetan Book of the Dead* contains three parts. The *Chikhai Bardo* describes the psychic happenings at the moment of death. The *Choenyid Bardo* deals with the dream-state that supervenes immediately after death and with what are called "karmic illusions." The third part is the *Sidpa Bardo,* which concerns itself with the onset of the birth instinct and prenatal events. It is a characteristic of the *Bardo Thodol* that supreme insight and illumination, and hence the greatest prospect of attaining liberation from a karmic "wheel of life," are vouchsafed during the actual process of dying. Soon afterward, according to the text, the "illusions" that eventually lead to reincarnation begin, the light grows dimmer and more varied, and the visions become all the more terrifying.

In Plato's tenth book of *The Republic*, the strange story is told of Er the Pamphylian. Er, as he was known to his friends, had been a Greek soldier at a battle where many of his comrades had been killed. When Er had also apparently died in battle, his countrymen had collected Er's body along with other fallen war dead and laid his body on a funeral pyre to be burned. Before the pyre was lit, Er revived (causing considerable surprise among his fellow soldiers) and began to describe his journey to a realm beyond.

Er told of his soul leaving his body, joining with other spirits, and proceeding through "openings" or "passageways" into the realms of the afterlife. He described the between-life or Bardo state in terms of timelessness, brilliant and warming light, reviews of past lives, and the existence of wise judges or advisors who oversaw such reviews. Er was not judged himself, but was told that he must return in order to inform the physical world what the other world was like. Er also described each soul selecting the form of its next incarnation and then drinking from the "River of Forgetfulness" in order to erase all conscious memories before reentering a physical body.

The various ancient descriptions of the Bardo, that life between lives, regardless of their source or culture, tend to repeat over and over again the same themes, the same events, and the same expectations. Noteworthy events in one tradition or teaching invariably crop up in other traditions, with differences only in name and terminology. Even more astounding is the fact that "evidence" and information accumulating today continue to repeat the same patterns. In addition to birth and near-death experiences, reports from past-life regressions provide a massive amount of documentation to support the wisdom of the ancients.

Past-Life Regressions

Instead of hypnotically regressing a patient or subject to the early part of his life or childhood (in an effort to discover a hidden trauma manifesting itself in the present), it has become rather commonplace to regress a subject into a past life as well. Such regressions were undertaken initially for the same therapeutic purposes as the more traditional regressions. However, the number of patients who have found the causes of their current problems stemming from what is apparently an event in a past life has led many psychologists and therapists to accept the technique of past-life regression therapy as a valid means of helping their patients.

This does not necessarily imply that the therapist believes in reincarnation, but that rapid and dramatic healing often result from bringing to the patient's conscious awareness what are apparently traumatic past-life memories. A multitude of serious mental and/or physical problems have virtually vanished as the patient has begun to understand the cause.

The fact that past-life regression therapy works as therapy is, of course, the great appeal of the method. As John Langdon-Davies has noted in his work *Man: Known and Unknown*, the great advantage of medicine over other branches of knowledge is that the only criterion of truth is that it works. At the same time, it must be noted that the thousands of cases of recoveries from serious disorders resulting from regressions into past lives does not constitute objective proof that the patients have in fact experienced a previous incarnation.

Dr. Edith Fiori is one of several psychologists who has discovered the efficacy of past-life regressions. Over a period of fifteen years, she has performed well over 20,000 past-life regressions. The patterns she has observed fit hand-in-glove with what others have learned from near-death experiences; there are just no inconsistencies. By taking thousands of subjects through their death experiences in their past lives, Dr. Fiori has consistently found the same events, feelings, and wonder that have been reported in near-death experiences.

These findings tend to be echoed by other therapists using past-life regressions as a technique. Remarkable cases of mental and physical healings have been reported by past-life therapists such as Dr. Helen Wambach, Dr. Morris Netherton, England's Joe Keeton, and others. All of these professionals have identified a "higher self," that transcends lifetimes and exerts influence in our daily thinking and behavior. Furthermore, this higher self maintains a more intense awareness of reality and the purpose of human existence.

In Dr. Wambach's *Reliving Past Lives*, for example, we learn of thousands of subjects undergoing regression who have gone through the death experience, reviewed their immediate past lives, gone to "temples of wisdom" to study and plan their next incarnation, spent time with their "guides," and chose the parameters of their next birth. In each case the higher self was dependent upon the earth experience for evolution and growth. Some proponents have gone so far as to note that apparently there is a big backlog of souls waiting patiently in line for their next opportunity to come to earth.

Dr. Joel L. Whitton, professor of psychiatry at the University of Toronto Medical School, has gone one step further and taken his subjects under deep hypnosis directly into the state of existence between lives. Because of the low percentage of subjects who are capable of entering a deep hypnotic trance (four to ten percent of the population, according to Dr. Whitton), he has been able to report on only thirty cases. This constitutes a relatively small number of cases and casts doubts on any possible statistical significance. Nevertheless, his reports have been internally consistent as well as consistent with the reports of other researchers and have provided us with additional and more complete information.

According to Dr. Whitton (in his book with Joe Fisher entitled *Life Between Life*), life after death is the same as life before death, and souls do in fact enter the space between lives as disembodied spirits. In fact, we are just as familiar with the state we have left behind as we are with the physical world in which we now find ourselves. Death is thus just the threshold between two forms of consciousness.

This clear verification of reincarnation as a fundamental by Dr. Whitton's subjects is noteworthy in that many of the subjects had religious backgrounds and initial prejudices against reincarnation, but these prior opinions were quickly dissipated. In addition, the space between lives appeared to these subjects as a place to evalute one's recent life on earth and then to plan the next, according to karmic requirements.

Activities Between Incarnations

If we were to attempt an agenda for a soul's activities in the Bardo, both the ancient and modern teachings would probably lead us to the following scenario upon death:

1. The progression to the discarnate existence through specific paths, with the choice of path dependent upon the soul's personal perception of what death is expected to be. Beliefs in various paths range from the "ferryman" who will ferry the soul across the River of Death for the price of a gold coin (please have the correct change ready), to the more secular version, common in today's views, of a tunnel-like conveyance leading from the earthly existence to the afterworld. Many of the variations include the deceased being met by friends, relatives, and other familiar souls, who have come to light the way–"and a host to greet you."

2. The presence of a nearby or more distant light, one beckoning the soul to approach it, and with the soul approaching the light, the sense of over-whelming envelopment in the brilliant light. Such light is often intense to the point of blinding, but never is it painful or capable of causing discomfort.

3. The release of pain and concerns for the world left behind. The intense feeling of unearthly bliss, a sense of all-permeating love, and an almost cosmic awareness of one's place in the universal scheme of things preside. Enlighten-ment is also present in many cases, and specific realizations or instant percep-tions may result from a soul's lifelong interests. Souls with preconceived ideas about the afterlife are sometimes rewarded in kind.

4. The necessity of the soul in the Bardo state to maintain its own sense of individuality. Descartes's statement, "I think, therefore I am" seems particu-larly appropriate, for without the soul's thoughts, there can be no experience of their existence. In *Life Between Life*, Whitton and Fisher reported that the amount of self-consciousness exhibited in the Bardo appeared to vary between individuals. Those eager to proceed vigorously with their spiritual develop-ment were more consciously active between incarnations. Those somewhat more bored with the evolutionary process were inclined to "sleep" for what would amount to large portions of earthbound time.

5. The appearance of the afterlife much in accord with the soul's expecta-tions. In effect, the contents of the soul's mind produces its own surroundings.

6. A detailed and *very* complete reliving of one's immediate past life. This "instant replay" appears to be more intense than a simple remembering of past events and is often accompanied with a greater understanding of how the events affect all other aspects of the previous life. Included with the review is an acute sense of self-judgment, as the soul critically evaluates the entirety of its past life.

7. The presence of others (wise men, advisors, judges, and others) who

either challenge or gently prod the recently arrived soul with questions of karma, good and evil acts done in life, and expectations of further lives to come. Many cultures and traditions think in terms of stern and uncompromising judges "weighing the soul" and possibily finding it wanting. Modern views tend to support the idea of judges acting in a less authoritarian manner, and more in terms of offering reassurance and encouragement. In fact, the judges tend to be more healers than anything else, fairly radiating understanding and a sense of caring.

8. The existence, in many cases, of temples of wisdom or learning, where further assessments of past lives and planning for future incarnations can be accomplished. There is a sense of choosing what the soul needs rather than what it wants. Or in one woman's view: "We have to be given obstacles in order to overcome those obstacles–to become stronger, more aware, more evolved, and more responsible." Other reports note that planning for the next incarnation is often done with other souls, with whom significant relationships have been established over many prior lifetimes.

9. The soul's ability to perceive its purpose in its many incarnations, gain detailed knowledge of its past lives, and determine the needs for further growth. Whitton and Fisher have noted, for example, that challenge is the price of advancement, as well as the reason why incarnations become progressively tougher as the soul evolves.

10. The specific decision by the soul (with perhaps the encouragement of guides and others) to reincarnate in a particular life for karmic and other purposes. Such planning might involve a specific soulmate, a detailed blueprint of the coming life, a more general outline, or the life might be just left to improvisation depending upon the maturity of the evolved soul. Furthermore, the planning can include more than one future life.

11. The partaking of some nourishment, resulting in the loss of all conscious memory of the Bardo and the past lives of the soul. Many believe that this amnesia is essential to prevent pining for the Bardo left behind and to remove possible confusion between past lives and the present one.

12. The opportunity for the soul to evade the tempting offer of the memory erasing nourishment. In this case, however, incarnated souls may, in a current lifetime, impose an amnesia upon themselves in order to avoid impairing the planned karmic events and purposes of the life.

13. To some degree, the presence of a knowledge of the Bardo and the soul's past lives continuing to reside in the subconscious memories of our incarnations. Furthermore, the belief that "guides" from the Bardo are available to help the souls in their present incarnation is also prevalent in many traditions and reported opinions.

Guides and Free Will

The idea of a soul receiving help and comfort from "guides" is found in a wide variety of traditions. For example, the very concept of guardian angels, patron saints, and the intercession of saints (a concept built into the canon of the Catholic Mass), all relate to this same belief. But just because *your* guides have taken an extended vacation at a heavenly spa for the terminally discouraged does not mean that they do not exist!

Incorporated with the belief in the existence of guides available to each and every soul is the concept that such help will not arrive unbidden. The sense is that help is available, but must be requested. If such requests (be they prayers, meditations, or demands) are made sincerely and often, results will follow. In effect, you get what you ask for, even if your requests may not be in your best interests. This latter point is important in that it very strongly implies free will, including the free choice of messing things up rather thoroughly.

Free will also surfaces in the fact that wishes and desires not specifically requested of a soul's guides will not arrive by virtue of anything the guides do. In other words, if the soul effectively maintains that "I'd rather do it myself!", the guides will definitely not interfere. For the guides to "inflict" help on some soul who does not request it would be to diminish that soul's free will to make its own choices for good or bad.

There is perhaps a great deal for all of us to learn from this wisdom of the guides. For example, praying for another to receive justice might turn out to be counterproductive, to say the least. While proponents of these ideas of guides, free will, and no help without request feel that it is proper to send unconditional love (unbidden) to another, they strongly believe that "gifts" of any other help infringe upon and often damage the integrity of those for whom prayers are being offered.

Planes of Existence

So what happens after you have evolved to a certain degree of perfection? Based on the correlation of the results from an impressive variety of sources, including past-life regressions, there are plenty of other existences to contemplate. The main difficulty seems to be in what to call them. Table 1 gives four versions.

Triune[1]	Theosophy[2]	George Meek[3]	Metaphsics[4]
Logoic	Mahaparanirvanic	Causal	Christ Consciousness
Monadic	Paranirvanic	Causal	Causal
Atmic	Nirvanic	Mental	Mental
Buddhic	Buddhic	Highest Astral	Highest Astral
Manasic	Mental	Middle Astral	Lower Astral
Astral	Astral	Lowest Astral	Emotional
Physical	Physical	Physical	Consciousness

[1] Triune Foundation's *The Rainbow Bridge.*
[2] C. W. Leadbeater's *Man Visible and Invisible.*
[3] George W. Meek's *After We Die, What Then?*
[4] School of Metaphysics, Windyville, Missouri.

The theory is that mineral and vegetable life is confined to the physical (or earth) plane of existence. This is also the only level where physical sense perceptions can operate. On the other hand, an animal may actually reach the astral plane (or lowest astral or emotional plane). A human personality is capable of reaching the third level without an accompanying loss of its sense of individuality. The spiritual being or soul, however, can reach to the fifth level, which is, in essence, heaven. Beyond that lie still higher planes. Meek, for example, describes the higher planes as:

8- Cosmic or Universal Sphere of At-One-Ment, the Godhead, and other
   levels of reality
9- End of Manifest Creation (Vibratory)
10- The Void, or Pure Consciousness (Nonvibratory)
11- Nirvana and other states of consciousness

How can we comprehend the higher levels? Actually we can't. But as a soul rises in these planes of existence, it can lose the ties that bind it to the physical plane and thereafter exist in higher planes. Supposedly then, this advanced soul can travel even further upward in the planes of existence until it can begin to understand, or at least describe, the essence of the still higher planes. The truly advanced soul may even, at some high level, begin to understand where lost socks go. Unfortunately, for such seekers of lost socks, that same advanced soul cannot come back and interact with those still on the earth (or physical) plane, but must interact only in an intermediate plane. Communications from the higher planes is, therefore, sort of a "bucket brigade" where word is passed from plane to plane with its subsequent loss in intelligible communication (which may explain why the mystery of lost socks is still with us).

Finally, many believe that after a while the advanced soul reaches the point where it is so close to a godlike energy level (with the same degree of perfection), that it can no longer reach even the intermediate planes (and where it no longer even cares about socks). What it does then is anybody's guess. As Greek philosopher Plotinus wrote: "The infinite can only be apprehended by a faculty superior to reason, by entering into a state from which the finite self must withdraw." Thus any knowledge of these planes of existence beyond our own must come from ever more esoteric sources, and with such sources our ability to judge the quality and usefulness of information being "passed down" will be severely tested.

Summary

The evidence for our understanding of the activities on the other side comes from birth experiences, near-death experiences, and hypnotic regressions directly into the Bardo state. Both the birth experiences and hypnotic regressions provide evidence only insofar as we are willing to accept information from subjects who are describing events while under hypnosis. Evidence from near-death experiences, of course, comes from descriptions after the fact.

Both forms of obtaining factual data have their serious and potentially fatal limitations. However, the consistency between these three forms of data gathering with literally thousands of subjects provides considerable credibility for the information so gathered. In addition, the reports and descriptions coincide with ancient and religious teachings with astounding accuracy. It becomes increasingly difficult to simply dismiss the reports. Accordingly, the general ingredients of the activities on the other side appear to have, at the very least, plausibility.

Our description of the activities on the other side supports reincarnation as a theory and provides considerable detail as to the precise chronologies and characteristics of the time between lives. (Obstensibly, we already have a fair idea of what happens during each of the lifetimes.) Nothing in the reports contradicts the basic idea of reincarnation, and instead, the reports consistently demonstrate the inherent plausibility of reincarnation. It is noteworthy that the reports essentially deny the possibility of a soul living only a single life. If all of the reports are to be believed, many lives is clearly the norm and a single incarnation for an individual soul would be a noteworthy exception.

Interestingly, the above descriptions of the activities on the other side and their relation to the concept of karma is less clear. For example, in the life review it is emphasized in some reports that as the individual relives the events of their past life, they feel every sensation and emotion, every pain and joy, and in general, relive all of the moments with all of the intensities of the participants. Essentially, a soul during the life review feels all of the pain and anguish it caused as well as all of the joys.

Therefore, if the life review is sufficiently intense, why do we need karma? Could not the life review constitute the soul's punishment for bad deeds as well as its rehabilitation? Do we need to return to earth to balance karma if in the life review we are directly experiencing the anguish and the joy we caused? If someone murdered a dozen people while on earth, and in the life review experienced the pains and anguish of his victims as well as their friends and relatives, is this not enough? Such a life review sounds pretty hellish and could conceivably be enough to satisfy karmic justice. In that case, do we need karma?

One can argue that the reexperiencing of all the relevant emotions for each event in the life review is insufficient for karmic justice. Alternatively, one could suggest that it is necessary to demonstrate that one has learned his or her lesson. An analogy is that not only does one have to serve his time, but in being released from prison, he also has to live a subsequent life that shows that he is, in fact, rehabilitated. The critical question that has not been answered in the descriptions of the activities on the other side is the extent of the joy and pain in reexperiencing the events in the life review.

There is also the possibility of karmic evolution. As souls progress in their own evolution, perhaps karma is also changing. The "eye for an eye" interpretation may become less important as the potential for karmic justice in the life reviews becomes more significant. We may have fewer or less-intense karmic obligations in succeeding lives, as our intervening life reviews take on greater significance.

Alternatively, karma may be a physical world phenomenon. In discussing his principles of yoga, Sachindra Majumdar specifies that karma belongs to the world of Mava, that is, what we call our practical world. Robert Monroe, in his book *Far Journeys*, states that karma exists only on the earthly plane. The implication is that karma exists only in our own egos, and that all guilt is shed as you reenter heaven. The life review and attendant self-judgment is not of great consequence. Furthermore, any karmic guilt would depart the ego at higher levels.

If this view is correct, then the subject of the last three chapters cannot provide a great deal of confirming or conflicting evidence for karma other than the possibility that planning for the next life involves karmic issues. While the reports of Dr. Joel Whitton's subjects (the hypnotic regressions) tend to mention such karmic planning as a matter of course, the reports of Dr. Wambach's subjects (the birth experiences) and the reports of near-death experiences almost never mention karmic considerations. This either implies something of a contradiction between methods, or that the karmic planning is done within the "depths" of the Bardo, not normally viewed from either the side of death or the opposite side of birth.

Note that the above discussions relate only to the effects of reincarnation and karma of the described activities on the other side; they do not consider the descriptions of the "planes of existence." Information on the planes of existence derives from totally different sources, and very few reports from the birth experiences, near-death experiences, and regressions touch on this significantly more esoteric subject. When such reports do broach the subject, they are invariably limited to the lower planes (i.e. nothing above the astral planes), and even then only indirect information is obtained.

More complete descriptions of celestial, causal, and astral planes derive primarily from "channeled" information (see Chapter 14). The adequacy of this means of gathering data will be discussed then. However, it is worthwhile at this point to note that the accuracy or inaccuracy of the information on the "Planes of Existence" has little or no effect on the questions of karma, reincarnation, and the related aspects of birth, death, and the Bardo state.

It may be comforting to know that a belief in reincarnation does not carry with it the implication that you have to know anything about the Mahaparanirvanic plane, nor for that matter even how to pronounce it.

Chapter 9:

Out of Body

Experiences

Ted Andrews still remembered the incident with extraordinary vividness. He had been ten years old at the time and living with his older brother in his uncle's house. His recollection of the event forty years ago was simple and to the point.

> One day, I was reclined on my bed, quite awake, and was looking at the ceiling beams of the old Spanish building where the living quarters were located. I was asking myself many questions, such as what was I doing there and who was I. All of the sudden, I got up from the bed and started walking towards the next room. At that moment, I felt a strange sensation in me: it was a sensation of weightlessness and a strange mix of a sense of a feeling of joy. I turned back in my steps in order to go back to bed when to my big surprise, I saw myself reclined on the bed. This surprising experience at that very small age, gave me the kind of a jerk which, so to say, shook me back to my body.

The idea of someone getting out of bed and inadvertently leaving their body in the bed may perhaps be a bit disconcerting to the average person (not to mention Ted, or even the unaverage person). Actually it may be more than disconcerting. Let's face it–the story has all the qualifications of the ramblings of someone who is crazy. The only question appears to be Was this fellow actually out-of-his-body, or was he just out of his mind?

A decade ago we could have dismissed this story as the ramblings of a prematurely senile fifty year-old man, but the mass of data on near-death experiences and the like should now give us pause. If we can leave our bodies at the time of death or near-death, why not at other times? Is there any reason why we could not achieve an out-of-body state without first having to suffer some sort of illness, accident, or other trauma, or even attempt suicide?

Why not?

The Astral Body

One of the oldest and most universal concepts of man's ideas about himself is the concept of the "astral body." This envelope of the soul is mentioned in ancient Egyptian, Indian, and Greek texts as well as the Christian Bible. During the Middle Ages, the concept was virtually a literary staple. It continues to be a powerful belief in many religious and cultural groups today, including most students of reincarnation and related phenomena.

The astral body is believed to be a perfect replica of the physical body in which it is housed. However, the astral body is composed of luminous, translucent materials. These far-lighter materials makes it ideally suited for out-of-body traveling. The astral body's function, supposedly, is to transport the soul at the moment of death into the white light. It is the astral body that allows for the travel of the soul in near-death experiences, pre-birth excursions in and out of the fetus, and during the time in the Bardo state.

However, there appears to be no reason to limit out-of-body travels to those associated with death and eventual rebirth. For those claiming to have had out-of-body experiences on numerous occasions, the state is considered no more unusual than dreaming. In *The Projection of the Astral Body*, Sylvan Muldoon and Hereward Carrington claimed to have been habitual astral travelers themselves, and that astral projection (a voluntary out-of-body experience) was within anyone's capability if they wanted it badly enough. In their words:

> The astral body, then, coincides with the physical body during the hours of full, waking consciousness, but in sleep the astral body withdraws to a greater or lesser degree, usually hovering just above it, neither conscious nor controlled. In trance, syncope, while fainting, when under the influence of an anaesthetic, etc., the astral body similarly withdraws from the physical. Such cases of withdrawal constitute instances of automatic or involuntary projection.
>
> As opposed to such cases we place those of conscious or voluntary projection, in which the subject "wills" to leave his physical body. He is then fully alert and conscious in his astral body; he can look upon his own physical mechanism, and travel about at will, perhaps viewing scenes and visiting places he has never seen before.
>
> The astral and physical bodies are connected by means of a cord, along which vital currents pass. Should this cord be severed, death instantly results. This cord–the "Silver Cord" spoken of in Ecclesiastes–is elastic and capable of great extension. It constitutes the essential link between the two bodies.

Belief in the concept of out-of-body experiences (commonly referred to as OBE, or ecsomatic state–whichever you prefer), appears in about ninety-five percent of non-Western cultures. In their book *With the Eyes of the Mind, An Empirical Analysis of Out-of-Body States*, Gabbard and Twenlow note that three separate surveys by independent researchers (covering a period from 1954 to 1983) have found that twenty-three to twenty-seven percent of college students have had at least one OBE. Furthermore, the descriptions of the experience from both the college students and a wide, diversified sampling of other people show remarkable similarity. In essence, something of the self leaves the body, often when the physical body is either asleep or unconscious, and is usually spontaneous. The occurrence is easily distinguishable from dreams.

The Experience

Richard Bach, in his novel *The Bridge Across Forever*, tells of the first time his hero discovers himself in an out-of-body state, when he could think about moving and move accordingly. There was no body, only the sense of one, something akin to a ghost's body. Bach also noted the extreme, razor-sharp consciousness in the out-of-body state, which comparatively makes ordinary consciousness feel like sleepwalking.

Another of Bach's observations was that of a faint thread of glowing life, the silver cord mentioned in the Bible, which linked his ghostlike body to his physical one. From Bach's viewpoint, a severing of the cord would mean the end of the incarnation. In this way he noted that near-death experiences were the same as out-of-body experiences, but that OBEs could be learned!

The editors of the *Reader's Digest* book *Into the Unknown* have described the OBE in less dramatic terms:

> During an OBE the "I" consciousness seems to be aware that it is in another vehicle, which may or may not be visible to an onlooker. Some subjects feel the second body to be an exact, if transparent, replica of the physical body; others liken it to a mist, a vapor, a white cloud, an eye, a glowing ball, or something like a magnetic or electric field. Not uncommonly, the out-of-body form is thought to give off its own light, and some subjects report seeing a luminous cord connecting the ecsomatic self with the physical body. Movement out of the physical body is often accompanied by a clicking sound, an apparent blackout or a journey down a long tunnel, and may seem to be assisted by some other disembodied entity.
>
> The pattern also suggests that the projected form is immune to gravity and may walk, glide, float or fly. It may hover lazily in the vicinity of the physical body, or it may seem to travel great distances beyond the limits of time and space. It may also be able to pass through matter with ease but is very seldom capable of touching or moving objects. The subject usually feels he is traveling in the world of everyday life but sometimes enters regions of otherworldly beauty or depression, and may see other apparitions during his experience. The out-of-body self may even seem to demonstrate some form of extrasensory perception.
>
> Skeptics, who are numerous, explain out-of-body accounts in terms of dreams, hallucinations, wishful self-delusions, ESP, gross misperception of natural events, psychotic episodes or deliberate hoax. No doubt each one of these factors might operate in a given instance, yet the mass of OBE cases is not so easily dealt with. For the sheer volume of anecdotal data does at least suggest that the OBE is a genuine phenomena; it suggests, indeed, that the consciousness apparently leaving the body may be the real self, one capable of functioning independently of the physical body's mass of bone, tissue and brain cells.

Ram Dass, a Harvard-educated guru with a decidedly Western background, has given a very simple description of the out-of-body state by describing the body as a spacesuit, with the eyes as the window of the spacesuit. Ram Dass goes on to note that you are *not* your spacesuit, and that an OBE is just leaving the spacesuit temporarily.

This viewpoint has the added benefit of implying that when you leave your spacesuit for good, you can be comforted by the fact that *this* spacesuit is biodegradable.

Robert Monroe is considered one of today's foremost authorities on out-of-body experiences. In his book *Far Journeys*, he describes the OBE as a condition where one is able to perceive and act as if physical, but with several major exceptions: One could move through space and time (and at speeds beyond the speed of light), and move through such physical barriers as walls, steel plates, concrete, earth, oceans, air, and even atomic radiation without effect. Monroe stressed that one was still fully conscious, able to observe, make decisions, and (to some degree) participate in events. Monore also noted that one could not only visit a friend across the country, but also explore the solar system and/or galaxy, or even enter into other reality systems or dimensions! Obviously, you could also skip the expense and inconvenience of traveling on airlines and other common carriers.

Preexisting Conditions

One might assume that the majority of OBEs reported derive from times of pain, stress, or other intolerable circumstances. It would be, in effect, an escape, and would probably be quite effective. Just as in near-death experiences, when the soul likewise leaves the body, the astral body would find itself totally free of pain and earthly worries, and capable of doing by merely thinking the thought.

However, near-death experiences account for only about ten percent of out-of-body experiences! Respondents to numerous surveys have indicated that in seventy-nine percent of OBEs, the subject was mentally calm and physically relaxed. "Flying or falling" dreams may include up to thirty-three percent, while twenty-seven percent of OBE subjects reported that they were meditating at the time of the experience. Cases of emotional stress or unusual fatigue only accounted for twenty-three and fifteen percent, respectively. An OBE occasioned by drugs, general anaesthesia, cardiac arrest, severe pain, childbirth, alcohol, and high fever each represented less than ten percent.

There is evidence to suggest that OBEs occur on a regular basis while sleeping. But like dreams, these events are seldom remembered after waking. Some proponents suggest that the "jerk" people often feel while sleeping, and which often awakens them, is the astral body returning abruptly to the physical body. If this is the case, the number of OBEs being experienced by many people is much larger than what might have been expected or has ever been reported by surveys.

Some Examples

Another class of OBEs include cases where a soul goes to the aid of a friend or relative. Sandra Johnson, a homemaker in North Carolina, was watching television with her husband when she suddenly found herself in a hospital emergency room looking down at her seriously injured father-in-law. After speaking with him for just a few moments, she abruptly found herself back in her own living room. Concerned, she then telephoned her in-laws, only to learn that her father-in-law had just been injured in a car accident. He died before Sandra could get to the hospital, but not before the dying man had told a nurse and his wife that he had been comforted by Sandra's presence in his room.

In a similar case an Indiana farmer went to the aid of his father in an out-of-body form. Even though concerned for his father's health, the farmer also sensed the presence of some sort of guide accompanying him to his father's bed. Interestingly, the father remembered his son's presence at the same time that his son had written down upon his return.

Equally dramatic is the case of Doris Sumner, who witnessed her husband, Paul's, apparent OBE. When she turned to him in bed she saw what looked like a person lying in a casket. A filmy, white substance surrounding his body was being drawn from the top of his head and the soles of his feet toward the solar plexus. When it came together in the middle, a small embryo figure that resembled a tiny albino man was formed. She couldn't see the eyes or guess the sex, but somehow she knew this figure, no more than two inches long, was Paul. Suddenly the tiny thing did a counter-clockwise motion, turned, and shot up at a forty-five-degree angle until there was nothing left except for a filmy, white cord still connected to his body. There was the smell of phosphorus, like someone striking a match, and everything disappeared. While shocking to Doris, Paul later readily admitted that he was out-of-body and in fact did it nightly.

Right! And he probably has to work late often as well! Paul's claim to routinely leave his body is supported by numerous other accounts. While many believe that anyone can go OBE on a regular basis, Robert Monroe has developed workshops that claim to teach the methods of accomplishing OBEs at will. Along with other experts, he suggests that people should not attempt to voluntarily leave their bodies without adequate instruction. While spontaneous cases of OBE seem to pose no problem (naturally occurring experiences seem to allow the people to instinctively return), conscious, willed out-of-body experiences without prior instruction are definitely not recommended by Monroe.

Nature of the Experience

Gabbard and Twenlow have utilized questionnaires to develop a prototype OBE. They have noted that physical relaxation or mental calmness precede a typical experience (i.e. stress is usually absent). The subject typically senses a state of peace and quiet, something that seems quite pleasant if not joyful. Unpleasant effects or a sense of going crazy is uncommon. The subject often finds himself or herself in a position spatially separate from the physical body (usually from a vantage point above the now inert physical body), but within the same environment. The experience is quite vivid (clearly more real than a dream state), and is usually sufficient to have a profound influence on the person's subsequent life. Views about life after death may be changed if the subject sees the event as a spiritual experience, and which they may even want to try it again. Some even view it as one of the greatest events of their lives.

According to Gabbard and Twemlow, ninety-four percent of OBEers describe the experience as more real than a dream. The form of the out-of-body figure was reported to be similar to the physical body by seventy-six percent of the subjects, while sixty-two percent considered the OB figure to be in the same environment as the physical body. Fifty percent felt their OB figure could pass through objects, while eighteen percent felt able to touch objects. Fourteen percent felt that people not out-of-body were aware of his or her presence. Thirty-three percent experienced a change in time sense. Thirty-seven percent heard noises in the early stages of the experience, thirty percent saw a brilliant white light, and twenty-six percent experienced being in a dark tunnel with a white light at the end of it. Thirty-seven percent of the subjects were aware of the presence of nonphysical beings. (In nineteen percent the beings were people close to the subject who had already died.) Twenty-six percent felt the presence of guides or helpers.

OBE Research

The American Society of Psychical Research located in New York has conducted numerous experiments in order to verify the reality of OBEs. In one case a subject was able to describe "targets" with sufficient accuracy that researchers calculated the odds against such success in identifications to be 40,000 to 1 against. Another subject made 114 hits out of 197 trials during twenty different sessions.

Gabbard and Twemlow conducted observations of Robert Monroe during a voluntary OBE. The psychiatrists concluded that while neurophysiological changes might be accompanying the out-of-body experience, there was no indication of a stable, external state existing. From their viewpoint, it was not even clear if the states were the cause or the effect of the out-of-body experience.

One aspect of the research has suggested that there is a measurable change in the physical body's weight during an OBE. In effect the astral body does possess some minute mass or weight, and its departure can register a slight loss in the physical body's weight. This weight loss has been estimated to range from one-half or three-quarters of an ounce to as much as thirteen ounces. But for the desperately diet-conscious, the possibility of shedding a pound very quickly is probably not worth the loss of one's soul. Try to keep that in mind.

Scoffers continue to suggest that an OBE is nothing more than a psychological mechanism to cope with the fear of dying. Given the existence of such fear, are OBEs still plausible? It would appear so. The fact remains that people who have undergone the experience of an OBE (either voluntary or involuntary, near-death, sleeping, or by any other means), invariably cease to be concerned with death. If OBEs are purely a construct of the mind to deal with a fear of dying, it is an amazingly effective method.

Isolation Research

Isolation research is the study of the effects on the mind and the body when an individual is isolated. This isolation can be in the form of removing all social contact with other humans (lone polar explorers, solitary shipwreck survivors, solitary confinement, and so on) or can involve sensory deprivation techniques. The latter techniques include the well-publicized cases of people being suspended in a water tank and being isolated from stimuli to any of the person's normal sensory channels.

Under these conditions, subjects have reported experiencing unusual psychological phenomena not unlike NDEs and OBEs. Dr. John Lilly, known for his isolation research, has reported in his book *The Center of the Cyclone*, that he considers the experiences under isolation to be real and not delusional. The implication is that isolation may well be another method of entering the new realms of consciousness that the OBEs and NDEs appear to be.

Mind/Body Problem

While Gabbard and Twemlow have done considerable research into OBEs and have shown that most common explanations of the phenomena are inadequate, they have not concluded that separation of the "astral body" and the physical body actually occurs. In fact, they do not even agree that separation is the logical object of research. In their view, they believe any attempt to prove an actual or artificial separation of the mind and body misses the point, and that instead the OBE should be viewed simply as a function of psychology. Since they are psychiatrists and psychoanalysts, this is the limit of their interest.

Gabbard and Twemlow go on to point out "substantial philosophical and semantic problems" with the "separationist" approach. Harold Widdison, in his article "Near-Death Experiences and the Unscientific Scientist," uses aspects of Kirlian research to dispute Gabbard and Twemlow's position. Dr. Widdison notes the case of the "phantom leaf effect." This occurs in Kirlian or corona discharge photography using high-voltage currents. The effect derives from the action of cutting from two to ten percent of the leaf away, and then photographing it using the Kirlian technique. Upon developing the film, the image of the entire leaf is sometimes seen. In effect the Kirlian photograph of the cut leaf shows the complete leaf, even though the cut portion has been removed before photographing it!

In effect, the phantom leaf effect suggests that living organisms may be composed of a nonbiological component as well as a biological one. The question that arises is whether or not these two separate components can exist separately as well as together. Thus the life-after-death question can be rephrased as the ability of the nonbiological aspect of the leaf to exist without the physical, biological leaf itself. More importantly, if the nonbiological aspect can exist, as in another dimension, is it possible for an individual approaching death to be able to glimpse that other dimension?

Gabbard and Twenlow, avoiding the issue of a separation between the mind and body, argue for a split between the soul ego and the physical ego. The split is purely psychological in their view. But why should a self-generated ego split result in the dramatic changes in one's view of life and death? What about the consistency of reports?

One has to wonder about the motivation of researchers who strive so earnestly to propose an alternative explanation. Why not assume the simpler hypothesis? Why not believe the hundreds of individuals who have reported the same vivid experiences? Alternative theories can certainly be useful, if only to make us continue to question, but any alternative theory must be pretty good to overcome the simplicity of just believing the voluminous reports of people who have experienced OBEs and NDEs.

I Spy?

Why would anyone want to voluntarily undergo an OBE? There seems little doubt that it would be a learning experience. There is no reason to suppose that two or more people could not take a trip together and find other, unique things to share. As a means to achieve guidance, to grasp the really incredible complexity and beauty of the universe, and to just take a first-class trip to parts unknown, an OBE would be unsurpassed. It might also be useful for military surveillance.

The latter idea is probably not that pleasant a thought, but there is reason to believe that both the Soviet Union and the United States have conducted research on OBE for just such purposes. It may seem that this is a rather dismal state of affairs, but there is also the suggestion that the research has not been all that successful. Whether or not this is due to our guides or other entities keeping us honest, or whether the clarity of the results has not warranted its implementation, is not clear.

Previous research has indicated that in most cases OBers have not seen things clearly enough for definite identification. The implication is that the other-than-physical eyes may have a less-than-physical perception, and we may very well be limited in our perceptions in the OBE state. From a military standpoint, an OBer might be able to tell you there is someone on the other side of the hill, but would be unable to identify the person, which is clearly a potentially serious limitation. On the other hand, locating a submarine with some reasonable precision might be all that would be required. Who knows?

An interesting aspect, however, is that how do you "control" an accomplished OBer? Death may not scare him, imprisonment may be a totally pointless effort (you've just taught him the ultimate escape technique), and he may be experiencing other things during his OBE that suggest to him that spying is hardly worth his time. The bad guys might have given the OBer religion (so to speak), and in the process lost their ability to direct their "agent" to do their bidding. (Isn't it amazing how much trouble we will go to in order to feel good about something?)

Why?

A question that needs to be asked is Why? Why are OBEs even possible? Is there an important distinction between an OBE that is voluntary and one that is involuntary?

Given the assumption that the soul departs a dying body and journeys to another plane of existence, it follows that an astral body exists in some form. OBEs occasioned by pain or intense discomfort, either in near-death experiences or otherwise, would also seem to be useful mechanisms for bodies attempting to secure relief. Clearly, if the separation of astral body and physical body occurs at death, the same effect at near-death or while under duress is not that hard to imagine.

Voluntary astral projection is less obviously beneficial. However, nature is notorious for allowing good and bad uses for virtually all of its benefits. This is not to imply that voluntary OBEs are bad, but there appears to be no logical or rational reason why astral projection would be limited to purely involuntary causes.

Certain belief structures may prefer to disallow the awesome possibilities, but invariably the universe provides ways around anything that man might construct. The first century philosopher, Seneca, perhaps phrased it best: "Our universe is a sorry little affair unless it has in it something for every age to investigate. Nature does not reveal her mysteries once and for all." In other words, the finite is fixed; the infinite is forever changing.

Questions and Answers

Out-of-Body Experiences may be a two edged sword, but this in no way should be construed as justification for discounting them. Consider, for example, the possibilities generated by Robert Monroe's answers to several questions related to OBEs (as discussed in his book, *Far Journeys*.)

1. Can anyone go out of body? 25 percent have already reported an OBE, and Robert Monroe claims that, with the appropriate psychological and/or philosophic preparation, anyone can consciously move into an out-of-body state.

2. Can you get back into the wrong physical body? Robert Monroe claims that he has in fact entered the wrong body before. He now suggests using a part of your physical body–such as your big toe–as a homing device by attempting to wiggle it before reentering.

3. Can someone get into your body? Robert Monroe believes that there is no more possibility of this taking place than there would be during normal

sleep. Furthermore, he notes that in 15 years of research there have been no incidents which could be remotely thought of as possession or anything destructive or uncontrollable. However, there is other evidence which suggests the occurrence may be surprisingly common (see Chapter X), but definitely not a good idea!! (Mr. Monroe is also contradicting himself between questions 2 and 3.)

4. Can you meet animals in the OBE state? Again Monroe has reported encountering domestic cats, including three cats which were favorites of his and which had died during the past three years.

5. Can you go anywhere? Apparently yes, as long as you have a specific address or identification.

6. Can you go to a particular person? This is supposedly easier than a place, particularly if you are close to that person emotionally.

7. Can you go forward and backward in time? According to Monroe, the answer is yes, because of the lack of time-space constraints while in the out-of-body state. However, Monroe warns that it is necessary to have a strong identification of your return location, which of course, must include a specific time. Monroe suggests you avoid "long" excursions until you have practiced near-time runs. Still others might suggest that you first have your head examined.

8. What is the relation of OBEs to reincarnation and karma? OBEs can be thought of as an extension of NDEs. As such there is nothing in OBEs to dispute reincarnation and/or karma. On the other hand, evidence for OBEs can be considered as contributing to the validity of NDEs and thus indirectly supports the theory of reincarnation. There is apparently no OBE evidence to support karma.

9. Can one ascend? Excuse me. I'll ask the question again. If one does not relish the possibility of sufferings the pangs of death, could an out-of-body excursion, followed by a severing of the "silver cord", allow the human soul to ascend to heaven directly and unimpeded by the unpleasant death of the physical body? Oh, that question! As for the answer . . . Why not?

One other intriguing thought: Robert Monroe, in his book *Journeys Out of the Body,* tells of one of his own experiences where he found himself out-of-body in a gray, non-descript place. While there he was accosted by an angry, sarcastic dead man, who demanded to know if Monroe was now ready to learn the secrets of the universe. It seemed as if the man was angry because no one had taken the trouble to tell him, when he was still incarnated.

Maybe it's time to learn to solo.

Chapter 10:

Earthbound

Entities

The therapist asked his client to describe the scene that seemed to repeat itself over and over in his mind.

"It's a trail. In Vietnam. It goes down the hill and then curves around to the left. There's a hill on the left and some kind of embankment on the right. I'm with five guys and there's lots of noise."

"What kind of noise?"

"Guns. M-16s. And helicopters. Hughies I think."

"What happens next?"

"We're going down this road, and I've got this feeling that somebody's going to get hurt. Maybe Jim. He's point man. I was supposed to be, but Jim's my best friend. He took point."

"Your friend's going to take point?"

"Yeah. But they're all my friends. We've been together a long time. Six or seven months. Anyway, we start down the trail and . . . Suddenly everything's coming apart. Mines are blowing! Everybody's blown to pieces! Jim's right side blown away!

"You see it?"

"I see it. I'm the medic and I grab all the morphine I can find and I'm just crawling around because I've got shrapnel in my hand, too, and I crawl (sob) around and I'm trying to help them and they're screaming. I'm trying to hold their bodies together. They're screaming. The VC opens up and they mow the rest of us down. Oh God! I shouldn't sent Jim out there!"

"Wayne, there was nothing you could do."

"I should have been the one. I should have been the one. I grabbed him, and I'm crawling up the side of the hill. I'm dragging him, we're gonna get out, we're gonna get out of there, somehow. Get to the top, this hill . . ."

"Who are you dragging up?"

"Jim, what's left of him."

"Is he still alive?"

"Still alive."

"Okay. You get to the top of the hill."

"I get to the top of the hill. There's a helicopter, he's coming down. The door's opening, and I . . . I don't have much strength left. It's just about all I can do. The CO's there. He's yelling at me, 'What happened, Wayne, what happened?' I don't give a damn. I pick what's left of Jim up and put it in the helicopter. He's bleeding. There's not much left of him. He's dying. He's dead."

"Jim's dead now, isn't he. You gave him morphine?"

"Yeah."

"You eased his pain in the last minutes, didn't you."

"The CO's screaming at me. He's asking me what happened. He thinks it's my fault."

"He thinks it's your fault?"

"Yeah. Smashed him right in the mouth."

"Good. What happens next?"

"Blacked out I guess. Next I knew I was in the hospital. They said I'd been there for three weeks."

"Do you remember anything during that time?"

"Sometimes. Like seeing my body from overhead. I wanted to help."

"You wanted to help?

"Yeah. Give him strength. So I went in."

"Give who strength? Who went in?"

"Me. Jim. Wayne was my buddy. I figured I could help him. All of us did. So we went in.

"You went into Wayne?"

"Yeah."

"You said, 'all of us'."

"All four of us. Tom, Jeff, Sammy. All of us."

"Who am I talking to?"

"Jim."

"Is Tom or Jeff or Sammy there with you now."

"Yeah. You want to talk to them?"

"Not yet. Jim, you were point man that day, weren't you?"

"Yeah."

"What happened?"

"It was pretty awful. Everybody was real tired. It was real hot. We got packed up, going down the road. We knew there might be mines, but we figured what the hell. Anything was better than where we were at. I just went on down, truckin' it down the road. All of sudden, man, there was a big ol' explosion. I didn't feel anything at first. Everybody else was yelling and I turned around and I wasn't all there. I started screaming. I couldn't help it. Oh, God, it hurt!"

"Where?"

"My whole right side's gone. Wayne comes barreling down the hill. Trying to help everybody. He was everywhere at once. And the road kept blowing up."

"The other guys . . ."

"He was trying to get to me. He was yelling, 'I'll be there in a minute, Jim, I'm coming. I'm coming. But it was too late. I knew I was, I was gone. I was gone. The last thing I saw was his face. He was crying."

"He drug you up the hill, to the helicopter."

"I was dead; he just didn't know."

"Were you watching him, drag you up?"

"Yeah."

"Were you in your own body?"

"No."

"Were you in pain?"

"No. The hurt was all gone."

"What happened next?"

"Well, I was, what was left of me, laying on the floor of the heelie, it was really a mess. The CO was laying in my blood. (laughter) The heelie went up and they landed. It was quite a ways from the base camp, about four clicks."

"What about the other guys on the road?"

"Well, they were, it was pretty ugly, man. They were just smashed everywhere. They'd have to look around trying to pick those guys up. They blew 'em everywhere."

"And you're still in the heelie watching all this happen?"

"Yeah. We were just like up on the ceiling or . . . weird!"

"We?"

"Yeah. Tom and Jeff and Sammy."

"And then what happened?"

"At base they take what's left of my carcass, it's pretty awful looking, and they just stick it in a bag. They take Wayne up to the hospital and I followed him."

"You followed Wayne?"

"I did!"

"Not your body, but Wayne?"

"Yeah. I was afraid. I didn't know what was gonna happen to him. I couldn't just let him think that it was his fault. It's not his fault."

"He thinks it is."

"I know."

"You heard him a few minutes ago?"

"Oh, yeah. I've been hearing him right regular for the last ten years."

"When did you enter Wayne?"

"When he was in the hospital. He's out. They're keeping him out. All he was doing was just screaming anyway. He's not making a lot of sense. They tried sending a shrink in there to talk to him, but he won't talk about it. He won't talk about it at all. It's gonna be OK though. Me and the guys are gonna help."

"All four of you go in?"

"Yeah. Been there ever since."

This incredible dialogue is taken from the actual transcript between a therapist and his client.[1] The implication is that a Vietnam veteran named Wayne, brought four of his dead buddies back to the States with him. All four were earthbound entities.

Missing the White Light

Unbelievable? Then consider what would happen if a dying person failed to see or decided to avoid the white light that we described in the near-death experiences? If a soul does not "go into the light" and thereby departs this earth upon death or sometime after death, where does the entity go? Hell? Earth? Purgatory? Some intermediate place?

Evidence is accumulating which suggests that many entities have gone on some rather severe detours on their way to heaven. One obvious possibility is the route supposedly taken by suicides – a detour we discussed in detail in Chapter 7 – but this is by no means the only possibility. Many people who have studied the subject have become convinced that entities can miss or avoid the white light, circle back and become "earthbound". According to some researchers, they may become ghosts and be responsible for hauntings and the like, or may in fact attach themselves to other living souls in what is referred to as possession.

Why would they miss the white light? Perhaps the entity was scared to death of it. For example, someone killed trying to escape from a concentration camp at night, might associate the white light with the spotlight that illuminated them and thus indirectly caused their death. The entity may have been frightened of the deceased friends and relatives they saw coming for them, or the entity may have refused to travel toward the bardo for any number of other reasons. If the person was killed abruptly on the battlefield or in a car accident, he might be too shocked or dazed to even realize that he had died. Other emotions, such as concern for a wounded buddy, might distract a soldier from leaving, and in fact, motivate him to stay around.

We cannot ignore the possibility that a recently departed soul might see the light and run the other way. There is some evidence that suggests that there may be souls which have been effectively running for years (if not centuries). Others may have committed such horrors in their lifetime, that the possibility of judgment day's imminent arrival may have justifiably prompted a flight response. These people may in fact already have found their own personal hell or purgatory.

It also seems reasonable that if such entities are indeed earthbound, they may from time to time interact with the living in a variety of ways. Such interactions can be grouped into two basic categories depending upon the attachment of the deceased to living beings. The first category consists of ghosts, spirits and poltergeist activities, while the second category is labeled

[1] William J. Baldwin, Ph.D., of Carmel, California

possession. Before we discuss these two categories, we should clarify one important point.

Nonbound Entities

It should be made clear that this discussion of earthbound entities does NOT include temporary visits from those already in the white light. For example, many people have felt a comforting presence after the death of a loved one. These people have sensed something that seems to be telling them not to worry and that the deceased is very happy and content; sort of a love-gram from the next stop (but without the traditional note of "Wish you were here").

There exists a multitude of reports where an already dead person has effectively said goodbye to loved ones, after their death – and it is important not to assume that such farewells in any way imply that the departed soul is earthbound. In fact they are clearly not "bound" to earth, but have considerable freedom of movement.

Ghosts and Spirits

Incorporated in virtually all of world's cultures throughout history is an awareness or insistence on the presence of beings or spirits that have no apparent reality in a material setting. These beings from an unseen realm have included deities, angels, demons, archangels, agents of evil, divas of the plant and animal kingdom, gods, demigods, healing spirits, and a vast menagerie of others, including the spirits of ordinary persons who have died.

But despite the persistence of beliefs in spirits, ghosts and poltergeists, and all the stories that have been collected and told, modern Western convictions about what constitutes reality invariably challenges these beliefs. The idea of the dead appearing among the living just doesn't seem possible to the mind enveloped in and committed to scientific thinking.

Imaginings of the Mind?

Modern psychiatry, for example, has tried to explain away ghosts and the like as manifestations of assorted unconscious wishes, patchwork imaginings, and unresolved guilts. Certainly such a view is rational, and in many cases is probably precisely the case. There seems little doubt that the mind is capable of a great many wondrous things. Dr. Ralph B. Allison, while accepting the very real possibility of spirits and the like, has noted that the human mind is capable of most anything. The only limitation seems to be our perception of what is or isn't possible. There is little disagreement with the belief that the mind is truly capable of astounding feats, given the motivation to do so.

An example of the mind's capabilities in this regard has been demonstrated by an experiment conducted in the 1970s by eight members of the Toronto Society for Psychical Research. As reported in the Reader's Digest book, *Into the Unknown*, these people proceeded to invent a nonexistent figure from the past, and then actively concentrated in making the purely fictitious ghost manifest itself. After several months, the ghost, named Philip, made his presence known by knocks on a table. Because the group clearly understood that there was no "spirit" behind the communications, they knew that the messages were coming from the group's subconscious. In fact knocks on the table seemed to be related or even activated by the knowledge, thoughts, wills, moods, and powers of concentration of each member of the group.

This unique experiment is, of course, as subject to fraud and misrepresentation (not to mention confusion) as any of many demonstrations of the actual reality of a spirit. Nevertheless, if true, it does point to the amazing powers of the mind – people can in fact manufacture their own reality. Even if the human mind is capable of conjuring up its own ghosts, does this fact eliminate the possibility of ghosts existing independently of the perceptions of living human beings? Of course not. With the proliferation of allegedly true ghost stories, the possibility of ghostly realities may not be that improbable.

Nathaniel Hawthorne, for one, believed his home was haunted by ghosts, one of which Hawthorne believed to be the Reverend Dr. Harris, an elderly clergyman who had shared a reading room with Hawthorne at the Boston Athenaeum. What was Hawthorne's possible motivation for this relatively casual acquaintance appearing in Hawthorne's life? Nothing obvious, and reasons to account for this tale may in fact become more esoteric than the acceptance of the tale as true. On the other hand, one woman reported seeing a gray-and-black-striped cat reappear at her doorstep, thinner and dripping with water, after the woman had decided to put the sick cat out of its misery by drowning it. Did the woman's guilt cause the appearance of the cat that no one else was able to see? Quite possibly. But not necessarily. As the editors of *Into the Unknown* viewed it; apparitions may exist only in the mind, or in fact the universe may be considerably more cluttered than we have hereto-before perceived or imagined.

Mediums

But if we can see or sense phantoms, why not talk to them? Some have claimed to do precisely that. Robert Leichtman, an internist, is just such a man. Dr. Leitchman considers himself to be a medium, and has documented much of his work in communicating with the spirit world. Dr. Leitchman thinks of mediumship as some discarnate human or non-physical intelligence assuming some degree of control over an incarnated body in order to communicate, hopefully something useful and meaningful, and/or to transmit some form of healing energies. Dr. Leitchman notes that mediumship may include varying degrees of trance, depending upon the process and quality of the medium. He also specifically notes that mediumship is not to be confused with the phenomenon of possession, inasmuch as mediumship involves the deliberate cooperation of the medium, and is intended to produce a constructive result.

Dr. Carl Wickland, in his book *Thirty Years Among the Dead*, describes the activities of his wife, who as a medium worked with literally hundreds of deceased persons communicating from the other side of the grave. These entities were often "attached" to another person. Dr. Wickland's method consisted of assembling a group of people, a "concentration circle," and the application of static electricity to the head and spine of the afflicted person, while Mrs. Wickland was in a trance. The entity would then incorporate into Mrs. Wickland (who presumably was not getting a charge out of her husband's apparatus). The voice from Mrs. Wickland would often complain about the "fire" running up its back, and would express considerable annoyance at being disturbed.

Dr. Wickland would then use the opportunity to strike up a conversation with the discarnate being. In the process Wickland would convince the entity (who often turned out to be someone identifiable) that he was in fact dead. Ignoring complaints from the being concerning his host's lack of hospitality, Dr. Wickland would gradually convince the entity of the desirability of "going into the white light". In most cases Dr. Wickland obtained the help of spirit guides, usually former loved ones of the earthbound entity, to lead the being into the light. Interestingly, many of the beings expressed profound gratitude to Dr. Wickland and his wife, for their guidance.

In those cases, however, when the being stubbornly refused to depart, Dr. Wickland would call for his "Mercy Band", a group of intelligent spirit guides who would remove the recalcitrant, ignorant earthbound entity to a condition simulating an impenetrable cell, from which there was no escape. Rehabilitation of the spirit could commence in this place, and eventually the being would be taken into the light.

Communicating with the Dead

Regardless of the gratitude of Dr. Wickland's earthbound entities who finally saw the light, the lot of the medium in the recent past has not been a cakewalk. People communicating with entities that other living people do not believe exist, are generally suspect of having mentally left this world themselves. This viewpoint, however, is not a consistent position throughout history.

The Bible contains a host of stories of people who heard voices, saw visions, told the future, and otherwise made inroads on our credulity. These people, who apparently were in contact or communicating with nonphysical entities, were called prophets or sages, or seers. In the early days of the American colonies, people with similar tendencies to tell of incredible things, were called witches and summarily burned at the stake. (My how times change. Obviously prophets were out of fashion in Puritan New England. Today we simply call many of these people crazy and let it go at that.)

We should at this juncture point out that it is preferable to distinguish between two different aspects of mediumship. In Chapter 14 we will discuss channeling, an alternate form of mediumship, whereby the nonphysical entity is presumably not earthbound, but is instead communicating from a higher plane (heaven or the equivalent). This is the stuff prophets are made of. For our purposes in this chapter, however, we have considered a medium to be someone communicating with an earthbound entity only (obstensibly a discarnate soul with all the characteristics of a ghost or "spirit").

Credibility

The difficulty of establishing credible proof for a medium communicating with the dead is difficult. Even the Great Houdini, who had gone to some trouble during his life to set up a means of checking the validity of communications between the living and dead, was never able to establish through his surviving widow evidence in support of such ideas. In more recent times, Dr. Leichtman has noted, the vast majority of communications through mediums falls into the categories of garbled, inconsequential, useless, mischievous, false, and harmful.

On the other hand, accumulating evidence for the existence of earthbound entities may be less difficult. Researchers in several diverse fields have encountered what is apparently earthbound entities in several different contexts. These entities are either in some sort of "intermediate place," or else attached to living human beings.

The "Intermediate Place"

According to Dr. Raymond Moody, in his book *Reflections on Life After Life*, many of his subjects reported that during their NDE, they saw others who appeared trapped in some form of earthbound existence. A consistent thread in their reports was that the beings seemed unable to surrender their attachment to the physical world (some particular object, person or habit), all of the beings appeared dull (with their consciousness limited in contrast to others), and that the beings were in their dismal state, apparently, only long enough for them to solve the problems that seemed to be detaining them there.

One of Dr. Moody's subjects described the people in some detail. It was noticed, for example, that their heads were bent downward, with sad, depressed looks, as they shuffled about as if on a chain gang. They seemed to have no idea of where they were going, who to follow, or what to look for. There was a crushed, hopeless demeanor; without the idea of ever even raising their heads to see what was happening. The subject also noted that the state they were caught in was neither spiritual nor physical. Any contact with the physical world was limited to just looking downward, trying to understand what had happened or what they were now to do.

The consistent thread of earthbound entities looking downward and thus not seeing the white light will be repeated again and again. Virtually everyone who believes in the possibilities of earthbound spirits, emphasizes the need for a dying person to look up and go into the white light.

Dr. Moody notes that other subjects had seen the same type of phenomenon, and these subjects had noticed some of the earthbound spirits apparently trying unsuccessfully to communicate with people still physically alive. Some appeared to be giving orders to living beings (obviously to no avail), while some seemed to be trying to atone for something they had done.

These reports from people involved in a NDE contains some similarities with a report from a participant in Robert Monroe's Gateway Program (i.e. the participant is involved in a voluntary OBE). Robert Monroe refers in his book, *Far Journeys*, to the participant's report. The participant noted many entities milling around, which looked like holograms, but seemed to be alive. Some of these entities ignored the participant, some moved away, and some seemed to think that he would be helping them find their way. One observation in particular, however, was that some of the entities were waiting for their bodies to die, so they could be free! Subsequently this same participant noted his overwhelming feeling of profoundness of his experience, and then pointed out that there were people in various institutions who were catatonic or comatose and whom medical science had not been able to reanimate.

The implications are indeed profound.

Possession

Possession is generally not a recognized branch of modern psychology; science today likes to think that it has progressed beyond witchcraft and spirit possession. The fact that belief in possession and rites of exorcism extend back in time at least to the Babylonians and possibly even earlier, does not carry much weight today. Little is made of ancient documentation such as clay tablets from the palace of Assurbanipal (dating to about 650 BC), wherein is inscribed the desperate appeal of a suffering man who asks his gods how he can rid himself of a tyrannical ghost who seems to possess his body and soul. Science has preferred to ignore such tales, as well as stories from the New Testament describing Christ's exorcism of sufferers (such as the Gadarene). On the other hand, the New Testament descriptions serve as a basis for the practice of exorcism by established churches.

Much of what we know of earthbound entities from present day efforts comes from exorcisms and depossessions. Such processes are often done as a form of therapy or healing for individuals who are suffering from what science terms dissociative disorders. Such "disorders" can be considered to arise from one of the following conditions:

1. Possession by an idea, an obsession, a compulsion, an involuntary act, or by an addiction to alcohol or drugs.

2. Possession due to the influence of one or more alternate personalities. This can be related to a Dr. Jekyll and Mr. Hyde situation where one personality has absolutely no memory of the other personality's activities; or to the condition of multiple personalities, where an individual can revert to a wide variety and number of different personalities.

3. Possession due to a controlling influence that appears to derive from the mind of another living human being. This is essentially witchcraft, voodoo, etc.

4. Possession by a spirit of a once-living human being.

5. Possession by a spirit that has never had its own life history and identifies itself as an agent of evil.

For the therapist it is essential to consider all five types as the potential source of a patient's mental or physical problem. In our discussion, however, we will be more interested in types four and five. [Multiple personalities will be discussed in some detail in Chapter 14.]

Some parapsychology researchers would also include: Thought forms (remember Phillip?), fragmentation (multiples, including possessing entities that are "not all here"), visitors from other planes of existence (and possibly other dimensions!), and extraterrestrials. But the bulk of the evidence is that a possessing entity is a fairly common sort of guy.

A survey in *Geriatics Today*, for example, indicated that two thirds of widowed women had sensed their deceased husbands, and that this occured even when using drugs to repress hallucinations. According to Anabel Chaplin, in her book *The Bright Light of Death,* many children whose parents die while they are very young, may end up with the parent attaching themselves to the child and continuing there while the child goes through its entire life. Robert Monroe, you may recall, notes that he has inadvertently entered the wrong body on at least one occasion. (I hope it was a friend.)

Poison Tree is a detailed account of a family in Wyoming who have undergone their own form of tragedy. According to the two children, the father had been severely abusing both of them for years. When authorities appeared to ignore their pleas, the son took matters into his own hands and killed the father from a well-planned ambush. A critical factor in the subsequent court case was the discrepancy between the daughter's testimony and her mother's concerning the daughter's insistence that the mother had witnessed on several occasions the father sexually molesting his daughter. Is it possible that the dying father attached himself to the mother, and was influencing her testimony in denying the alleged sexual assaults? Can you imagine the legal implications of such a possibility?

Characteristics of Possession

One of the most knowledgeable therapists and researchers in the field of possessing, earthbound entities is William J. Baldwin, Ph.D., of Carmel, California. He has described in detail much of what is currently known about the subject:

"Earthbound spirits, that is, the personalities or psyches of people who once lived on earth, are the most prevalent possessing entities to be found. The emotions and feelings connected with a sudden, traumatic death can become the force which binds a spirit to the earth plane. Anger, fear, jealousy, resentment, guilt, remorse, even strong ties of love, can interfere with the normal transition. Confusion and disbelief concerning religion and spirituality can prevent the spirit from moving into the Light. Obsession with food or sex can detain a spirit, and it must attach to someone in order to indulge its needs through the physical sense of a living being. Drug and alcohol habituation exert a powerful hold on a being, even after death, and these appetites can only be satisfied by attaching to a person who already uses the substances, or can be induced to use them.

"A discarnate spirit may attach itself to anyone who is available and open for whatever reason. The choice may be completely random. It may occur because of close physical proximity to a person at the time of the death. Victims of an air crash, or fatal automobile accident can be drawn to a bystander who is deeply compassionate or sympathetic. One who dies in a hospital of a condition with certain symptoms, may be attracted to another patient with similar symptoms.

"In well over half of the cases of spirit attachment I have dealt with, the connection stems from other lifetimes, when both beings inhabited their own physical bodies. They may have been parent and child, brothers or sisters, most often lovers. Jealousy can be a strong link. The early, untimely death, with unexpressed feelings and emotions, guilt over leaving the other alone, the promises and vows to be together forever, all these can truly be the tie that binds.

"The disembodied consciousness seems to attach itself and merge with the consciousness of a living person, exerting full or partial control over the mentality, as well as the physical body. The physical, mental, and emotional conditions that characterized the entity when it was alive, may be imposed on the host. The entity can speak through the voice of the host, often with dramatic changes in tone, timbre, even accent. Dr. Ian Stevenson, of the University of Virginia has studied cases of responsive xenoglossy and has published two books on the subject. A person in an altered state of consciousness can respond logically, intelligently, and reasonably to questions posed by the therapist but in a language which could not possibly be known by the subject.

"Dr. Stevenson suggests this phenomenon indicates the influence of a separate consciousness, or spirit possession. The attached spirits may not cause noticeable symptoms, but they do use the energy of the person. In some cases, the only indication of an attachment is chronic fatigue. However, in cases of very recent attachment, obsession, or possession, personality changes may occur, physical appetites for food, sex, alcohol, and drugs can increase drastically. Personal behavior and attitudes may change quite noticeably. Symptoms of physical ailments may suddenly appear. The voice and even facial features and appearance can change dramatically. A victim of this phenomenon can be totally amnesic about episodes of complete takeover.

"Physical sensations and symptoms, in the absence of a medically sound cause, can indicate an attached entity. These sensations often move about in the body, especially during a session when the client is in a light hypnotic trance. A client may report hearing voices, originating outside themselves or from within, and have no other psychotic symptoms or behavior. Dreams or spontaneous visual images of faces, sometimes grotesque and frightening, may indicate the presence of an entity. Severe stress may cause susceptibility to the influence of an intrusive spirit. Personality changes after surgery or accident, the sudden onset of drug or alcohol usage, inappropriate speech and behavior patterns, may signal the newly formed attachment of a discarnate being."

Depossession

Assuming one is possessed by an earthbound entity, is there a means of detaching that entity and sending him on his way? Why not? If you can buy possession, depossession should be a piece of cake.

Depossession can be accomplished, according to Dr. Baldwin and others, through therapy. Dr. Baldwin notes that:

> "The spirit helpers and guides always come to meet the soul consciousness after the death of the physical body. Strong feelings and emotions, often accompanying drug related, violent, or untimely deaths, seem to block the connection necessary for the soul to be guided into the Light. Lack of religious beliefs, or strong incorrect thought forms regarding the afterlife, can also prevent contact. The spirit helpers simply can't be seen. After resolution of the strong emotional feelings, the new awareness of its own condition will allow the entity to see the helpers. Firmly clasping hands with the guides assures that the entity will be securely placed on the path of transition. If, after the release of a discarnate being, the Light is still visible to the client, it may mean there is another entity present. The process is begun again."

Such "therapy" can be said to have been practiced for centuries. Catholic theology has recognized the reality of people being earthbound for various reasons. The church's response has been to pray for the deceased, conduct masses for the dead, perform last rites, and include usually the sacrament of reconciliation and communion (which is understood as food for the journey).

For those with a strong earth attachment, this can be good news. Earthbound entities may spend literally hundreds of years in this state of hell. These souls can be helped by prayers and ceremonies, and when the departed reaches the appropriate frame of mind, guides can be beckoned to receive the individual, and together they can make it into the white light.

Anabel Chaplin, in her book *The Bright Light of Death*, tells of her efforts to utilize a therapeutic, prayerful session with the possessed individual in order to release an attached entity to the Light. Ms. Chaplin, however, may also, under very special circumstances (e.g. with a spouse's permission and cooperation), attempt to depossess someone without their conscious knowledge. In both cases, Ms. Chaplin enters into prayer-like and highly creative visualization. She then proceeds to try to convince the attaching entity to vacate the premises and go to the Light. As in most modern depossession therapies, every effort is made to ensure the possessing entity makes it into the Light. In this way the attaching entity does not simply go to some intermediate place and thereafter, possibly attach itself to another victim.

Post Traumatic Stress Disorder

Post Traumatic Stress Disorder (PTSD) is a psychological disorder stemming from continuing and severe stress such as that associated with combat, concentration camps, and other horrors. Killing, sustained exposure to the possibility of sudden death, and witnessing the violent death of friends can have a lasting, traumatic consequence for a high percentage of survivors. PTSD has been very prevalent among Vietnam War veterans, even several decades after the war. Of the approximate 1,600,000 American soldiers who served in Vietnam, 800,000 have had severe emotional and psychological problems since the war, and 200,000 have been diagnosed as having PTSD.

Symptoms of PTSD in Vietnam veterans who have returned to the U. S. include dramatic personality changes, increased levels of drug abuse and criminal activities, continuing nightmares of having died in combat, and a grotesquely high rate of post combat suicides. It has been estimated that the number of casualties from suicides of veterans who returned to the United States now exceeds the number of combat-related casualties! Truly this is one of the most horrifying statistics of that ill-fated war.

In Hendin and Haas' excellent book, *Wounds of War*, Vietnam vets describe many of their dreams and nightmares. For example, the authors write that veterans "mourn for friends who have died, but they also mourn for what they have lost themselves, and often perceive themselves as *having died in combat*." [emphasis added] One of their patients said that "he recurrently dreamed that he was back in Vietnam and someone would sneak up behind him and cut his throat. Periodically he would be overcome with a desire to end his life and had made several suicide attempts. He had no idea why he sometimes became suicidal . . ."

Yet another veteran suffering from PTSD had nightmares in which he would see himself in combat fatigues, lying dead in a coffin draped by an American flag, while members of his family, including his wife and sister, would be seated around the coffin, crying. Other therapists, such as J. O. Brende and I. L. McCann, have reported on one veteran who claimed that since his return, something had changed inside of him. "*Something was locked up within me.*" [emphasis added]

Still another veteran was preoccupied with friends who had died in an ambush. He dreamed of them frequently, but when he did, it was as if they were not dead. Another vet had dreams of a similar nature. In the latter's recurring nightmare, he would be turning over the bodies of soldiers who had been killed, and one of the bodies would turn out to be his own. Invariably the dream image involved finding his own body and sensing that part of him had died in Vietnam.

Hendin and Haas have noted that "this theme has a striking parallel with many Vietnam veterans with post-traumatic stress whose words and lives express a sense that their survival of combat is an illusion and that *they have in reality died in the war*." [emphasis added]

The conclusion seems tantalizingly easy. In some form or another the memories of other personalities who have died still continue to reside in a living person. The possibility is best described by a veteran who continually relived the experience of being shot by a Vietcong woman, felt the impact of the bullets, fell backward, and died. Hendin and Haas have noted that in many of the episodes where the veteran relived the experience, the vet seemed to "dissociate from his present life. He was absorbed with the death of his friends in combat, Vietnamese civilians, enemy soldiers, and *his own sense of having died*. [emphasis added]

After his tour, he wrote [taken from *Wounds of War*]:

"Even dead men
Ours and theirs - reside inside,
rotting in my head."

Can we interpret the words in this poem in a literal fashion? Do they mean precisely what they say? Are many cases of PTSD but instances of possession? Hendin and Haas, who apparently have not even considered possession as a possibility, describe one veteran's recurrent nightmare in which the vet "would be shot and killed, but he would be *like a spirit outside of his body* looking at what happened." [emphasis added] Do we need further evidence?

At the beginning of this chapter, we included material from an actual transcript of a Vietnam veteran suffering from PTSD. In the process of the hypnosis, the therapist, Dr. William J. Baldwin, talked to several entities, including four of the G.I.'s friends, a Klu Klux Klan member (attached to one black G.I.), and a Vietnamese boy. The therapist was told of "several" Viet Cong, a baby, and "several others," all residing within one living person. By the end of the session, the therapist had sent all possessing entities into the Light. In a subsequent visit to his therapist, the veteran reported that he no longer was having any symptoms of PTSD.

Several other Vietnam Veteran PTSD sufferers have found similar relief. The idea that PTSD may be possession in some cases is no doubt incredible. But if depossession therapy works, not using it because it sounds fanciful and nonscientific would constitute nothing short of malpractice. Surely it is time to try any means necessary to "heal the wounds of war."

Demonic Possessions?

It does not appear that all possessions are due to an entity that had a prior life as a human being. In Dr. Baldwin's words:

"Several types of entities can influence or possess a human being. A strong thought form, such as fear, anger, guilt, resentment, jealousy or revenge, can take on an independent existence of its own, and may interfere with either the one who created it or another person altogether. In this way, voodoo, black magic, witchcraft, or curse can produce very real effects, even without the victim's knowledge of the attack. A spirit can be conjured into being, literally created, to do the bidding of the one commanding it.

"There have been cases of takeover by a being or beings claiming to be extraterrestrials. A more dangerous form of possession is caused by a spirit which identifies itself as an agent of evil, a demon or devil, with no history of earth life. They profess a total hatred for humans and express their intentions to cause harm, destruction and death whenever and wherever they can. These cases are uncommon. Interestingly, these entities seem to be bound by the religious beliefs of the culture and can be exorcised by a member of the appropriate clergy."

Demons? Isn't there a simpler explanation?

In the *Reader's Digest* publication entitled *Mysteries of the Unexplained*, three other possibilities are considered. They include epilepsy, hysteria, and multiple personality. Each of these disorders have medical and psychological symptoms which are similar to those encountered with demonic possession. The book concludes that there were distinguishing characteristics, such as the hatred of religious objects and paranormal phenomena, often observed in demonic possession. Obviously we're not out of the woods yet.

Exorcisms

In psychological terms, the rite of exorcism appears to bring about the equivalent of a mental and emotional catharsis. In such a state, some experts would suggest that buried memories of deeply traumatic events, neurotic conflicts, infantile or adult guilts, compulsive-obsessive notions, may all be subjected to some degree of release. Because these interpretations are not without support, ecclesiastical authorities are extremely careful in seeking to rule out all possible psychological and physiological conditions before proceeding with an exorcism or depossession. Nevertheless, in the 1970s over 600 solemn exorcisms were performed by the Catholic Church on victims of demonic possession. This is equivalent to about one each week!

Catholic seminarians, on their way to the priesthood, also discover the church's recognition of the reality of possessions. There the would-be priests are introduced to an order of exorcism that is built into the progression of the priesthood. There may be no "official" public recognition, but apparently practical heads have kept the rituals and knowledge available... just in case.

Hanz Holzer, writing in *Possession,* includes a list of things every exorcist should know. This list of pointers include the nonuse of force, having the exorcist not become a party to the case, strict adherence to the ritual, absolute belief in the ritual, recognition that the victim's personality and beliefs are not shared by the possessor, and a lack of fear or hesitation on the part of the exorcist.

Holzer's concern that the act of exorcism might be taken too lightly is echoed by Scott Peck in his book, *People of the Lie, The Hope for Healing Human Evil.* Peck considered the differences between exorcism and psychotherapy as equivalent to the differences between radical surgery and lancing a boil. Peck also noted that it is essential to use a team of three or more in attempting to conduct an exorcism.

Do Demons Exist?

Are these exorcisms, no matter how solemn, just another form of depossessing a victim from a misguided soul who has not been able to find his way to heaven? Do we have to have demons and evil spirits, or can we content ourselves with run-of-the-mill, rotten-to-the-core, deceased human beings? Surely the human being is capable of carrying it off. Or, is it necessary to have, for real, a being who is the "Devil" or "Satan" or "Lucifer"?

Scott Peck, in *People of the Lie*, describes the demonic influence that he encountered in an exorcism in which he participated. Peck was particularly struck by the patient resembling a writhing, vicious snake of great power, ready to bite the team members. The reptilian's eyes seemed to alternate between a lazy reptilian torpor and active, blazing hatred, whenever it might dart out in attack. Even more extraordinary to Peck was the sense of an ancient heaviness from the eyes, which had caused Peck to feel that there was no hope for the exorcism. From Peck's viewpoint, he was convinced of being in the presence of something horribly inhuman and alien.

Peck, a psychiatrist, noted that he had found nothing which failed to support the Judeo-Christian myth and doctrine about Satan. But at the same time, Peck believed that there were real limitations to Satan's powers. The psychiatrist noted that Satan's only power lay in his ability to deceive humans and to act through the human body. Peck also noted that Satan's intelligence was afflicted with two blind spots: One being that Satan could not comprehend the phenomenon of love, and the other being that Satan assumed that all humans would naturally want to deceive themselves. Peck also observed that extraordinary demonic stupidity occured occasionally in addition to demonic intelligence.

Dr. Ralph Allison has reported on one case of possession in which the victim heard a voice announcing the victim's imminent death. The victim was put under hypnosis, wherein a voice came forth, claiming to be Satan. When a local priest was called for consultation, the priest was able to meet Satan, without hypnosis, by reciting certain rituals. After a relatively mild exorcism, the priest expressed the opinion that the exorcised entity was not Satan, as known in theology, but that he was an evil spirit who was so stupid, he actually thought he was Satan!

I love that story! More than just entertaining, the story points out that evil spirits may think they're devils and demons, but they can be wrong. It would be only natural for a thoroughly evil but dead human being to attempt to increase his status by claiming to be Satan, or if he were a bit more clever, claim to be only in the second echelon of evil beings (sounds more believable that way). We can probably expect that an evil entity would not hesitate to lie about its nature.

The question of the reality of Satan's existence is not likely to be answered by depossessions and exorcisms. Clearly the question is a bit more profound. For our purposes, let us content ourselves with some notable quotes and opinions:

"Certain tyrannical demons require for their enjoyment some soul still incarnate; being unable to satisfy their passions in any other way, to incite to sedition, lust, wars or conquest, and get what they lust for." -Plutarch

"A sick man pining away is one upon whom an evil spirit has gazed." -Homer

"Demons are the spirits of wicked men." -Josephus

"And it came to pass, when the evil spirit from God was upon Saul, that David took an harp, and played with his hand; so Saul was refreshed, and was well, and the evil spirit was departed from him." - I Samuel 16:23

"And when he had called unto Him his twelve disciples, he gave them power against unclean spirits, to cast them out, and to heal all manner of sickness and all manner of disease."   - Matthew 10:1

"And he preached in their synagogues throughout all Galilee, and cast out devils." -Mark 1:39

"And God wrought special miracles by the hands of Paul.
"So that from his body were brought unto the sick handkerchiefs or aprons, and the diseases departed from them, and the evil spirits went out of them." -Acts 19:11-12

"The result of modern 'enlightenment' to treat 'possession' as a hypothesis to be spoken of as even possible, in spite of the massive human tradition based on concrete experience in its favor, has always seemed to me a curious example of the power of fashion in things scientific. That the demon-theory will have its innings again is to my mind absolutely certain. One has to be 'scientific' indeed to be blind and ignorant enough to suspect no such possibility." -William James (1896)

"It is not at all likely that sane and intelligent spirits are the only ones to exert influence from a transcendental world. If they can act on the living there is no reason why others cannot do so as well. The process in either case would be the same; we should have to possess adequate proof that nature puts more restrictions upon ignorance and evil in the next life than in this in order to establish the certainty that mischievous personalities do not or cannot perform nefarious deeds.
"In a number of cases, persons whose condition would ordinarily be described as due to hysteria, dual, or multiple personality, dementia praecox, paranoia, or some other form of mental disturbance, showed unmistakable indications of invasion by foreign and discarnate agencies." -Dr. James Hyslop (1919)

"It is impossible to prove the existence of possessing spirits, if "prove" is meant to be a kind of mathematical or logical certainty. But that is possible only in relating symbols with stipulated meanings. In matters of fact, law, history, medicine, and life in general we must be satisfied with a preponderance of evidence or conclusive evidence beyond reasonable doubt. On the basis of high probability we often act with moral responsibility and psychological certitude. In matters related to the influence of spirits, we can hope for no higher probability than in other matters of fact and experience." -Lewis (1976)

If we cannot "prove" the case one way of the other, it still might be useful to remember one thing: If you die, or you think you might be dead, look around for a white light. If you see it, don't hesitate –
GO FOR IT!!

Consolidation

Are possession and demons necessary to reincarnation theory? They do not appear to be. The possibility of earthbound out-of-body entities attaching themselves to living beings would seem plausible, but would not be a necessary condition for proving reincarnation. The existence of Satan and/or lesser demons would appear to be even less necessary.

At the same time, possessions appear to be a logical extension of the evidence for NDEs and OBEs. Post Traumatic Stress Disorder (PTSD) emphasizes the potential importance of possession, and possession in turn argues for an open-minded approach by modern psychology in treating PTSD. Exorcisms continue to be conducted (there's nothing like witnessing an actual event in order to become a believer!), and demonic influences appear to be real. The reality of demons would appear to be more involved with good and evil, but it might be observed that the mind of man is capable of some rather extraordinary feats, including perhaps the creation of demons.

It must be noted that reincarnation theory does not dispute the possibilities of possession or demonic influences. In fact, the phenomena of possession and demons merely extends the range of possibilities in which reincarnation theory operates. Having earthbound spirits wandering around in an intermediate place, just makes the transition into the light more "eventful".

It is important to remember that when you die and go toward the light, you may meet beings from the light sent to guide you along the way. These "light beings" invariably wear white (there seems to be a decided lack of fashion on the other side), and will likely take your hand. If their hands are warm, that's good.[2] But if not . . . or if the beings you meet are wearing gray or black, pass them by. The guys in levis and designer jeans are more likely from the "intermediate place," and these guys you can safely ignore.

---

[2] Interestingly enough, they no longer appear to be wearing "white hats."

Chapter 11:

Changing

Paradigms

Her name was Helena and she was a multiple personality. In describing her many personalities and their respective talents, Helena casually mentioned that each of her personalities could read minds. This rather surprising revelation suggested to Scott, one of the enterprising interviewers discussing her case, that he should perhaps test her claim of telepathy.

When Helena was speaking in the guise of a ten year old girl, complete with blushes and giddiness, Scott turned and asked if she could truly read minds. Helena's young alter ego simply said, "Yes." Scott then asked her to read his mind.

Scott had not thought in great detail what he should think about in order to have his mind read, but inasmuch as Helena was a very attractive lady, Scott decided to think about the fact that he would like to kiss her. The ten year old personality in a grown woman's body looked at him for just a moment. Then, suddenly horrified, she jumped back and exclaimed, "Stop that! I'm just a little girl!"

While this impromptu experiment was hardly conclusive, the other interviewers in the room did make an effort, thereafter, to think good thoughts (and all strictly platonic). Later, as if to emphasize the point, Helena began a one way conversation with one interviewer by answering several of his unspoken questions. It was a very interesting conversation to witness.

Observing the possibility of telepathic communication tends to put one in a rather interesting frame of mind. Should one be jealous of such talents? Or maybe suspicious? The emotional reaction to such displays can range from paranoia to delight. Which would you choose? Does the answer depend on whether or not you truly believe someone can read your mind? Is such a thing even possible? Why not? An inevitable result of accepting reincarnation and the idea of there being not only life after death, but a life with which we might be able to communicate, is in its very essence, profound. In previous chapters we saw that many people have either contacted the "other side", OR that their minds were capable of some wondrous imagination. In either case, our view of human mental capabilities may require some drastic changes.

Reincarnation, in fact, requires a different view of our world, a change in our paradigm. In the next chapter we will be exposed to how our concepts of time might require change. Now, however, with our changing perceptions, is there anything that is not possible, including extrasensory perceptions such as telepathy?

Don't count on it.

Changing Paradigms

Willis Harman, in his book, *Global Mind Change*, argues that "the real action today is changing fundamental assumptions. " We are, in fact, being asked in these last decades of the millenium, to review and reconsider the most basic assumptions under which we live our lives. And if these basic assumptions fail to measure up, we may have to change them, i.e. change our paradigm, our most fundamental view of life, in order to account for what can no longer be denied.

If reincarnation makes sense, if reincarnation represents our best and most accurate description of the universe, then reincarnation requires a new paradim. (Actually, belief in an afterlife requires the same type of change, inasmuch as, among other things, the afterlife is not considered reality by western science.) Among many other things, reincarnation suggests the mind (or soul) may have some effects in the physical world, other than through traditional avenues of physical expression. Dr. Harmon goes on to describe three basics kinds of metaphysics i.e. three ways in which we perceive our world. The first is a Materialistic Monism, in which the basic stuff of the universe is matter-energy.

> "Whatever consciousness is, it emerges out of matter (that is, the brain) when the evolutionary process has progressed sufficiently far. Whatever we can learn about consciousness must ultimately be reconciled with the kind of knowledge we get from studying the brain, for consciousness apart from a living physical organism is not only unknown, *it is inconceivable*." [emphasis added]

This first metaphysics, which Dr. Harmon calls "M-1", is the current reigning champ of western society. It is the basis of our view of science and technology, where if you can't measure it with some form of mechanical or electronic apparatus, it doesn't exist. Reincarnation, on the other hand, implicitly assumes that there is a mind (or soul) separate from the physical (and that in fact, there is a great deal of the universe, not being observed under either the microscope or telescope). Reincarnation raises doubts concerning one of our most fundamental tenants of our society! Furthermore, reincarnation suggests that it is time to look at an alternative metaphysics!

The other two metaphysical perspectives Dr. Harmon discusses include: Dualism and Transcendental Monism. The first of these alternatives, which Dr.

Harmon calls "M-2", assumes that "there are two fundamentally different kinds of stuff in the universe: matter-energy stuff and mind-spirit stuff." The Transcendental Monism, ("M-3"), on the other hand, assumes that the basic fundamental stuff of the universe is mind-spirit stuff, or more simply, consciousness. On the one hand, M-3 is the contrary view of M-1, where all of the universe arises from consciousness (as opposed to matter-energy stuff). As such, M-3 can be considered to be the paradigm espoused by reincarnationists, particularly those who believe that all of "physical reality" is an illusion. Note that this illusion includes death, sickness, and all manner of "reality", over which we assume that we have no control. M-3, for example, assumes that essentially all sickness is psychosomatic! In other words, everything is just in your mind! This would include cancer, heart disease, and AIDS! The mind controls it all.

M-2, on the other hand, assumes that there's room in the universe for both M-1 and M-3. In this case, we can have a little of each. The cancer may very well be "real", but the stomach ache might be only in your head (which, when you think about it, would be a funny place for your stomach to ache). Another way of looking at it, might be that the physical universe of matter-energy stuff is the combined stuff of all the minds or souls (perhaps including God's), but that what we do with it, is pretty much how we decide to perceive it. In this latter case, you may be carrying a flu virus (which could exist without the benefit of your consciousness), but until your mind decides it's time to have the flu, the virus has no effect over you.

While Dr. Harmon ultimately chooses M-3 as his choice for the ultimate reality, it is not necessary for our purposes to choose either the all-consciousness mode of existence (M-3), or allow some matter-energy stuff to exist independently of and simultaneously with our consciousness (i.e. M-2). Rather, we can assume, based upon the requirements of reincarnation and a between lives state (or even just an "after life"), to simply recognize that the mind/soul is capable of vast capabilities, including creating much of its own reality.

With that in mind, we can now go back to Scott and Helena and consider of just what things Helena's mind might be capable. (We can assume that we already know what Scott's thinking! Just like a man, right!?)

Extrasensory Perception

Extrasensory perception (ESP) is perception that is assumed to be totally independent of the five known senses. As such, it includes:

> – Telepathy: direct mental communication between two or more persons, either as a one-way communication or multidirected.

> – Clairvoyance: the ability to perceive things that are not in sight or cannot be seen by the sense of sight.

– Clairaudience: the ability to perceive and understand sounds without actually hearing them with the sense of hearing.

– Precognition: the perceiving of future events without deducing their occurence from existing knowledge.

– Psychokinesis: the use of the mind to effect changes in external matter.

ESP Research

Efforts to validate or disprove the existence of ESP have been occurring with increasing frequency ever since the 1930s when psychology professor J. B. Rhine began his research into finding statistical evidence. While the concept of ESP was more or less accepted in many cultures throughout the world, the Duke University Professor's research was one of the first major research efforts in the United States.

The difficulty of proving or disproving ESP is complicated by several factors. One such factor is that in many cases of ESP research, the very act of scientific investigation may influence the thing under study. (Remember, the mind may be capable of many things!) Another major concern was the ability to replicate a particular experiment and obtain similiar results in each and every case, regardless of the investigators involved.

An early experimenter was J. G. Pratt, who tested Hubert Pearce, a divinity student at the Duke School of Religion, on Pearce's ability to predict which card Pratt would turn over next. In some of the experiments, Pearce operated in a room located 100 or 250 yards from Pratt's laboratory. In the course of 1,850 trials, Pearce was able to demonstrate truly amazing results. His clairvoyant ability achieved so many hits that the odds against his doing so were ten thousand trillion, trillion to 1!

Russell Targ and Dr. Harold Puthoff conducted remote-viewing experiments in 1972 through 1975, by asking subjects to describe what experimenters were seeing at a distant location. The odds against one subject's successes were caluculated at 500,000 to 1; comparatively paltry odds. Targ and Puthoff also concluded that distance and electrical shielding had no effect, and that the skill apparently was a function of the brain's right hemisphere. Other investigators have suggested that such clairvoyant ability might be within the grasp of anyone, but that overdevelopment of the left brain might be responsible for the apparent lack.

So what were you teaching your child the other day?

Psychic Candidates

Subjects who seem to be likely candidates for ESP abilities have been found to be younger, better educated, sensitive to events and emotions around them, and more open minded in social and religious matters; but there is apparently no evidence that suggests that anyone could not exercise some form(s) of ESP. ESP proponents think that babies may have it as a natural ability, then lose it as a result of their acquiring language skills. The important point here is that telepathic communication would no longer be needed for survival once language was learned.

Many people who have multiple personalities have been found to have a strong tendency to possess some ESP abilities. This fact of telepathy or ESP abilities being demonstrated among people with multiple personalities is noteworthy. A child undergoing severe child abuse might literally grab at any straw in order to discover the intentions of an approaching adult whose behavior was unpredictable and therefore uncontrollable. Such desperation could explain the initiation of the ability. And the maintenance of ESP abilities into adulthood may simply be due to their having been "locked in" during the child's early and dramatic physiological development.

Potency

Researchers have also noted a "potency" factor. If danger is a significant part of an ESP event, there seems to be a greater likelihood that the news will break through to the conscious mind. Ian Stevenson, for example, found 19 instances of apparent telepathy, clairvoyance and precognition in relation to the sinking of the Titanic in 1912. Clearly an abused child concerned about the next possible round of immense pain would qualify under the potency factor. Alternatively, when monotonous experiments are conducted over and over again, researchers note a drop in scores, what they called the "decline effect."

The factor of potency (or lack thereof) can apparently be eliminated by an altered state. The alpha state (normal dream state) appears to be an optimal mental state for obtaining the best results in experiments involving ESP. Many psychics have noted this state is one in which no two entities are separate because everything flows into everything else.

Psychokinesis

As an aspect of ESP, psychokinesis stands alone. For unlike extra-sensory perception, psychokinesis (PK) is an outward extension of power. Instead of the equivalent of a radar tracking beam, we have a "tractor beam", capable of changing what we perceive.

J. B. Rhine conducted tests on psychokinesis with the use of dice. At first, allowing subjects to throw dice, Rhine obtained successful results despite odds of only one chance in a billion. In one case he used opposing teams, one known for its ability to throw dice, and one using prayer or meditation as its motivating force. The teams achieved virtually identical results and, in both cases, against odds of one in several billion.

More recently, Brenda J. Dunne, Roger D. Nelson, and Robert G. Jahn, of Princeton University, have reported clear evidence of "significant anomalous" events, indicative of psychokinesis. These experimenters noted specific variations between subjects, lack of inhibition of the PK effect by separating the experimental apparatus and the subject by several thousand miles, and the observation of radically different results between individual subjects, and the cooperative effort to two or more subjects. These results are now being reported in respected scientific journals.[1]

Individuals with PK

By the 1960s many parapshololgists had begun to feel that the possibility of PK's existence was sufficiently demonstrated. However, the experimental evidence was easily defendable only for mental influence over moving targets. When tested with the idea of modifying nonmoving targets, such famed PK subjects as Ted Serios and Uri Geller failed to demonstrate clearcut abilities under laboratory controlled conditions. Only Nina Kulagina of the Soviet Union had consistently produced exceptional psychokinetic effects (according to Russian sources). These abilities included causing movement of objects toward or away from her and in circular patterns, and were said to affect metal, fabric and plastics. Ms. Kulagina was able to alter positions of objects even with intervening screens (but not in a vacuum), and in one case caused a burn-like mark on a British researcher that took over a week to heal.

Many investigators believe an involuntary or an unconscious form of psychokinesis may be at the heart of much poltergeist activity. Dr. William Roll, project director of the Psychical Research Foundation in Durham, North Carolina, and Gaither Pratt, an experienced Duke University ESP researcher, have observed subjects (who were obviously unhappy) at the very center of poltergeist activities. But when these same subjects were then tested in the laboratory, they apparently had no conscious control over their supposed ability to influence objects at a distance. Roll and Pratt, subsequently, postulated that PK acts as a safety valve for venting pent up emotions. Adding fuel to this fire is the fact that Roll noted a disproportionate number of subjects with apparent involuntary PK powers suffering from symptoms not unlike those of epilepsy.

Joel Whitton reported in *Life Between Life* that one of his subjects also demonstrated an apparent unconscious form of PK due in part to her traumatic history of child abuse. In this case the lady was not even aware of the possibility that she was in fact causing the problem. Apparently, this is not an uncommon symptom with many such subjects.

Conflicting Theories

By the time of Professor Rhine's death in 1980, hundreds of volumes of experimental data exhibiting significant scores in telepathy, clairvoyance, precognition or psychokinesis had been collected. The evidence was then deemed so overwhelming by the Parapsychological Association that this group concluded that further tests were both superfluous and boring. The fact that ex-

---

[1] *Journal of Scientific Exploration*, Vol 2, #2, 1988.

perimental evidence has continued to accumulate and support various forms of ESP only goes to show that many scientists need to see some things for themselves.

Critics, in the face of overwhelming documentary evidence, have now retreated to the charge that parapsychology has yet to develop a plausible theory to account for the phenomena. The key word seems to be "plausible", for if you have been reading this book, a theory appears to be already emerging. One possible view, for example, is that ESP phenomena transcend time and space by going into a state where time and space pose no constraints on the mind. Whether such a view is plausible or not, the evidence that ESP exists is becoming undeniable. One Nobel Prize-winning physiologist, Charles Richet, has remarked on the evidence for precognition, for example, by noting that while he might not say it was possible, he was constrained to say it was true.

One theory of telepathic reception could be based on morphogenetic fields. A morphogenetic field is one which shapes a growing plant or animal (or even chemical systems such as crystals), based on the forms of previous organisms (or crystals) of the same species (or chemical form). An embryo, for example, might "tune in" to the forms of past members of the species. In their instinctive behavior, animals might draw upon some sort of species "pooled memory" or "memory bank".

In his paper, "Can Our Memories Survive the Death of Our Brains? (*The Proceedings of the Symposium on Consciousness and Survival*), Dr. Rupert Sheldrake, one of the main proponents for morphogenetic fields, says:

> "If we pick up our own memories by tuning into our own past states, and these memories are not stored inside our brains, then why don't we tune into other people's memories? Perhaps we do. If we tune into the memories of large numbers of people in the past, we would not be aware of all the specific memories of particular events in their lives, but rather a kind of composite of pooled memory which would contain the basic forms or patterns of their experience and thought. This idea closely corresponds with C. G. Jung's theory of the archetypes in the collective unconscious; and Jung's approach to psychology harmonizes well with the notion of morphic resonance.
>
> "It might also be possible to pick up particular people's memories which are very recent – only a few seconds old. In this case there might be a transference of thoughts, or in other words, a process which is equivalent to telepathy. In this way the hypothesis of formative causation might provide a bridge between science and at least some of the phenomena of parapsychology."

As a last vestige of hope, skeptics might point out that there is no evidence for the existence of a morphogenetic field. This last ditch effort, however, is also flawed. Consider the following idea: If we wanted to establish the existence of an electromagnetic field, we would almost certainly fail if we used a mechanical apparatus to measure some aspect of the EM field. It would be as if we were attempting to use apparatus designed to measure gravitational fields, to measure an electromagnetic field. Obviously such a measurement would likely fail. Equally obvious, any attempt to measure a morphogenetic field with electromagnetic apparatus will also fail. If you want to establish the existence of morphogenetic fields (i.e. "mind" fields), you must use... you guessed it!. a mind.

But there is more to it than that. If we purchase a radio kit with which to build a radio and fail to assemble the set properly, we may very well find that we cannot find any evidence of the alleged electromagnetic fields associated with radio waves. Even if we assemble the set properly, there is still the chance that we may still obtain only static. In other words, we have to be able to tune our receiver in order to get meaningful results!

Thus if the mind being used to find the morphogenetic field is not properly "tuned," it is unlikely that that mind will get anything but static. Furthermore, the first necessity of "tuning the mind" might be the presence of an "open mind." (Small wonder that many researchers may have great difficulty in finding any evidence of a morphogenetic field.) Thereafter, and depending upon experience and training, one can become more or less adept at tuning into the morphogenetic fields and effectively display a whole host of ESP abilities. The loss of potency with ESP subjects might be simply that they do not have an automatic frequency control (AFC), as do FM radio tuners, and thus may sometimes lose their "station." It would appear that "a theory of ESP phenomena", using Sheldrake's morphogenetic fields, may in fact now exist!

Finally if incredibly strange and unexplainable events occur in other areas and are accepted by scientists, why should ESP be so hard to explain? Neutrinos, for example, were postulated only because there was the need to account for momentum in certain forms of radioactive decay. Quantum physics' "weak force" has had particles imagined by science in order to explain this little understood phenomenon. But the idea of two minds communicating without the use of normal sensory channels, haunts the scientific establishment as surely as do ghosts and spirits. There is little justification for such narrow-mindedness in science. It's really time for science to get its act together.

William James wrote (after taking laughing gas), that the one conclusion which he was forced to come to, and which he had ever since found unshakeable, was that one's normal waking consciousness was only one form of consciousness, while parted from it by the flimsiest of screens were, potentially, entirely unknown forms of consciousness. A century later we are attempting to penetrate the "flimsiest of screens". In dreams, altered states, hypnosis, insanity, and trances, sensory deprivation and overload, psychedelic states and even simple relaxation, we may have the means of piercing the screen.

Into the Unknown, by the editors of *Reader's Digest*, makes the noteworthy comment that, if ESP does in fact exist and can be proven to the scientific establishment to exist, science will feel its most basic tenets to suddenly be in question, and that this situation is one that few scientists wish to face, or, in particular, contribute to. All new knowledge invariably faces the same challenges. The originator of the concept of continental drift, Alfred Weggener, was literally laughed off the stage when he first presented his theories in 1915. Since then, continental drift has become a basic tenet of geologic and related sciences.

From Galileo to Einstein, science and society have always resisted radically new ideas. Let's face it: it's tough on the scientist when he or she discovers that everything that person has learned or taught during the last fifty years, is wrong. Or at the very least, inadequate. The potential for ESP and psychic phenomena to upset the scientific applecart is enormous. With the number of scientists who have so vociferously resisted the possibilitites, crow could become an endangered species.

The Mind-Body Connection

Holistic medicine is simply the consideration of mental and physical processes in determining health. In effect, illness can be construed to be a mind-body problem. If you are upset, you effectively tell your brain, perhaps through some form of ESP, that you're upset, and the brain, being a highly litteral computer, will provide physical ailments to match your upset emotional state. The brain can be thought of as a combination of a problem solver/goal seeker/maintenance man, under the direction of the mind. If the mind conceives of a problem, the brain will solve it (one way or the other). If the mind has no problems, the brain will often manufacture one in order to keep busy and to be able to solve yet another problem.

Worried about what will happen tomorrow? Emotional concern may trigger the brain to provide appropriate physical problems for you to solve as well. The brain is always very amenable to suggestion. Give it a hint, and it'll take you for miles. It's also noncontroversial, so that there's no chance it will say, "Hey man, that's not what you want." The brain cannot even distinguish between real and imaginary, so it doesn't know that the terrible worry with which you are spending so much time, is probably illusory. As Mark Twain once said, "I've had many problems in my life, most of which never came true."

On the other hand, holistic medicine proponents claim that if you tell the brain you're fine, it will cure whatever problems that might arise and in the process make you well. The brain is a computer, afterall, and computers always do what you tell them. Tell the brain you're feeling great and the brain will so inform the rest of the body. (But don't get cute; remember that the brain has no sense of humor -- it does what you tell it to do, and not necessarily what you want it to do.)

Psychomatics

Dr. Norman Cousins, in his books *Anatomy of an Illness* and *The Healing Heart*, desribes his own experience with what he sees as the healing powers of laughter and emotional well-being and the killing potential of panic and depression. As chairman of UCLA's Task Force on Psychoneuroimmunology, he is exploring the possible ESP connection between the mind and the body's healing powers.

In doing so, he has noted that while the negative effects of emotions, such as depression, panic, anger, hate, rage and frustration, are well documented with medical evidence, there is no comparable body of knowledge on hope, purpose, creativity, laughter, and the will to live. This becomes particularly important when people's attitudes about health and life itself may have biochemical effects, i.e. what you think, ultimately shows up in the biochemistry of your body.

Cousins has noticed, for example, that when told of a diagnosis, the patients' illness intensified at that precise moment. The panic and fear that occurred, in fact, set the stage for the advance of the disease by producing hormones, constricting the blood vessels, and so forth. From his viewpoint, there is a major conflict of interest with the attending physicians, who for legal liability reasons must lay it on the line, but who by telling the patient the worst, may contribute to bringing on the worst!

Scientists and medical practitioners, such as Dr. Cousins, are coming to the conclusion that one cannot have an emotional action without a physical action. Such a conclusion, however, can be good news just as well as bad news. For example, if your emotions and mental state can cause psychosomatic ills, why can't the same psychological factors cause psychomatic benefits? In other words, if you have the power to think yourself into ignorance, disease, and death, then it follows that you also have the power to become grander – simply by opening yourself up to the immense possibilities, which can allow you to have greater genius, greater creativity, and possibly, life for a much longer time, if not forever.

Brendan O'Regan of the Institute for Noetic Sciences has collected over 3,000 cases of spontaneous remission. (Spontaneous remission is the medical term for cases where the patient gets well, and the medical establishment has no earthly idea how.) In effect, the patient decides on their own to get well and do. Terminal cases become non-terminal, and quickly thereafter, non-cases. One well known medical doctor specializing in terminal cancer, has taken to telling his cancer patients (when appropriate) that they have, for example, only 3 chances in 10 to survive their particular cancer. Then he asks the patient if they would like to be one of the 3! This medical doctor, recognizing the immense power of the mind to heal the body, has concluded that if a patient really wants to be healed and believes that they will be, then they will in fact be healed!

The key, of course, is to believe one will be healed. Witch doctors did a thriving business when the natives believed in their powers. Modern man has had much the same relationship with the modern medical doctor. But today, when patients are coming to the conclusion that medical doctors are not omniscience, doubts have started to creep in, and thus the medical community's ability to facilitate healing has decreased.

Consequently, modern man must make their own decisions to heal themselves, and at the same time, believe that they are capable of doing so! Inasmuch as the mind may very well rule the body, and if healing is to be effective in whatever diverse form it is practiced, it is therefore essential to heal the mind as well as the body. It no longer seems plausible that psychological problems can be ignored when trying to heal the physical ills. With this holistic approach to medicine, surgeons may have to learn bedside manners, doctors, in general, learn psychological counseling, and patients learn that they themselves are the only ones really doing the healing.

At the same time, it must be noted that a psychological problem manifesting itself in the present might not necessarily have originated in this life. There is always the possibility that the psychological basis for an illness may have originated in a past life. Apparently, medical doctors may have even more considerations to contemplate (such as reincarnation theory) in their continuing quest to adhere to the Hippocratic oath.

Dr. Edith Fiore, who conducted 20,000 past-life regressions in 15 years, states in her book *You Have Been Here Before*, that 98 percent of the problems with which she has been presented, originated in past lives. Dr. William J. Baldwin of Carmel, California, has come to a nearly similar conclusion:

> "89 percent of all ailments treated by physicians are psychosomatic in origin. That means the source of most illnesses lie in the subconscious mind. The subconscious contains the complete record of everything you have ever experienced, seen, heard, tasted, touched, smelled, felt, said, thought. Must the basis of our problems be limited to just one life?"

If healing is indeed largely psychosomatic (and the evidence appears to be almost overwhelming), and in turn, psychosomatic ills may have their origin in past-lives (considerable evidence here as well), the connection between healing and reincarnation then becomes obvious. Not only does reincarnation support many of the aspects of healing discussed above, directly and indirectly, but healing has provided considerable evidence for reincarnation through the medium of past-life regressions done to cure or heal psychological and psychosomatic problems.

Mind Control

If the mind is capable of telepathy, precognition, psychokinesis, and healing it's physical body, what next?

Consider for a moment the following idea: A mind or soul controls the physical body in which it resides (albeit maybe only temporarily, like during an incarnation) through some form of psychokinesis. This then neatly ties in with the fact that a soul existing separately from the body (and thus capable of occupying a wide variety of bodies over time) can still manage control over the body. Not only manage control, but determine its state of health. In this way healing and ESP can be intimately linked with reincarnation.

Note also that the mind-body connection, the psychokinesis between soul and body, may require specific vibrations or tuning. But that in some cases, another soul can, using its own powers of psychokinesis, manage to tune itself into someone else's body and take over, at least partial control. Thus possession connects with all the other things of which we've just discussed.

That same psychokinetic power of a soul wandering in the space between physical reality and heaven, might also be utilized to effect poltergeist activities, or even allow itself to appear in some ghostly fashion. An incarnated being, only visiting the intermediate space while out-of-body, would maintain its psychokinetic connections with its body through the "Silver Cord", that transcendental-umbilical cord, with which the life force of the soul could be conducted to the body.

Strangely and weirdly, everything begins to connect and individual paranormal phenomena begin to be perceived as simply implications of a broader theory of life and death. Slowly it becomes apparent why reincarnation is, in fact, making a comeback, and suggests that perhaps reincarnation may very well, also have a future.

Or then again, maybe not. Maybe, even the idea of a future, might be in question. For this cheery thought, consult the next chapter.

Chapter 12:

It's About

Time

Shari already regretted her decision. Asking advice from the very weird lady across the table from her did not seem to be the best idea in Shari's young life. Paying forty dollars for the session seemed wildly extravagant, especially when the potential for worthless advice seemed so likely. Of course, it was too late now.

The lady smiled as she looked over the cards. "I see a long trip for you. Possibly near a great body of water. And very soon, I think."

Shari frowned. "I'm going back to school in three weeks. Long Beach, California. Maybe that's it."

"Possibly." The weird lady was apparently not yet convinced.

Shari wasn't either. The old lady probably knew that Shari was a student, and she might well have seen her college sticker on her car when she arrived. But Shari had already paid her; she'd have to get her money's worth somehow. "What else?"

"Don't go riding in a red pickup for the next month."

"Excuse me?"

"Especially with a short, balding man. He is a careless driver."

No sweat, Shari thought, I don't like short men, bald men, and/or pickups. "No red pickups . . . right!"

"And avoid the short, balding man."

"No problem."

"However, I do see a tall, six foot man, whom you will soon meet."

"Oh?" Shari was suddenly interested.

"I see you in some sort of class room together."

Wonderful! Shari thought, One tall six foot man in a class of about two hundred students! Good luck meeting him! Shari's momentary enthusiasm waned as quickly as it had occured.

"He will be wearing a blue suit, when you meet. I see him with a neatly trimmed beard, and light brown hair. You will know him when he says 'I'm in communications.' He's very nice looking. You will be immediately attracted to him."

"Is he rich?" Shari asked, with just a hint of interest.

"I see you with him in a convertible. A Mercedes I think."

Shari was now definitely interested. "Great! I'll take him! What's his name?"

"I am not sure the car is his. Might be his parents."

"No problem. I'll take him either way. Just tell me his name!!

Predicting the Future

How can an otherwise intelligent young lady go from critical skepticism to eager anticipation of a highly improbable future event? Is it her eagerness to find a desirable mate, or just simple gullibility? More importantly, is it possible for someone such as a psychic to predict Shari's future? Would you change your mind if the events predicted actually came true?

Obviously, there are plenty of short, balding men and even a few with red pickups. There is even a reasonable supply of tall, nice looking bearded men driving Mercedes. If Shari manages to avoid the former and actually meet the latter, does this prove anything? Probably not. Shari may beat the odds, but it may have little to do with a foreknowledge of the future.

Mind you, predicting the future is not always that hard. Forecasting that the sun will rise in the east tomorrow morning is easy enough. Forecasting rain is simple, if you have access to the right kind of information. Predictions of other people entering one's life is not that difficult either, unless the person is a serious recluse. The fact of the matter is that many predictions are odds on favorites to begin with.

In other cases, the predictions may be self-fulfilling. If you are told you will take a trip to Hawaii and then subsequently do exactly that, is the prediction itself partly responsible for your actions? Did it give you the idea, which you later acted on? Conversely, if you avoid driving a red pickup in order to avoid an accident, can you ever know if the accident that didn't happen, would have happened if you had not taken steps to avoid it?

The difficulty is in the statistics. The odds of two people meeting and falling in love is quite good, if you are working with a large number of people. On the other hand, if the entire sample of people all met and fell in love, that a different story. Isolated statistics simply don't prove much of anything, whereas 100 percent predictions being correct might very well prove at least the possibility of predicting the future. Alternatively, predictions which effect large groups of people or the entire world are more noteworthy in that they are seldom "self-fulfilling prophecies" and may occur for reasons other than simple statistical probability.

A good example of this larger scale forecasting is provided by Dr. Helen Wambach. Dr. Wambach, in addition to regressing her subjects into the past, has also taken them under hypnosis into the future. In separate efforts, Dr.

Wambach told her subjects to go to the years 2100 and 2300, and then describe what they sensed. The accounts of her subjects seemed to follow four basic scenarios, but otherwise were quite consistent. At the same time, all of the accounts indicated that the population of the earth in 2100 would be about 5 percent of today's population, while the year 2300's population was about 15 percent.[1]

The obvious implication of a worldwide catastrophe wiping out 95 percent to 99 percent of the population of the earth, sometime in the next hundred years or so, is obviously the sort of thing to catch one's attention. The potential for near-term or not-so-near-term disaster is certainly a legitimate topic for discussion, and as a consequence, the idea will be discussed in some detail in chapter 15. For the present, however, our interest will be directed toward the very existence of a predictable future. In other words, is the very nature of the future such that it can be predicted? To consider this question, we must first consider the more fundamental issue of time. Is time a chronological necessity (providing for maximal free will), are we in fact limited by "the arrow of time", or some other confining structure?

The Nature of Time

On the one hand, Fisher and Whitton, in their book, *Life Between Life*, noted that their subjects were invariably confused by the lack of time and space dimensions in the bardo. There seemed to be no logic, order, or normal progression, as if everything was happening at once. (Of course, a lot of reincarnationists are invariably confused. And, of course, a lot of the single life advocates.)

Stranger still, in *Life Before Life*, Helen Wambach has reported on people being counseled prior to their birth, by fathers, mothers and relatives who had either died prior to their birth, or in some cases, those whom they would know later in the coming lifetime. Ms. Wambach observed that the distinction between people alive at the time of birth (when the future life was being planned), and people who were dead or not yet born, was essentially absent. In effect, the chronological time sequence of who is alive and who is dead is of apparently little importance.

Dr. Wambach then notes that space and time are indeed different in a dream than when awake, and that in a dream we seem to have no constraints of time and space (we can be a child at our parent's home one minute, and in our office in present time the next). She also notes that right brain time is experienced differently–daydreaming or involved in creative work, time rushes by us. Time also slows when one is stoned on marijuana. Finally, memory is also indifferent to real world time, an experience twenty years ago often being more vivid than what happened at last week's lecture.

Of course, anything would be more vivid than last week's lecture!

---

[1] One of Dr. Wambach's associates, Chet Snow, has recently published a detailed account of these and other predictions, entitled *Mass Dreams of the Future*. If you like to worry about the future, this may be the ideal book for you!

This lack of temporal sequence may seem a bit disquieting at first, especially to someone still attached to the comfortable time sequences of earth. The idea of making plans before your birth with parents who were currently incarnated, might seen a little difficult at first, but this seems perfectly plausible in reincarnation theory. You just have to readjust your idea of time.

In order to do that and, perhaps, better visualize this new concept of time, it might be desirable to consider Richard Bach's description, from his book, *Illusions, The Adventures of a Reluctant Messiah*. Bach describes what we call reality as a reel of film, one which is finished and "in the can". Everything already exists in the same precise second. In effect, the film exists outside of time, and you may already know what the move is about before you even enter the theater. But in order to enjoy the movie, to really get into it, it's necessary for the projector to show you, frame by frame, the exact sequence of events. In effect, the illusion the movie provides requires space and time to be experienced.

Fred Hoyle, one of the worlds most famous astrophysicists, has described time as a multitude of pigeon holes, with a light periodically shining on one hole, then another, and so forth. The concept is that time derives from the progress of the light across pigeon holes, one at a time and in a specific sequence. However, one never knows which pigeon hole will be next in the light, or whether or not, in fact, each and every pigeon hole will be lit by the progressing light.

These theories of "simultaneity" are quite prevalent in the views of most reincarnationists, but is such a concept of time necessary to the theory of reincarnation? Probably yes. In fact, the idea of living simultaneous lives is routinely considered, as well.

In this case, an individual incarnated today might remember separate past lives when he fought for the Union in one, and fought for the Confederacy in another. The two past lives could even have ended up shooting at each other! (Talk about a split personality!)

Robert Monroe has reported that the question of living two lives simultaneously relative to time, has been asked of the beings encountered in the out-of-body state, and that the answer appears to be that it's not only possible but happens frequently. Monroe goes on to note that physical lifetimes are not sequential in time, but may be simultaneous.

In *Far Journeys*, for example, Monroe describes a report by one of his subjects, who is allegedly in an out-of-body state. The OBE subject, supposedly communicating with beings on the other side of consciousness, reports back the gist of his otherworld conversation. In it, the OBEer notes several interesting facts: Any soul may have several personalities going at the same time in physical time and space, (e.g. one old, one male, one female, etc) and that such personalities are not limited to earth, but may be in very different physical bodies on very different planets. In one case, the OBEer notes that one is a slimy, gelatine kind of thing, living a "life" thousands of light years from earth!

Just think. . . the next time you call someone a "slime", you may be referring to one of his soul-siblings. On the other hand, for safety's sake, don't expect him to take the time to figure out this perfectly rational chain of logic. Particularly, if he's big and mean, and thirsty for blood.

Monroe later states quite explicitly that one can go forward and backward in time during OBEs. Monroe goes on to suggest a few helpful pointers in doing so. He suggests, for example, that in one's first attempts one should "travel" only short distances in time. The concern is that one might have some difficulty in returning to the proper time! For example, you could be out to lunch on an OBE, and when you returned, find yourself in time for breakfast on the same day. This sort of thing could completely blow your diet!

Oops. Paradox time. Consider just briefly the possibility of reliving a morning. What would your friends think, if you insisted on doing it over again, perhaps with a few noteworthy changes?

Is Time Essential?

Is there a contradiction here? Proponents of the theory that everything is happening at once, invariably also believe in the concept of the evolution of the soul. Reincarnation exists in order to allow for successive lives of experience as a means of evolving the soul from one state of being to another. Even in the case of living simultaneous lives, the soul is simply allowing for more experiences to be gained by providing for more and varied experiences.

However, such evolution of the soul, particularly from a strictly biological point of view, virtually insists on a chronological sequence. How can one evolve except over time?

Evolution, as defined by Webster, is an unfolding, opening out, or working out; process of development, as from a simple to a complex form, or of gradual, progressive change. Process is even more specific, namely "course (of time, etc)." If in fact our time(s) on earth are for the evolution of our soul, then it appears that some form of time is vitally needed.

At the same time, it seems clear that our physical world depends rather heavily on time. As Richard Bach has noted, in order to experience any illusion, space and time is required. Presumably any of our illusions within the bardo would also require time and space. More importantly perhaps, it may be that when we are in the bardo or in an altered state of consciousness (dream, out-of-body, etc) our souls *may not be bound or constrained* by the confines of time and space, but that this does not imply that neither time nor space exists in those realms.

Paradoxes

Many reincarnationists also believe that we can select our lives for specific purposes and can as easily select a 16th century experience following a 20th century experience, as the other way around. The difficulty with this idea concerns the inevitable time paradoxes that arise. Science Fiction, for example, has belabored these paradoxes thru a hundred years of novels, short stories, and other forms of narrative writing. Serious students of science fiction will find it difficult to give any credence to the ability to take a step back in time in order to accomplish something you forgot during the first time around.

There is, of course, the exception. In order to eliminate the inevitable paradox, everything to occur in the future might already be set in concrete, so to speak. A classic example of this is the recent movie, The Terminator, where Arnold Shwarzenegger gets to prove he has brains as well as brawn. (Just kidding, Arnie!)

In the movie (and amazingly enough, in the book as well) a revolutionary from the future has returned to the present day in order to save the life of the woman destined to give birth to the future hero of the revolution. The future dictatorship, supposedly a very smart but thoroughly evil computer, has initiated the action of the freedom fighters by sending The Terminator to kill the woman before she is able to give birth to the hero who will eventually overthrow the computerized dictatorship. The computer is thus attempting to change a single aspect of the past in order to arrive at a very different future. Rather clever of the computer, don't you think? Our revolutionary is of course, trying to outdo the computer and its agent, The Terminator, by saving the woman's life.

Naturally the good guys win (the computer loses). But the critical factor is that the revolutionary sent back to foil the computer's terminator, turns out to be the father of the future hero who will overturn the computer's dictatorship! The initiation by the computer of sending their hit-man back in time, was the cause of the revolutionary returning in order to spawn the future nemesis of the computer! In effect the attempt to change the past was thwarted by everything being fixed before hand – sort of a rigged game against the computer. Obviously the mechanical-electronic monster seriously erred when it attempted to change the past. But perhaps, the error was foreordained.

The Arrow of Time/Entropy

Related to this limitation on times past is the concept of cause and effect. A fundamental aspect of most proponents' views of reincarnation is karma, in effect a direct result of cause and effect. Any action taken in the past (the cause) will result in a specific condition (the effect) in the future. The reference to past and future for the exercise of cause and effect, thus implies time. There is, in fact, no way around time, if cause and effect are involved.

Furthermore, time seems to be an absolute requirement of a physical world. Modern physics has, in fact, found the need for "an arrow of time." This point is heavily stressed in one of the most fundamental laws of physics, the Second Law of Thermodynamics. The second law establishes a very one-directional process for something referred to as entropy, a quantity which measures the degree of disorder in any given system. In effect the Second

Law, of which there has never been a single conflicting piece of physical evidence, decrees that the entropy of any closed system must increase, i.e. the disorder of a system must increase.

Order can be thought of as a drop of liquid red dye and a separate glass of water. Initially the dye drop and the water are ordered, in the sense that they are readily distinguishable. But once the dye is dropped into the water, it mixes and becomes indistinguishable. This latter state is disorder. The Second Law implies that no matter how long we wait, the red dye will never return to its nonmixed state with the water, a fact easily conceivable to our everyday experiences.

If the system is not closed, i.e. we impart energy to it in some appropriate way, the entropy can then decrease (order is restored). However, if we consider the imparted energy and its source to be part of a larger "closed system", the entropy of the larger system will always increase. If the universe is considered the ultimate in larger closed systems, the entropy of the universe must always increase. In other words, the universe must eventually lose all order and in effect, die. Physically, this can be thought of as the entire universe reaching the same temperature.

Lest anyone should become overly concerned about this, it should be noted that the universe is not expected to cease its functioning next week, or even next month. Current estimates place it at about 10 billion years in the future. Hopefully this will be enough time to allow you to finish this book. Among other things.

[However, predictions concerning other significant interruptions of life on the Planet Earth, place the time frame in a matter of years. For more on this, refer to the doomsday predictions in chapter 15.]

More Paradoxes

While we may have difficulty eliminating our concept of time from the physical world, is it conceivable that in the bardo, time can in fact be simultaneous? Can we not in fact have our cake and eat it as well? Can the bardo state be equivalent to seeing everything at once, while the physical state exists alongside, happily complete with time and space as essential ingredients? Perhaps we can in fact have it both ways - sounds just like something that perverse old nature would allow.

The critical question comes down to: Is the timelessness of the bardo real? Are the reports of non-time in the space between lives, an accurate perception? Or is the confusion of those visiting the wonderland of white lights responsible for the illusion of being unable to sense time (not to mention space)?

Interestingly enough there is physical evidence suggesting that our traditional concept of time may be less than self-evident. In the Einstein-Podolsky-Rosen paradox, an experiment generates two elementary particles (particles on the order of electrons and protons) which are moving apart at the speed of light. An experimenter, who takes action to alter a characteristic of one particle, will then find that the other particle changes its corresponding characteristic as well. The paradox arises from the unknown, non-local connection between the particles. With the speed of light being, theoretically, the universe's absolute speed limit (although generally ignored on the West German Autobahn), the question arises as to how the second particle becomes aware of what happened to the first particle.

We have no clever answers for this one.

Free Will

Clearly time is more complicated than we might have thought. In fact, as Professor J.B.S. Haldane has remarked, "The universe is not only queerer than we think, but queerer than we can think". Nevertheless, our concept of time, no matter how incomplete, must include reference to another staple of our existence: Free will.

If time is a non sequitur during our stays in the bardo, and if in fact the future is already determined (or in Richard Bach's analogy, filmed and "in the can"), can we have free will? It is obvious that if everything is predetermined, then we will not have choices, free will, or even decisions to be made.

If that is the case, why are we here? Without free will, any alleged "evolution of the soul" would be pretty cut and dried. (Not to mention boring.) There would, in fact, be no point in an earthly existence, other than to act out a drama for the benefit of some unearthly audience. But even in a play, there is ample opportunity for ad-libs and dropped lines. With predetermined futures, we would not even have the solace of being allowed to forget one's entrance. Or exit!

Recall also that the multitude of reports from the bardo all involve the concept of planning our next reincarnation - not just the selection of parents and sex, but the intention of meeting others in the coming life for any number of purposes. Planning in the bardo apparently includes the possibility of determining in large part all the events of a future life.

As one of Dr. Whitton's subjects reported, the basic outline of our lives is predestined, and we specifically chose that outline. The details, however, we fill in as we live our lives, proceeding toward our own selected destiny. Whitton subsequently concluded that such self responsibility ultimately leads to self-determination. Accepting the concept of reincarnation implies the acceptance of responsibility for ourselves in growing through a series of successive births.

Limitations on Free Will

Clearly our ability to plan our own reincarnations would imply the existence of a soul's free will. If we are making our own choices, we are exercising free will. But are there limitations on our free will? Is free will available during our time in a physical body? If so, to what degree?

In choosing our future lives, we are clearly limited by the plans of other souls. We may cooperate with others in planning for a future life, but the act of cooperation is inherently an act of limiting our own choices. Free will of the soul is thus not unlike what one might expect from what we apparently have in our physical state of being.

Once on earth, however, are we locked into a particular script? The answer would appear to be no. Or perhaps more accurately, the answer is probability.

Future Probabilities

Consider for example a radioactive uranium atom (obviously the sort of thing to which you've been looking forward for years). This atom plans to go through the process of decay, transforming itself into an atom of thorium by emitting an alpha particle, i.e. the nucleus of a helium atom. The only question is when? If we have millions of similarly-minded uranium atoms, we can predict with great certainty that half of these atoms will fall prey to their inclinations and decay in precisely four-and-one-half billion years. The decay of a specific atom, however, is indeterminable. The best modern physics can do for a single atom is to assign a probability that the atom will decay at some specified, precise time.

The idea is not too far removed from our experiences in an everyday world. We can assign a probability to virtually any future occurrence. Most, for example, would be willing to risk their money on the probability of the sun rising in the east tomorrow morning at a specified time (this is not a guaranteed bet inasmuch as there have been notable exceptions - see chapter 15). There is also a significant probability that on a very icy day, a specific person will manage to fall on his or her keesters. (Keisters, if you prefer.)

From this point of view, we are all capable of predicting the future, or at least assigning a probability to the occurrence of particular events. It would not be tough for example, to predict that a particular person will meet and fall in love with someone within the next few months, particularly when our subject has been known to fall in and out of love at the drop of a hat.

Uncertainties

However, there seem to be significant limitations in our ability to absolutely determine specific events. Electrons, for example, impose severe restraints on our ability to determine this elementary particle's precise energy at any specific time. This limitation, known as the Heisenberg Uncertainty Principle, states that an electron's energy (within a specified range of energies dE) during a specified interval of time (dT) is limited by Planck's constant, h, by the equation:

$$h \text{ is less than } [\, (dE) \times (dT)\,]$$

The implication of this famous equation is that if we try to be more specific in our time interval (decrease dT), we will be confronted with the necessity of increasing our uncertainty in the electron's energy (i.e. increase dE). And vice versa.

Admittedly, Planck's constant, h, is a teeny, tiny number (h = 6.622 x 10^{-27} erg sec), but with respect to an electron, it is quite significant. From our viewpoint it establishes a physical principle that limits our abilities to precisely define a time-energy relationship for certain aspects of the physical world. From a macroscopic world viewpoint, we can imagine a corresponding theory, the Inadequacy of the Wild Guess Principle.

Probabilities and Free Will

More to the point is the apparent fact that predictions of future events, whether by psychics, scientists, or any other venturesome sort, must rely for their reasonable accuracy on probabilities. Probabilities, in turn, allow for a substantial latitude in the exercise of free will. A soul may not be able to effect whether or not the sun rises tomorrow morning, but he or she may be able to determine if that soul witnesses the event.

It appears reasonable to assume that each soul exercises free will in the bardo, limited only by universal or natural laws (physical and non-physical) and the free will of others. In our earthly and other physical incarnations, free will appears to continue to exist, but is still limited by the universal laws, the free will of others, and to a lesser degree by the self-imposed limitations of every soul's planning while in the bardo.

Summary

In summary, it appears that time can continue to exist. We may not be constrained by time (and/or space) while in the bardo or in an altered state of consciousness, but time will continue to exist, in some form or another, even in an otherworldly state. At the same time, future events can be predicted on the basis of assigning probabilities and without infringing upon free will, or our traditional view of time.

When time is viewed in this way, it becomes an essential ingredient in reincarnation theory. As such, it supports the theory, and, in fact, is required by the theory. Conversely, without this view of time, some of the supporting experiences of reincarnation would have to be considered as invalid. Karma, being the law of cause of effect, requires time as a fundamental tenet.

Time and space seem essential to our ability to experience events necessary for our soul's evolution. Time may not be felt or sensed by our soul while in the bardo, but some form of time in the nonphysical world would seem to be a critical ingredient if a soul does in fact evolve. Undoubtedly, our concept of time, based on our physical experiences, is a narrow and incomplete view, but nature has generously managed to provide little clues that tweak our imaginations and keep our attempts to understand time always interesting.

Chapter 13:

Divination, Astrology
and Dreams

"A couple of hours ago, I was getting ready to go down and pick up my airline tickets. The trip's not until next week, but you know me, I never like to wait until the last minute. But when I hopped in my car, guess what? My battery was dead. A brand new battery and not enough juice to start a motorscooter. Naturally, no one was around with a set of jumper cables. But I figured, 'no problem!' So I grabbed my bike. I know you won't believe this, but both tires were flat. And of course I had loaned my pump to a neighbor. Inasmuch as he was out of town for the week, I was flat out-of-luck. I thought about hitching a ride with Sarah across the way, but when I looked over at her house, she was just pulling out and driving off. Just missed her!" I mean the whole thing was weird! It was like I was not meant to pick up those airline tickets." Alex smiled slightly. With his story finished, he looked at Marie for her reaction. When she said nothing, Alex became a little anxious. "Well?"

Marie was hesitant. "I'm not too good at omens, and that's what that sounds like."

"A what?"

"An omen. Something that happens which foretells the future. Can be good or evil."

"What do you think it means?"

"Maybe you should avoid travel."

"And not go to Seattle next week?"

"Maybe that's what it's telling you. I'm not sure."

Alex frowned at the lack of direction from Marie. Then he tried to make light of it. "I really need to go to Seattle next week."

"Then go."

"Well . . ."

"Well what?"

"I probably wouldn't have paid much attention to what you're calling an omen, but it reminded me of my dream."

"Oh? Tell me about your dream. I'm better at dreams."

"It was about three nights ago. I dreamed I was going to the airport, and kept going down the wrong streets. I could see the airplanes taking off and landing, but I could never find the entrance. I must have been to that airport a hundred times, but in my dream I just couldn't find my way. At one point I thought about climbing over the fence, but when I started toward the fence, it seemed to grow taller."

"Definitely sounds like you shouldn't go to Seattle."

"But if I don't go next week, I won't get another chance."

"Let me look at your astrological chart for a moment?"

"Yes, but what's that got to do with anything?"

"It depends on where Saturn is right now, in relation to your natal planets. Ah yes, here it is: 'Good time to stay home and avoid traveling.' Just as I thought. You'd better cancel the trip."

Alex looked very hesitant. With little conviction in his voice, he replied, "Right."

If Alex cancels his trip, we may never know if by doing so he saved himself from some disaster or merely saved the cost of an airline ticket to Seattle. If nothing happens to his flight, we can all smile smugly and dismiss his fears as nothing more than superstitious drivel. On the other hand, if his flight ends up a crumpled heap on the side of a mountain, we might want to investigate a little more carefully as to the meaning of his omen, dream, and/or astrological chart, particularly before we take another airplane trip.

We have seen in the previous chapter that given the nature of time, it is possible to predict the future, if only, at the very least, in terms of probabilities. It follows that it should be entirely possible for one to predict their own future, or at least certain probable events. On a personal basis, each of us might be able to base our decisions on our own psychic foreknowledge of the future.

Psychic potentials may be thought of as the ability of human beings to predict the future, understand the present, and clarify the past; and then to modify or change the future. The latter point is very important in that it allows free will and the ability to avoid an undesirable future and/or to create a preferred future. These psychic potentials that we supposedly all possess, fall into a wide variety of different areas, of which we will in this chapter briefly discuss divination, dreams, and astrology.

Divination

Divination can be thought of as the ability to "know" the present and predict the future. As such, it has been practiced throughout the world since the dawn of history (if not before). The question is, of course, does it work? Can it be relied on? Is it even a good idea? Let us not forget that in Dante's Hell, fortunetellers were doomed to look forever backward. Obviously, Dante was not a big fan of divination.

Nevertheless, there exists a multitude of stories that give us pause to wonder. King Croesus of Lydia, famous for his wealth ("as rich as Croesus"), was said to have checked with the Delphic oracle prior to his launching a military campaign against Persia in the sixth century B.C. According to the Greek historian Herodotus, Croesus first tested the oracle with several requests, and then when he had become a believer, he asked for a prediction concerning his planned attack on the Persians. The oracle told Croesus that if he did launch such an attack, the king would "destroy a great empire." Croesus, quite pleased with the news, happily charged into Persia. Unfortunately, the Persians were no pushovers and Croesus ended up succeeding only in destroying his own empire. Naturally the Delphic oracle took full credit for another accurate prediction.

Omens

Omens, ill and otherwise, have also come to haunt many a man and his plans. A black raven, such as celebrated by Edgar Allen Poe, was often thought to signify the imminent arrival of bad luck. The royal house of Hesse with its links to the British and Russian royal families, has become thoroughly disgusted with the appearance of black ravens, as each appearance has always been an omen of impending ill fortune or death.

Birds, dogs, cats, goats, sheep, fish, rats, mice, and even spiders have been known to bode good and ill fortunes to come. They have also shown an ability to perceive the onset of specific large-scale weather changes or natural calamities. In attempting to predict earthquakes and the like, scientists have noted, with some wonderment, the abilities of animals and insects to sense the coming event, hours or even days ahead of time. Such ability may, of course, be the result of the animals simply using their five senses, with special sensitivities to early warning signs, or it may be something else. The "something else" is the item in which we're interested.

Science seems capable of handling an animal's ability to sense an earthquake, but the arrival of a raven signifying the imminent death of a relation is not something for which modern theories can account. If the arrival of the raven and the early departure of the relation were not coincidence, how do we explain the raven's arrival? Did the raven know what he was doing? Do ravens get advance word about human deaths? Was the raven merely a pawn sent by someone else? Is there a central dispatcher for ravens? Did the raven sense something from one or more of us that prompted the raven's extracurricular flight?

Of all the "non-coincidence" possibilities, the latter idea seems the most plausible and is typically the alternative given the most credence by non-traditional thinkers. There is, for example, the well known fact of vultures arriving at the scene of an expectant death. The vultures are either very keen observers, or else they may be reacting to the thoughts or actions of the weary traveler. Are omens of death just another form of a vulture with a keen eye or is there more to it?

If you have a pet dog, try this experiment. Sit down to read a paper and when the dog has settled down to merely watching you, start thinking about taking him for a walk. In most cases the dog will pick up on the idea (without any apparent action on your part) and will be ready to go. Some dogs will even retrieve their leash as a convenience to you. Alternatively, if you rise in order to turn on the TV, the dog will probably ignore you.

The obvious question is how did the dog know? Was the dog a student of divination? Better yet, is it possible for a human to develop or utilize some sort of latent talent and thereby devise his own divinations? Is there a way that a human being could regularly use his senses, a sixth sense, or something akin to intuition in order to "sense" the future? Don't bet the farm on the answer being "no."

History is replete with such possibilities. When Julius Caesar was told to "beware the ides of march," the soothsayer was either an astute political observer, someone with "inside information," or a person capable of divination. While Julius' soothsayer was fictional, there are a fair number of people today who believe divination to be a very real possibility. These proponents would suggest that the soothsayers of yesterday, as well as today, might be simply "tuning in" to other sources of information via an altered state of consciousness. Given the predictability of the future, such altered states might be just the ticket for divination.

Altered States

It should be noted that one's ability to achieve an altered state of consciousness is relatively straightforward. Besides the use of some forms of meditation or drugs, practitioners have used everything from intense staring into a bright light (a fire, candle, or crystal ball), to tarot cards, pyramids, and various forms of numerology. Virtually all of these methods appear to use exotic and not-so-exotic equipment as simple tools with which to tap into their subconscious mind.

The *I Ching*, or *Book of Changes*, dates back to the third millennium B.C. of very ancient China. The basic technique of the *I Ching* is the throwing of sticks – the divination is linked through a series of complex philosophic principles. The use of the *I Ching* requires deep thought and self-examination, and may be used to induce a deeply meditative state. Concentration by the subject appears to be essential, because of the potentially obscure nature of the sayings. Carl Jung, utilizing his concept of synchronicity has thought of the *I Ching*'s ability to parallel events in space and time as implying something more than mere chance, potentially an interdependence of objective events among themselves.

Similar to the *I Ching* is the deck of tarot cards. These cards may have originated in Egypt or northern Africa as early as A.D. 1200. Divining by tarot cards is as individual as crystal gazing, because the cards tend to indicate something other than the interpretations of the diviner who is utilizing an altered state of consciousness.

Don't assume that an altered state of consciousness is some deeply hypnotic state. It can be, but such a deep state is not necessary. Many tarot card readers, for example, appear normal, even while in the midst of predicting future events. At the same time, altered states can include hypnotic, waking, sleeping, fear or shock (traumatic), somnambulist, or trance states. Children in their teenage years, for example, move in and out of a variety of trances. That you might have already suspected.

Dowsing

Dowsing, the ability to locate underground sources of water has been around since the Middle Ages. The sheer strangeness of the event is often enough to send critics into a state of total bewilderment. The American Society of Dowsers has pointed out that the reasons the procedures work, are entirely unknown. This lack of a guiding set of principles has not endeared the concept to its critics.

Nevertheless, dowsing has claimed credit for giving the Occidental Petroleum Company (currently a multibillion dollar corporation) its start in the petroleum industry by helping to bring in ten producing oil wells, which had been successfully dowsed. Even the U. S. Marine Corps has used dowsing at its Camp Pendleton base in California. As the editors of Reader's Digest pointed out in their book, *Into the Unknown*, on the basis of performance, no other form of divination has so thoroughly challenged its scientific skeptics.

Decision Making

The multitude of successful prophecies and predictions that have been made over the ages, has stretched the imagination of many a skeptic. The key ingredient has always been the diviner himself. The tools of trade appear to be nothing more than a means to stimulate the diviner's unconscious or as a focus for his "intuition." The ability of humans to read the future lies almost certainly in their own minds and not in any external symbols. Or as Shakespeare put it, "not in our stars, but in ourselves."

With the array of successful predictions has come the realization by many modern executives of the need for psychic assistance. Most executives appreciate fully the necessity to make critical decisions on what is often insufficient data. If divination can clear up some of the mysteries, it will certainly be welcomed. Whether "operating by the seat of their pants" or asking for a reading of the cards, businesses and individuals may have taken divination and renamed it decision-making.

Astrology

Policeman, firemen, and ambulance drivers have often noted that the busiest days, or more specifically the busiest nights, occur when the moon is full or new. During these two nights, all manner of murder, mayhem, suicides, crimes of passion and other aberrant behavior seem to crest. Arnold Lieber, author of

The Lunar Effect, in reviewing the homicides occuring in Dade County, Florida, between 1956 and 1970, found a statistically significant lunar periodicity in that more murders took place at times of new and full moons than at any other times.

The movement of sunspots toward the sun's central meridian has been correlated with measured changes in men's blood by Maki Takata, a Japanese doctor. Furthermore the extent of the change was greater when the man was closer to the sun. John Nelson, an engineer for RCA in 1950, noted that whenever two or more planets formed a 90 or 180 degree angle with the earth (what astrology deems to be bad omens), disturbances in radio transmission always occurred; but that radio transmissions were much improved when the planets were in the angular relationships that astrologers consider to have a benign influence.

The idea that the sun and planets somehow influence man in his day-to-day life is not a new one. Evidence indicates that the Chaldeans were using astrological studies of the skies to make predictions for their kings as long ago as 4000 years. Some believe that the earlier Sumerian civilization may also have practiced an early form of astrology. Early Egyptians, Indian religion and philosophy, and the emperors of China were already fine tuning the art as long ago as 2000 B.C. Even the Mayan civilization in the western hemisphere had produced its own class of astronomer priests.

Astrological Predictions

The use of astrology to predict the fate of nations, kings, and harvests, is called mundane astrology. It was left to the ancient Greeks to make the science available to the common man (provided of course the common man was willing to pay for it). In true democratic fashion, the Greeks insisted that the portents of astrology could influence human actions, but did not rule them! In effect this catarchic astrology avoided conflict with later theologians and philosophers by indicating favorable times for projects, but not guaranteeing their success. The idea was, "The stars impel; they do not compel."

This latter view has turned out to be quite convenient in explaining why some predictions go sour. It also allows for free will. For example, if during the next full moon you feel like punching someone's lights out, you always have the choice of refraining from doing so. Maybe just a low growl would be sufficient.

The question remains, however, can astrology predict the future? On the night of a given full moon, is it really going to make a difference if you are a Scorpio born on the 19th of November or a Sagittarius born on the 23rd of the same month? What can the moment of birth have to do with predicting what you will do in the future?

Electromagnetic Fields

Physics has slowly come to realize in the last several decades that the solar system is virtually awash in an electro-magnetic field. The discovery of the Van Allen Belts around the earth was one of the first indicators, but it has now become clear that all planets have their own electromagnetic signatures. The sun, of course, has a much more intense and stronger field and as a consequence allows the planets to make only slight modifications to the solar system's overall EM field.

A multitude of experiments have shown that microwaves and other electromagnetic wavelengths can have observable effects on the health and mental development of human beings. At one point the Russians were directing intense microwave broadcasts toward the American Embassy in Moscow and causing a rash of headaches among the personnel. Is it possible that the solar system's electromagnetic field could have some effect on the early, very rapid changes in infants as they enter this world and begin to develop? With the planets modifying this same field by their positions with respect to earth, could such a modified field cause certain "alignments" in the basic blueprints of DNA, and could this in turn tend to establish definite personality characteristics? Why not?

The why not, from traditional science's point of view, is that the magnitude of the electromagnetic fields involved would be insufficient to accomplish anything. Roger Culver, in his book, *The Gemini Syndrome*, makes an excellent argument against the idea of EM fields being the connecting link between the sun and planets, and the actions of men.[1] Unfortunately, the act of dowsing may use similar fields and the fact of dowsing's success might suggest that traditional science's inability to detect such fields is science's problem!

Precession of the Axis

Reader's Digest, in its book, *Into the Unknown*, describes what it believes is a serious contradiction in astrology. They point out that the precession of the earth's axis (a gradual shifting) over the last two thousand years has resulted in the fact that the first day of spring arrives when the sun is entering Pisces, and not Aries (as was the case in ancient times). In effect the whole sequence of the sun entering each constellation is off by about one month now. Thus if astrologers today are now dealing with the zodiac as it was determined thousands of years ago, things must be seriously wrong.

The flaw in this argument is that our lives are not "ruled by the stars," but according to astrology, are governed in part by the sun and to a lesser degree the planets. The sun's electromagnetic field will be influenced by the relatively nearby planets, but the effect of other stars trillions and trillions of miles away can be considered to be virtually nil. Astrology considers the relative position of the sun and the planets, but never the stars. The precession of the earth's axis would have virtually no effect on the solar system's field. The fact that the Sun Signs are named after star groups, in no way implies that it is essential for

[1] Interestingly, Dr. Culver is now very involved (romantically) with a professional astrologer. Some professors really get into their research!

the sun to be in the constellation Cancer, for a person to be born with the personality of a Crab.

Shakespeare and Augustine

From the viewpoint of the ability of astrology to predict the future, it would appear that a knowledge of a person's personality could give some clues as to future actions and events. If astrologers are simply tapping into the plans for a soul's current incarnation, then the predictions may potentially take on even further authenticity. Furthermore the fact that astrology provides only probable futures (as do other forms of forecasting) is clearly in its favor.

Shakespeare, in King Lear, takes a jab at astrology, when his Edmund says, "This is the excellent foppery of the world, that when we are sick in fortune – often the surfeit of our own behavior – we make guilty of our disasters the sun, the moon, and the stars . . . an admirable evasion of whoremaster man, to lay his goatish disposition to the charge of a star."[2]

It is noteworthy that William attributed much of our fortune to the "surfeit of our own behavior." Reincarnation, and to some extent, astrology readily acknowledges the responsibility of the self in determining our fortunes.

Perhaps the bard had taken his cue from Saint Augustine, who found it impossible to reconcile the fact that two people born at identical times (which astrology calls astral twins), could lead such dissimilar lives as that of a nobleman and a peasant. Of course, Saint Augustine was also having trouble with the idea of reincarnation or that that same nobleman and peasant may have switched places in a past life.

Know Thyself

Another use of astrology is in what can often be a precise determination of an individual's characteristics based on the date of his or her birth. An astrological natal chart can provide a relatively nice description, which allows a person to "know thyself." It might even come in handy in attempting to explain to someone else, your point of view. As a matter of fact, if you just mention that you're a Scorpio, they'll probably know. And run in the other direction.

One advantage, which should not be dismissed too easily, is the ability of perhaps understanding other people. For example, a stubborn Taurus father will have a much better chance of understanding and dealing with his Leo daughter, if he is willing to accept her as having the characteristics of a Leo. She'll probably want to be a princess, and he might as well accept that inevitable fact. For the Cancer husband, whose wife is a Gemini, it will help a great deal, if during those times when the "depressed twin" is in charge of her mood, that he just back off and wait for the "vivacious twin" to once again reappear.

If nothing else, the twelve signs of the zodiac tell each of us that as a bare

---

[2] Of course, Edmund was the most thoroughly evil and dastardly character in the play! Perhaps we shouldn't assume that he speaks for Shakespeare.

minimum,11/12ths of the human race is not like us and cannot be expected to have the same goals and priorities. Astrology may, if nothing else, breed tolerance of others and their different personalities.

Nostradamus

No discussion of divination or astrological predictions would be complete without some mention of Nostradamus. Born on December 14, 1503 in St. Remy, France, Nostradamus became a well known doctor of medicine, herbalist, magician, creator of fruit preservatives and cosmetics, "celestial scientist" (i.e. astrologer), and prophet. His name has come down to us through the last four hundred years because of *The Centuries*, written by Nostradamus in the years from 1554 to 1564. In this remarkable document, Nostradamus predicted critical events occuring in the next several thousand years. His predictions were based, apparently, on astrology and some form of prophetic trance, and were normally written in cryptic poems called Quatrains.

Many researchers have attempted to interpret Nostradamus' predictions, but are often unable to do so *before the fact*, due to what is believed to be Nostradamus' intentionally cryptic and subtle manner of writing. Some of these researchers believe that because of the sensitive nature of many of the predictions, Nostradamus specifically avoided a clear and definitive language in his work. At the same time, these researchers also believe that Nostradamus utilized certain conventions in his writings which would allow others to discover the specific dates and events to which a particular Quatrain referred.

Not all of Nostradamus' predictions were cryptic and difficult to interpret before the fact, however. One example is what has come to be known as, perhaps, Nostradamus' most famous Quatrain:

> "The young lion will overcome the older one
> On the field of combat in a single battle
> He will pierce his eyes through a golden cage
> Two wounds made one, then he dies a cruel death"

It was understood, even in Nostradamus' day, that the prophecy concerned King Henry II. In 1559, the King, carrying his great lion-decorated shield, had his golden visor pierced by the splinters on a broken lance in a joust. He died after ten days of agony. The Count of Montgomery, with his own lion-decorated shield, had tried to avoid the joust, knowing of the prophecy.

Nostradamus subsequently predicted the fates of virtually all of Henry's remaining royal family members and all of the predictions were fulfilled. Nostradamus, who died in 1566, even predicted his own death and wrote a Quatrain warning against desecrating his grave. In 1700, the city fathers decided to move his illustrious corpse to a more prominent wall of the church. Knowing of Nostradamus' warning, they nevertheless took a quick look inside, being careful, naturally, not to disturb the body. There they found, around the skeleton's neck a medallion inscribed simply with "1700."

John Hogue, in *Nostradamus and the Millenium*, has credited Nostradamus with accurately predicting, among other things:

1. The death of Mary, Queen of Scots,

2. The rise and fall of Charles I of England,

3. The London fire of 1666 ("the year 66"),

4. Numerous details of the French Revolution,

5. The rise and fall of Napoleon (whom Nostradamus referred to as the first of the three "anti-Christs"),

6. World War I,

7. The electric lightbulb, newspapers, the 1929 crash,

8. Hitler (the second "anti-Christ"),

9. Mussolini, Franco, and DeGaulle,

10. The atomic bombing of Hiroshima and Nagasaki,

11. The assassination of John Kennedy,

12. The space shuttle Challenger disaster,

13. The fall of the Shah of Iran, and

14. The Russian invasion of Afghanistan.

It is important to realize that many of the predictions were fairly specific, but many were much more open to interpretation. The London fire of 1666 was predicted in terms of "the year 66", which gives some leeway. Hitler was spelled Histler, while Kennedy was referred to only as "the great man." Others, such as those relating to predictions 13 and 14, you may wish to judge for yourself.

> Rain, famine and war will not cease in Persia
> Religious fanaticism – and too great a trust in his allies
> Will betray the Shah whose end was planned and conceived in France
> A secret sign for one to be more moderate.

Persia is the older name for Iran, and Khomeini, had been exiled to Paris for years before the Iranian Revolution actually succeeded in overthrowing the Shah.

> The Russians will enter Afghanistan
> The Moslems will find these areas open
> The Afghans would like to keep Afghanistan
> But the resistance will be buried.

The latter quatrain not only predicts the invasion, but also goes on to suggest the ultimate defeat of the Afghan resistance. While it is true that the Afghan resistance was "buried" for many years, recent events might suggest that the Afghan resistance has won the day. At the same time, the jury may still be out on that one! Meanwhile, in Chapter 15, we will be dealing with more of Nostradamus' predictions, all of which may make the predictions thus far, seem rather tame!

Dreams

For ten nights in a row, David Booth had the same nightmare: an American Airlines passenger plane swerving, rolling in the air, and then plunging to the ground inverted, where it burst into an inferno. On May 22, 1979 he contacted in turn: The Federal Aviation Administration (FAA), a psychiatrist, and American Airlines. The FAA took Mr. Booth seriously enough to guess that the description of the airliner was that of a DC-10, but could not identify the airport. On May 26, an American Airlines DC-10 departing O'Hare International Airport, lost an engine, causing the jet to roll over and crash inverted. The accident killed 275 people in the worst aviation accident in U. S. history.

Just before his 1947 welterweight title fight with Jimmy Doyle, Sugar Ray Robinson had a vivid dream of hitting Doyle with a few good punches and then watching Doyle on his back, to all appearances, dead. Even though Robinson wanted to call off the fight, it proceeded after a hastily summoned priest eased Sugar Ray's concerns. In the eighth round, Robinson dropped Doyle with a left hook to the jaw. Doyle fell, hitting the back of his head on the mat. Doyle died the next afternoon.

Samuel Taylor Coleridge gives credit for the inspiration of his famous poem, Kubla Khan, to a vivid dream. After waking with 200 to 300 lines of poetry in his head, Coleridge quickly begin writing it down. Interrupted after 54, he returned later to discover that his inspiration had vanished like the images on the surface of a stream.

Giuseppe Tartini tried in vain to compose a magnificent musical composition after dreaming that he had made a pact with the devil in return for the devil's playing of a sonata of exquisite beauty. The piece he did compose, The Devil's Sonata, was what Tartini considered to be the best he ever wrote, but far below the one he had dreamed.

Dreams of impending disaster have involved Abraham Lincoln, Archduke Francis Ferdinand, and Adolph Hitler; and have been included by Shakespeare in haunting dreams of Richard III and Julius Caesar's wife, Calpurnia. The ancient Egyptians developed a papyrus dream book about 1350 B.C. as a means of interpreting good and bad messages (apparently Joseph's success inspired the Egyptian scholars). Greek philosophers such as Heraclitus and

Plato viewed dreams as a product of an individual's own private creation.

In the 2nd century A.D. a Greek soothsayer, Artemidorous, considered dreams to be very individualistic, complicated, and varied. Because of this, Artemidorous carefully studied the dreamer as well as the dream and viewed dreams as either the product of day-to-day living or as a means of predicting the future. His books on dreams have continued to serve as a basic reference for almost two thousand years.

In 1968 the Central Premonition Registry was established for prophetic dreams. Of over eight thousand dreams registered, the registry had found 48 that were sufficiently detailed and clear to allow correlation with actual events. Nearly half of these correlations were found to have originated from just six people. Many of these "heavy hitters" have claimed that a prophetic dream is easily distinguishable from other dreams by the unmistakable, almost oppressive impact and the repetition of the dream night after night.

Dreams of Prediction

Any attempt to explain prophecy (dreams, psychic "knowings," etc.) must ultimately depend upon our ideas of the future. If the future does not yet exist, it seems unlikely that the future can affect the present. If, on the other hand, the future does exist (as many proponents of reincarnation maintain), then it seems a simple if not esoteric concept that one could easily predict major events. If future events are based on probability (and thus allow for free will), then predictions are still possible, but with somewhat fewer guarantees.

Is the contrary argument viable? Does the very existence of prophetic dreams imply that the future already exists (at least in probabilities)? Not necessarily. It may be that events cause a slight probability change at a subatomic level, in the form of what Cambridge mathematical physicist Adrian Dobbs has termed a psitronic wavefront. As the waves spread out and impinge on a person, the brain's neurons may actually register their impact in such a way as to allow interpretation. Not unexpectedly, no one has ever found any physical evidence of any so-called psitronic wave. The question remains moot.

Dream Communications

Dreams are not necessarily the stuff of prophecy. They can also provide insight and understanding of one's own psyche. If we in fact have guides (who can see the "big picture" from their heavenly viewpoint), dreams would seem to be a perfect means with which to communicate with the physically bound souls still on earth. (If nothing else, in a dreamstate we're less likely to talk back.)

Many proponents of psychic potentials strongly emphasize the desirability of recording our dreams. Over a period of time, they believe that a wealth of information can be gained. (It might also help during lulls in party conversation.) But, if you are so inclined, please be aware of one problem: Dreams are fleeting at best - write them down immediately upon awakening and without any delay or interruption. Otherwise your next poetic masterpiece may be as short as Coleridge's "Kubla Khan."

One other piece of advice from someone who might even know: "It's much better for someone to interpret their own dreams, rather than have someone else do it."

Summary

How are divinations, dreams, and astrological predictions related to reincarnation? Consider two possible rationales:

Reincarnation theory describes a series of lives for each soul. From the details of birth experiences and other evidence, we can conclude that each soul, while in the bardo, plans to some degree his future life. These future plans are prepared in order to provide certain learning experiences during the incarnation. In our discussion of time, we saw that all such future plans may be based more on probabilities than clear certainties. It would therefore be possible that chance events could interfere with our achieving the preplanned learning experiences.

Many reincarnationists have also strongly suggested the possibility that each soul has a "Higher Self" (or some type of "guide" or "oversoul") who monitors and assists the soul while that soul is incarnated. In order for the Higher Self to be able to assist the incarnated soul, some form of communications would appear to be necessary. Divinations, dreams, and astrological predictions may indeed be the means by which the Higher Self can communicate with the incarnated soul.

Given that our plans may be influenced by probabilities, and that occasionally the improbable may occur (and thus cause the best laid plans of mice and men to go astray), it would appear desirable to allow for Higher Self prompting in order to get back to a life's plan. Dreams, astrology, and divination (DAD) may just be one of several means to remind each soul of "who knows best."

Secondly, such arts as astrology may be nothing more than a basic script under which all souls operate. In planning their lives in the space between lives, astrology would provide the general framework, with which each soul could follow. Thereafter, on the planet, that same soul could stay with the script, interact with others as preplanned, and also ad-lib, forget entrances, and on more than a few occasions, get into all sorts of unplanned situations.

DAD therefore appears to complement reincarnation and again to provide details on the operating conditions. Belief in DAD is not a requirement for reincarnation, and reincarnation may not be essential to DAD. Nevertheless they do fit together well.

Chapter 14:

Communications with the Other Side

Scott watched the woman, who claimed to be a psychic, as her eyes rolled up and then closed. She took a long deep breath and held it. After a brief silence, the woman began to speak in a deep voice: "My name is Pue-ton. I am channeling through this woman to bring you enlightenment. You have a question?"

Scott swallowed slightly before he spoke. "There have been predictions of world wide catastrophes. Are these predictions true?"

"Yes. The problem is negativity. Negative thoughts will weigh heavily on the continents. As your scientists are aware, the earth's surface is covered with tectonic plates. These plates are mirrors of all the energy patterns that occur above them. Furthermore, these energy patterns are cumulative of all the civilizations that have lived on a particular plate. The effects on the North American plate, for example, includes the thought patterns of the first peoples who crossed the Bering Strait to North America, the civilization of Atlantis (which was located off the southeast coast of the United States), Central American civilizations, early Indian cultures, and emigrants from other parts of the world from the Mayflower to the present day.

"At the same time, the negativity of individual thought patterns can combine with other individual thought patterns to cause a physical imbalance within the molecular structure of the ionosphere, resulting in mass density depletion. This depletion has been occuring since the beginning of man's time on earth and is now becoming critical.

"The ionosphere is, in essence, earth's aura. As the aura is weakened, greater amounts of outer space pressure can be exerted on the earth's surface, drastically increasing the gravitational pull of the earth. The atmosphere's added tension combined with the weight of the accumulating negative energies on each of the tectonic plates will eventually result in the gravitational pull inward to the earth's core increasing to the point that the outer crust of the earth will buckle, causing an implosion."

Scott was amazed. This was really incredible! "Can we expect massive land shifts?"

"Yes. First there will be lesser disturbances and eruptions occurring before the more catastrophic earth changes, especially in the latitudes between 27 degrees North and 38 degrees North."

"Does that include Seattle, where we are?"

"No."

Scott's relief was obvious. "That's comforting."

"We of the Andromedean galaxy have spent many of your years in traveling here to witness the coming earth changes."

Scott looked shocked. "Andromeda?"

"Yes. We are extraterrestrials."

"But the Andromedean galaxy is so far!"

"The distance that light would take to travel in two million years. Approximately six billion billion miles."

"Couldn't you have found an event equally exiting in your own neighborhood?

The above is adapted from actual remarks by several people who claim to have received information from unique energy sources and who are now attempting to "warn" the earth's populace. These individuals claim access to massive amounts of information and are prone to liberally dispense their advice. Such enthusiasm and earnest desires are not that new. (Doomsday warnings are, of course, old hat as well, but we will wait until chapter 15 to discuss the possibilities of catastrophes.)

It is worth noting that nothing in the above "conversation" is considered frivolous or incredible by the psychics and/or channels that gave the information. The channels themselves and their supporters believe that the above aspects of negativity, ionosphere changes, and the like, are quite real and that worldwide changes are quite plausible. Even the reference to visitors from Andromeda is taken from writings of people who firmly believe this assertion to be true. In other words, the author has not taken "dramatic license" with the above basic assertions. These predictions are considered by some to be absolutely serious.

Prophets, et al.

History is chock full of prophets, seers, sages, and others who obtain their knowledge and understanding from parts unknown. Are there prophets today, vainly trying to point out the obvious? Of course. But considering the advice of an old Turkish proverb ("He who tells the truth should have one foot in the stirrup."), it may be that the modern day versions are attempting to show slightly more sophistication in what they call themselves and the manner in which they supposedly gather and disseminate their profound philosophies.

Much of our present-day understanding of reincarnation and related psychic phenomena derives from the near-death and birth experiences, past-life and "between-life" regressions, and the experimental and statistical analysis of numerous case studies. The vast majority of these methods have relied on hypnosis and/or intentionally induced, altered states of consciousness in the selected subjects. The reports from these altered states have in most cases, verified or substantiated ancient and near-ancient historical teachings. This should not be too surprising in view of the fact that the ancients were apparently very much involved in inducing altered states of consciousness of their own by the use of drugs and other means.

The use of hypnosis and altered states has unquestionably allowed us to peek into a variety of universal cubby holes. We have been able to ask a variety of questions and receive answers. While most of the information gathered in this manner has been consistent, there have also been significant differences, such that the method employed to gather the information becomes more and more important.

In previous chapters, we noted the possibility of beings who had departed their physical bodies, possessing a living being. In some cases, this possession was without the permission of the still-living being, and in some cases, the living entity purposefully allowed the temporary use of its body. The first case is, of course, possession, while the second is mediumship. In both cases, it was possible to communicate with recently departed souls. And with the potential reality of telepathy and the incredible resources of the human mind, communications with the other side seem quite likely.

The knowledge gained through mediums and possessed persons is, of course, very informative. On both cases, however, we are dealing with earth-bound spirits. It seems reasonable to believe that the trustworthiness of their information might be suspect. For if these entities are confused about death, unaware of the light, and in general making a nuisance of themselves, there is little reason to accept their apparently unenlightened opinions about anything. Of course, we have already determined to ignore the opinions of demons, no matter how energetically such opinions are propounded. Why should we make a bigger fuss about hearing from our deceased Uncle Harry, who was bound and determined to never leave home?

What is needed instead is a living being who can act as the equivalent of a medium, but with the guest entity being from the "higher planes of existence." Our information will obviously be a bit more accurate if we have an entity who is now "living in the light" and can in fact see what is going on.

The good news is there are now living beings who are able to provide the critical communications link and allow their fellow living beings to talk with entities from the light. (The bad news will be discussed shortly). These living communication links are called "channels".

Channels

Channels obtain their information in a very interesting way. The channel allows an entity or entities (but usually one at a time) to use their physical form in order to communicate their information to the physical world. A channel is distinguished from a medium by the fact that the entity or entities providing the information are "living in the light" and are therefore, not earthbound. Theoretically the entities communicating through the physical being of a living person have access to a vast amount of correct and profound information and are eager to help out the poor wandering souls still attached to the earth. It is also important to note that, at least in theory, a channel is merely "channeling" information (passing it on) and is not relying on its own knowledge or understanding. This is, however, not always the case.

The means by which information is channeled shows up in a variety of ways. Usually the discarnate entity simply talks using the physical abilities of the channel, but some channels limit their output to written or typed messages. Other channels may only see visualizations provided by the entities and at a later time commit the perceived information to canvas or paper.

Those channels using the spoken word often converse directly with those around them. Others merely expound at great length. Virtually all use audio or video tapes to keep a record of their conversations (not to mention selling them for fun and profit), or write books on their possibly enlightened views of life.

Types of Channeling

There are two basic types of channeling which deserve to be clearly delineated. These two types are "trance channeling" and "thought plane transfer." The distinguishing characteristic of a trance channeler is that the individual typically does not remember what was said while the channeling entity was "in" the physical body. The channeler may be asleep, unconscious, or has left its body for parts unknown. The trance channeler, while channeling, will usually do so with very different facial expressions, tones of voice, and/or other personality characteristics.

In distinct contrast to trance channelers, thought plane transfer (TBT) channelers remain conscious during those times when the information is being channeled, although they may be in an altered state. These TBT channelers usually write books in lieu of public demonstrations of their channeling technique, but several noteworthy TBT channelers utilize a variety of means to get their message across.

The distinction between trance and TBT channelers may be important. If the trance channeler is unconscious and unaware of what information is being disseminated, it would seem less likely that the channeler's own ego and philosophical point of view would interfere in the transmittal of information. Thus the trance channeler might be considered to be more "accurate" than the TBT channeler. But don't count too heavily on it.

Edgar Cayce

In the world of ESP, channels, clairvoyants, and psychics, the one name that stands above the rest is Edgar Cayce, easily considered to be the modern world's most important clairvoyant or channel. Mr. Cayce slept through his channeling sessions (thus earning him the title of "The Sleeping Prophet"), and over a period of forty years, provided 14,246 "Life Readings". Such output represents a feat of amazing dedication considering the fact that upon awakening from his sleep or trance, Mr. Cayce had no conscious recall of anything he had said.

Cayce's credibility derives from several sources. For one thing, he never accepted monetary rewards other than those necessary for his modest family needs. Secondly, his trance channeling method is considered more reliable, particularly because the views that he expounded as a channeler often contradicted his own firmly held, fundamentalist Christian beliefs. While Cayce never detracted from the biblical Jesus, he did add much to the dimensional concepts of Jesus, such that Cayce himself must have wondered about his sources.

In the vast majority of Life Readings given by Cayce, his source of information was obstensibly the Akashic Records. The Akashic Records, according to seers and others familiar with their alleged existence, are the indelible impressions on the fabric of the universe of everything that has ever happened. A channel may refer to this cosmic memory as a vast, non-molecular library, complete with a full understanding of each and every event in the universal record. In this respect, the Akashic Records may be likened to Carl Jung's Collective Unconscious, or Rupert Sheldrake's Morphogenetic Fields. In all cases, these collection of all memories, not only exist, but are accessible by anyone capable of properly tuning their mind-receiver. (These records may also be available even though one is not consciously aware that they are tuning in!)

Cayce's normal mode was to simply visit the Akashic Records, as if going to the local library. In this way, he could answer virtually any question that might be posed to him. At the same time, there were occasions when Cayce was apparently not speaking in the first person, but was in fact channeling another entity. While Cayce never attempted this feat of performing as a channel or medium, there were apparently occasions when other entities did spontaneously speak through him. One notable example was John of the Revelation.

Edgar Cayce simply cannot be dismissed out of hand. There is simply too much credibility to justify a wholesale rejection. On the other hand, there is no a priori reason to accept all of his readings at their face value. For example, Cayce's references in his readings to Atlantis, the Pyramid of Gizeh, and the Land of Mu (among other things) may indeed justify criticism. Thus, while three fourths of Cayce's work may be correct, the remaining fourth may be simply misinterpreted or just plain wrong. The sheer bulk of data from Edgar

Cayce should not be construed as evidence for its accuracy in all readings.

Other Celebrity Channels

Another trance channeler is Ms. Taryn Krive, a former legal secretary, who channels Bell Bell, a giggly six-year old from Atlantis, Barking Tree, a Hopi Indian spirit, and Aeffra, a man who once lived in Eastern Europe. (Yes, a channeler can channel more than one entity.)   Other channelers include Darryl Anka, a 40-year-old entrepreneur, who channels Bashar, an extraterrestrial from a planet 500 light years away (who among other things is obviously quick-witted); David Swetland, who channels Matea, a 35,000-year-old six-foot-eight-inch black female spice trader; and Diana Hoerig, who channels Merlin of Camelot. No kidding.

TBT channelers appear to be in even greater abundance than trance channelers. This may be due to the fact that anyone who is "inspired" may consider themselves a TBT channeler. There are several TBTers, however, who are well known in their own right. These include such personalities as Ruth Montgomery and Norma Green, both of whom have written several books.

Often the entities being channeled become more famous than the channelers themselves. Some of the better known channeled entities include Ramtha, Seth, Lazarus (pronounced La-czar-us), Raphael, Bartholomew, Mentor, Menos, James, etc. The lesser known channeled entities include Tom, Dick, and Harry. There are apparently hundreds if not thousands of channels currently plying their trade; the country now has probably more "channels" than TV stations. There are even channels who are attempting to acquire the blueprints for an electronic device to communicate with the other side without the use of channels!

Consistency of Channeled Information

There is certainly some consistency in the teachings from different channels. However, most teachings boil down to emphasizing the capability of anyone to love themselves, direct their own lives, and to ultimately assume total responsibility for all of their actions. While such "teachings" might be excellent advice, their consistency does not necessarily add to their credibility.

Thus while the teachings of various channels may be consistent, there is, however, no assurance that what they are saying is correct. The consistency may imply nothing more than the fact that channels tend to say what other channels have already said. Presumably they occasionally read each other's work, and certainly they have access to the same wise sayings of ancient channels. But the statistical correlations of past life regressions, which gave the method more credibility, are apparently not available for channels. At the same time, what the channels are saying is often of such an esoteric nature that there is no way of checking the information.

In many respects, different channels, particularly those who have published books and provided video tapes, are like different prophets. They all have very individual characteristics, propound very specific philosophies, and describe varying paths with which to reach the light. Yet all of these modern-day prophets have essentially the same messages, the same basic view of the universe, and describe the same basic wisdom to their respective followers. Jesus Christ said, "In my Father's house, there are many mansions." Apparently there are also many paths a soul may travel in order to reach those mansions.

One notable channeled book is *The Course in Miracles*. This book and its teachings have acquired a following, although in far fewer numbers, not unlike the Bible. Study groups throughout the country are now diligently and religiously pouring through "the course", and attempting to live day-to-day with its daily teachings. *The Course in Miracles* goes on to note that "the course" is mandatory/required (a prerequisite of some kind?), but that when it is taken, is left to the individual.

Unfortunately, more than one channeled book has claimed to be absolutely essential to enlightenment. That in itself, should make you pause and wonder about its credibility.

Sources

Another tactic of channelers used to obtain greater credibility has been to claim a very credible source. These sources have included every saint, prophet, great thinker and philosopher, including Jesus Christ and God. The implication is that if they said it, it must be true.

Of course, at last count, there have been at least six different channels speaking for Jesus Christ and two for God. Inasmuch as they are in many respects telling us significantly different things, it is important not to assume that any teaching is true because of its alleged source, its claim to be essential for enlightenment, or the fact that it is channeled.

We might also crudely note that when someone goes into the "channeling business" (a profession that has become highly lucrative for several famed channels), they tend to look for an entity to channel who has the "clout" to make things believable. The selection of Jesus Christ might be challenged on the basis of Christ's own disclaimers:

> "And Jesus answered and said unto them, Take heed that no man deceive you.
> "For many shall come in my name, saying, I am Christ; and shall deceive many." (Matthew 24: 4-5)

> "Then if any man shall say unto you, Lo, here is Christ, or there; believe it not"
> "For there shall arise false Christs, and false prophets, and shall shew great signs and wonders; insomuch that, if it were possible, they shall deceive the very elect." (Matthew 24: 23-24)

Changing Personalities

The transfer of bodily control from a trance channel to an incoming entity is of particular interest. For purposes of discussion we can briefly describe the transformation when Ms. J.Z. Knight becomes "Ramtha, the Enlightened One".

Sitting in a comfortable chair, Ms. Knight goes into what could be an altered state of consciousness, her eyes closed and her breathing regular. Then as the breathing becomes heavier and indicates a few apparent discontinuities, the body's stance changes slightly, the eyes open and Ramtha arrives. The whole process is accomplished in less than a minute, and is in itself rather dramatic. Subsequently, Ramtha moves about the room like a man who is accustomed to command, constantly stroking "his" imaginary beard, and speaking with a low and comforting voice.

This transfer of personalities is also very like the changes of personality of someone with multiple personalities. Because of this similarity, it is worth describing what psychologists call multiple personality disorder (MPD).

Multiple Personalities

MPD is a condition where an alter personality often assumes the control of a physical body in lieu of control by what might be considered the prime personality. The switch is often sudden, sometimes dramatic, and invariably involves substantial changes in voice pitch, body stance, and overall outward appearance.

Major physiological changes may occur. A particularly striking example is a wound, suffered when a specific alter personality was in control of the body, suddenly reappearing when that same alter personality again takes over control, and then fading away when the alter personality relinquishes control. The overall effect in the change is the sudden realization by an observer that the person now appears to be a totally different person.

Alter personalities can be of different sex, widely different ages, usually do not age, and can be very different in temperament, strength, viewpoint, and maturity. Usually the alter personalities are aware of the other personalities, and may in many cases have very definite feelings of likes and dislikes toward the other personalities.

Unlike the alter personalities, the prime personality is often amnesiac and suffers from a complete lack of knowledge of the alter personalities. Often the only symptom the prime personality is aware of is the unexplainable losses or blanks of time (during those times when an alter personality surreptitiously assumes control of the body). Many MPD's are now aware of their alter personalities, but usually only through therapists and others informing them of the fact. The news is often traumatic in itself.

MPDs are invariably the result of severe child abuse. It is believed that critical to the formation of a multiple personality is the total lack of control that the child senses concerning its own safety and well being, and the utter lack of predictability of the abusing adult (usually a parent). Current evidence suggests that both the lack of control and lack of predictability are essential in order for an individual to develop a multiple personality.

A common characteristic of MPDs is the presence of what is apparently extrasensory powers. An MPD often displays telepathic powers or very highly developed intuition. From the viewpoint of the cause of multiple personalities, such extrasensory abilities may be more of a defense reaction than a disorder. If a child, for example, is unsure of a beckoning parent's intentions as to whether that child will be hugged or hurt, the child's mind (not knowing of society's bias against accepting telepathy as real) might develop extrasensory powers purely in order to survive.

In this regard, some researchers have suggested that MPD is more likely an advanced species than a mental problem. This rather radical concept has some merit. While it is unmistakably true that child abuse is a serious and traumatic event in one's life, it is also true that once the trauma of child abuse has been dealt with, the multiple personality may in fact have some distinct advantages over the more common single personality. If one believes in the advantages of teamwork, clearly a multiple personality who has its act together could be a formidable foe.

Most psychologists, psychiatrists, and therapists find the idea of healthy multiples to be a contradiction in terms. This inability of "learned profession-als" to consider the possibility of mentally healthy people with a number of personalities other than one, strikes many people as rather ironic; we certainly know of many psychiatrists and the like who have zero personalities.

But I digress. For the present discussion, let us consider the possibility of channels being nothing more than reasonably-healthy, multiple personalities.

Channels vs. Multiples

Channels and multiples display several characteristics in common. The switching of personalities is one. Another is the diversity of the personality traits, whether or not the "second" personality is another entity or simple an alter personality. Channels often have entities purportedly from different eras and widely different cultures, while MPDs have a wide diversity but usually within components of the MPDs various stages of maturity. The question of the sex of the alter personalities or entities is virtually irrelevant. Some cases have been observed where an MPD has "invited" other entities; such that in addition to having alter personalities, the person now has attached entities as well. Such situations further complicate the lack of distinction between chan-nels and MPDs.

One characteristic of a channel which is usually sufficient to WOW the crowd is the ability to provide information of which only the audience is aware. There is the sense that if the channel knows a hidden secret you wouldn't have told your grandmother, then that channel, supposedly, must have access to some very powerful sources of information. However, a channel with substantial telepathic or intuitive powers would also have access to such "inside" information. The fact that some of the information is contained in the subconscious of the audience would make little or no difference. With occasional demonstrations of such telepathic or intuitive powers by multiple personalities, the distinction between channels and multiples is further eroded.

Child abuse, the apparent cause of multiple personalities, is now believed to be much more prevalent than previously thought. Some researchers estimate that as many as one in three women are abused as a child (usually sexually). Men apparently suffer less incidents, but nonetheless account for as many as one in seven. Obviously there is a large population from which to draw in our recruitment of people who can be multiples or channels.

It is probably essential that a person capable of channeling be reasonably stable in mental matters. If a channel is an MPD, then it seems likely that they have somehow managed to deal with their childhood trauma (a not insignificant feat), and have managed to integrate any alter personalities into a team whose primary interests are on behalf of the integrated multiple. As this integration is difficult at best, it would allow for the substantial differences in numbers of channels and "healthy multiples."

When asked if they were a multiple, one channel quickly responded with "no." However, psychologists who are experienced with multiples have found them to be extremely sophisticated and clever in avoiding the vast majority of psychological tricks used by professionals in their quest to learn what is happening inside the multiple's mind. The chances of a multiple admitting to being a multiple are very slim.

But the same channel who disclaimed being a multiple, also displayed a strong correlation between what her channeling entities knew and what she knew. In other words, if the channel was unaware of some technical terminology in what was being transmitted, her "entities" were similarly disadvantaged. The entities seemed entirely incapable of providing any more information than the channel was capable of providing out of her own imagination and experience. This lack places some rather severe restrictions on what this particular channel could hope to convey or the value of this information to others.

An inherent assumption by many proponents in listening to a channel is that the channel is somehow tapping into sources of information which are valuable. In many cases, the assumption is that the channel has access to the Akashic Records. However, if an alter personality of an MPD has telepathic powers and thus has access to altered states, it may be that the alter personality also has access to the Akashic Records. Effectively, the alter personality may have information of equal value to that of the channeling entity (assuming, of course, that either personality's information is of any value). In this case, from a purely practical viewpoint, it may not make any difference if the individual is a channel or a multiple personality.

There is one potentially critical distinction between MPDs, channels, and people with attached entities. Alter personalities are created by a multiple as needed and, as a consequence, seldom have a history. The alter personality may have been "around" for a long time, but they will have no history of being born or any memory of events prior to their creation. Channeling entities and attached entities will often have full histories (including rank, serial number, date of birth, etc), although it is worth noting that many channeling entities do not provide any details of their prior history which could be substantiated. When in doubt as to whether an entity is a multiple's alter personality or an attached or channeling entity, ask for a history. To then distinguish between attached and channeling entities, ask the entity if they are from the Light. Channeling entities will say "yes," while the attached entity will more than likely describe only his history.

Real or Imaginary?

Are channels a figment of their own imagination? The very definitive answer is: Not necessarily. There is certainly some evidence supporting the existence of channels, which is not so easily explained. There is also a strong case for many channels being MPDs in disguise – even to the point of the channel not knowing the difference. But there is also other evidence that tends to discount the value of channeling still further.

For one thing, relying on an altered state of consciousness for receiving accurate information from the other side is fraught with peril. Inside a trance-like state, the fine line between imagination and enlightenment is often blurred and very nearly indistinct. Recall, for example, that entities channeling from the other side, often literally do not know what time it is. As viewed by one hydraulic engineer, "Information from a channel that doesn't hold water is worthless." There has been more than one episode of a channel bringing through technical information on which investors relied to build everything from a flying saucer to a radically new and much more efficient solar energy system. All such episodes have ended as technical failures, i.e. the information either was insufficiently technically accurate, or just plain garbage.

The process whereby channelers receive their information is also of note. In one case, when asked how he got back after a channeling entity had left his physical body, the channeler said, "The same way I leave. I feel like I'm going through a paper-towel tube. It's like w-o-o-s-h and then pop! And I'm back." This description may ring a few bells. It sounds much like the near-death experience. Margot Gray has noted the connection between the biological processes attending death and the ones necessary to reach higher state of consciousness. Essentially the life force is withdrawn from bodily sensations. It can be deliberately induced by centering inwardly away from the sensory world, in effect simulating a death-like state, and thus experience union with the Christ Consciousness.

Instead of thinking of the "tunnel experience" as a near-death aspect, it may be more appropriate to think of it as an out-of-body aspect. If, for example, a trance channeler leaves the body to make room for anther entity, it is reasonable to assume that they might do so in an out-of-body state. This possible correlation between trance channels and many of the other aspects of reincarnation-related phenomenon should not be dismissed lightly.

What Difference Does It Make?

Channels themselves, along with proponents of the concept, have expressed their own reservations about channeling. One well known channel, Norma Green, has noted that some sources are better than others. Ms. Green also suggests that one always ask channels which level they are from – obstensibly the higher the level, the better the information.

This idea may be very important in that channeling entities appear to be limited in their "enlightened views" by their own past-life experiences, egos, and stage of evolution of their own souls. Candy Tsuchiya, a metaphysical bookstore owner, believes that channels are for real, but she has reservations about the integrity of many of the channeling entities, noting that good motives are not necessarily a consequence of the channeled entity being from the astral-plane. Ms. Tsuchiya suggests that some channeling entities may be on their very own ego trip, deliberately passing along incorrect or faulty information for reasons entirely their own. She has even expressed concern that after gaining a channel's confidence with a correct prediction or two, the channeling entity may take over the channel physically and spiritually.

Ms. Tsuchiya's concerns would appear to be well founded.

The principle danger in any philosophy is to place too much credence on the prophet. The value of a philosophy should be in the inherent value of its principles in directing one's life, and not in the charisma or popularity of its teacher. Richard Alpert, a one time Harvard psychology professor and who has since become renowned as the New Age star and lecturer, Ram Dass, has expressed such reservations about channeling. In his introduction to Pat Rodegast's channeled book, *Emmanuel's Book*, Ram Dass writes:

> "I have been asked again and again . . . whether I really believe that Emmanuel is a separate being from Pat or whether he is another part of Pat's personality with which she does not consciously identify . . . From my point of view as a psychologist, I allow for the theoretical possibility that Emmanuel is a deeper part of Pat. In the final analysis, what difference does it really make? What I treasure is the wisdom Emmanuel conveys . . ."

So what are we to make of channeled information? Are these people claiming to be channels real? This possibility cannot just simply be dismissed. Channels may still have some good answers. Any out-right denunciation of all channels is likely to be pure folly, but the idea that the majority of so-called channels are deluding people (and perhaps themselves as well), is probably a pretty good bet. As one pundit put it, "Channels may have access to all the answers; but it seems unlikely they will always be able to connect them with the right questions."

Perhaps the wiser course is to take Clyde Reid's advice to always test channeled information. Perhaps the very reason for having channels is to remind us that we must always question. Everything. In detail, and not let the idea that 80% of the stuff being right necessarily imply that the other 20% is also true. The same argument can probably also apply to psychics and anyone who claims to find truth in an altered state or otherwise.

Walk-Ins

A "Walk-in" is a person who has taken over the body of a living being on a permanent basis, while the original resident of the body has gone off to do other and possibly more interesting things, and who has no expectations of ever returning to that body. Walk-in's thus provide for a whole new realm of strange and very mysterious beings wandering about the earth. According to Ruth Montgomery, "A Walk-in is a high minded entity who is permitted to take over the body of another human being who wishes to depart." In Ms. Montgomery's book, *Strangers Among Us*, we learn of a vast menagerie of souls who have supposedly "walked-in" and taken over the use of another's physical body.

Obstensibly, "the motivation for a Walk-in is humanitarian. He returns to physical being in order to help others help themselves, planting seed-concepts that will grow and flourish for the benefit of mankind." Such generosity, as advocated by Ruth Montgomery, can hardly be questioned. Surely, Walk-ins can be considered by many to be quite a bit more knowledgeable than the average soul arriving by more conventional means, if only because the Walk-in has the decided advantage (at least, in most cases) of not having to go through adolescence again. The avoidance of the teenage years has got to be a blessing which can only bode for the best.

The question of whether Walk-ins are in fact more knowledgeable and possess a greater understanding of the big picture, is, like channeling entities, dependent upon the individual Walk-in. One can even consider the question of whether or not one should even bother with the concept. Clearly, if someone has something worthwhile to say, their status as a Walk-in should not be the controlling factor as to the value of their sayings. Frankly, there does not appear at first blush a good reason to have Walk- ins, but the claims persists.

Unfortunately, much of the evidence of such irreversible changing of the guard involves nothing more than sudden and very distinctive personality changes in an individual. Such changes are supposedly substantially greater, for example, than that observed during menopause, or other such traumatic times in the life of an individual, so that we can hopefully disregard these possibilities. However, the question of whether or not a dramatic personality change indicates a switching of souls is still questionable (despite the fact that a change could be an improvement in some cases).

Adding further confusion is the fact that as Ruth Montgomery points out, "You yourself may be a Walk-in! Since the memory pattern of the departing entity survives intact, Walk-ins are sometimes unaware of their altered status for several years after the substitution as been effected." Is she kidding us? Why be a high minded and "enlightened" Walk-in, if you don't know it? Wouldn't that tend to negate the whole point? Is, perhaps, the concept beginning to show a few cracks in its foundation?

There is another, perhaps more devastating, problem. What is the difference between a soul deciding to sublet his body, and simply checking out? What distinguishes a suicide and a "Walk-out?" Apparently the only difference between suicide and walking-out, according to Ms. Montgomery, is that for the Walk-out, the physical body, the "flame of life," is not "quenched." This idea also has some problems.

Recall, for example, that in the near-death experiences, there is a consistent reference by those experiencing the phenomenon, to their having little regard for the physical body that they have left behind them. In effect, their physical body or "spacesuit" is of little concern . Arguments against suicide suggest that it is not the physical body that is of value, but the fact that a refusal to face your problems this time around will mean that you get to face them again in the next life, after a possible detour for retribution purposes for failing the first time. Walk-outs continue to sound suspiciously like suicides, although there may be other justification for walking-out, other than having problems. One could, for example, have finished with the business of this life successfully and now feel the need to incarnate in another body for the next life-project.

Meditation

The predictions made by channels, clairvoyants, psychics, and others in recent years are sufficient to give anyone concern for the future. We might be able to laugh at the bearded fellow on the street carrying the sign, "The End of the World is at Hand", but the consistency of many of the more recent prophets of doom must make us at least pause for a moment. Many of the more noteworthy of the predicted catastrophes from channels and the like, are discussed in detail in Chapter 15, but for now, we might question the apparent need to rely on these rather strange people for foreseeing our future. Is there no other way to predict what will happen, what our health and fortunes will be? Must we always confine ourselves to listening intently to the rather imprecise ramblings of some would-be prophet?

The good news is: Yes, Virginia, there is another way. And the name of this means to an end (pardon the pun) is meditation.

Meditation, as defined in our handy dictionary, implies the dwelling in thought on some feeling, idea, or object. Here the mind may be gathered and focused, or diffused, discursive and merely revolving around an object. Instead of the brain looking for new problems to solve, it becomes quiet and motionless. Meditation is often an attempt to achieve a mind steady and free from fluctuation. Contemplation might be a better word, since in its original Greek sense it meant the steady viewing (without a flicker) of a single object like a candle's flame.

This narrower view of meditation can be thought of as a way of achieving a self-controlled, altered state of consciousness, without the use of hypnosis or drugs. This meditative state is nothing more than a dream-like condition, where alpha waves predominate, but where the subject in not asleep or unconscious.

Reasons for Meditation

Most people associate meditation with eastern religions and such things as Yoga. Certainly meditation is the very heart of Yoga practice (particularly Raja Yoga), but meditation does not require any specific beliefs or dogmas. Virtually all that is required is a faith in one's own self, an expectation of truth, and a sincere desire to find both self and truth through the process.

The proponents of meditation claim that the practice offers substantial benefits, particularly as part of one's daily life. The endless distractions and restlessness of society, constantly draw people away from simply knowing and understanding themselves. Meditation opens the door to subtle perceptions, which can change both convictions and character. It can calm emotions, strengthen nerves, heal tensions, and help a person attain a greater self-mastery of themselves. Day-to-day repetitions seem to nourish their practitioners by making them healthier, stronger, and happier.

In many respects meditation can give us the power to view life and its activities in perspective and with enough detachment to allow us to judge things in their proper dimensions and true character. Meditation can theoretically give poise and clarity of vision.

The purpose of meditation for many of its proponents is to discover the Truth of our Self, in Yogic parlance, samadhi. The spiritual greatness of a soul is supposedly revealed through meditation. When we speak of individuals being reduced to some sort of "thing" or "object", of becoming estranged from their own self by the pressures of an industrial and exploitative society, we may be stating the best need for meditation.

Higher Self

Meditation is also considered the supreme method of learning about the Self (that "Higher Self" or "Oversoul" we all supposedly have within our reach). The Higher Self is theoretically, that portion of your soul or spirit still residing in the space between lives, knowing of the divine plans and destinies, and attempting to guide you such that the incarnated portion of yourself gains the most from the experiences encountered on earth. The Higher Self is also that entity that could provide each of us with guidance and comfort.

So why does it seem that your Higher Self is off vacationing in some heavenly equivalent to Hawaii? Don't worry about that. According to reincarnationists of the spiritual persuasion, time and space mean nothing on the other side, and thus your Higher Self is always available. Maybe just not quite available at your beck and call.

The description of a Higher Self tends to vary, depending upon whom you ask. But most would agree with the basics of the following description given by Jacqueline Damgaard (writing in *Consciousness and Survival*, her paper on "The Inner Self Helper: Transcendent Life Within Life?"). Dr. Damgaard's remarks are directed to a discussion of multiple personalities, and are not necessarily an indication that the ISH (Dr. Damgaard's "Inner Self Helper") is viewed by her as one's Higher Self. But the description is nevertheless very much to the point:

> "There is no date of origin or formation ('I have always been with her'). The ISH is not created to handle a patient's unexpressed anger or other feelings from a violent trauma. The ISH is present from birth as a separate ego state. There is no capacity for hate. The ISH feels only love and good will. The ISH expresses both awareness and belief in God and may also believe in the Devil. The ISH serves as a conduit for God's healing power and love. The ISH sometimes calls on a higher power for help. It never expresses a desire to lead a separate life – rather it wants to become one with the others. The ISH knows that the condition of multiplicity exists, and understands the patient's entire past history, which is available for easy recall. The ISH can usually predict future actions with great accuracy. The ISH has no conception of gender, referring to the self equally as male or female. Other than love and goodwill, the ISH lacks emotions, seeming to be pure intellect. The ISH answers questions and communicates in the manner of a computer repeating programmed information, and expects to be a working partner with the therapist and can see the therapists errors and help correct them. Often the ISH believes in reincarnation and often speaks of being next to God and consequently difficult to summon directly. The ISH is usually not known by the presenting personality. It can often be suppressed by the other ego states, and comes through usually by request of the therapist, unless an emergency is occurring – then the ISH will influence another ego state to call the therapist. Finally the ISH is able to bring memories through to the different ego states, as those are ready to process them."

And you thought you had no one to talk to when you meditate!

Hopefully, it is clear that the presence of an ISH may not be limited to individuals with multiple personalities. If, in fact, the above description of an ISH is equivalent to that of a Higher Self, then the effort to meditate and make contact may be a very beneficial activity. One assumes that you can always ignore their advice – with all your practice at ignoring your parents' advice, you should be accomplished at that by now.

All kidding aside, there is no reason to believe that you would not continue to exercise free will. Consequently, it might be time to contact your Higher Self, or at least make the attempt, sort of "reach out and touch your Higher Self". Such communications could eliminate the need for channels and prophets of doom (surely a worthwhile goal), provide guidance and direction in your own life (someone has to tell you where to go), and perhaps allow you to foresee and understand the implications of our joint future, whatever that may be.

With respect to reincarnation, life after physical death, and all of the things about which we've talked thus far, the concept of a Higher Self, seems to be extremely important. Sufficiently important, in fact, that you might want to reread Dr. Damgaard's description of the ISH. During this review, you might also want to consider not only the idea that her description accurately describes the Higher Self and that a Higher Self exists for each and everyone of us, but also consider how that description of a Higher Self ties in with our emerging theory of reincarnation. You may find it a useful exercise.

Chapter 15:

Predictions of

the Future

She was the greatest psychic known. In her trances she was able to tell of past-lives, explain current problems, and predict the future. She had been uncannily accurate in every verifiable pronouncement she had ever made. She had made many a believer out of skeptics, and now she was being tested once again.

"What predictions do you have for the world in the next 15 years?" The skeptical investigator watched the psychic as she drew in a deep breath, seemed to hold it for just a moment, and then began to talk in a forceful and intense manner.

"I've got some good news and some bad news. The bad news is that the world is going to undergo the most massive destruction imaginable; the poles will shift abruptly, whole continents will be innundated, lands will appear, volcanos and earthquakes will set new records for destruction, and the vast majority (i.e. 95 to 99 percent) of the earth's population will be killed in fire storms, bitter cold, wrenching earth shifts, and other clever and very violent natural means. To put it mildly, all hell's going to break loose.

"That's the bad news. The good news is that in the "New Age," everything's gonna be all better."

Say what?

Prophecies of Doom

From time immemorial doomsayers have been prophesying the early end to the earth, man, the stock market, and bad breath. In only one case did the predictions come true (albeit, predictions of the 1929 stock market debacle were few and far between). On a more positive note, religions and prophets have been heralding the coming of a new and glorious age (with appropriate appearances of religious figures) for just as long. Interestingly enough, they too have managed to come up with a few correct predictions. Occasionally. Maybe.

Predictions of doom are almost always newsworthy. Telling the world that this week will be a lot like last week is seldom going to make the six o'clock news, whereas stories of the coming market crash and depression (recently predicted for 1982, 1983, 1984, 1985, 1986, 1987 – at least it was close! – 1988, 1989, and so forth), always manage to catch someone's eye. It seems as if mankind relishes the idea of its forthcoming demise or destruction, but would rather not hear about how good things are. If one has problems, they certainly don't want to hear that everyone else is doing great; and since everyone has problems of one kind or another, no one appears eager to hear of another's good fortune.

Accordingly the market for terrifying predictions has been and is currently enjoying considerable interest. In terms of dollars there is tremendous speculation in the stocks of prophets of doom and gloom. The interesting aspect now is that we are hearing from a much wider group of doomsayers. No longer limited to the down-trodden (who would just as soon forget their current troubles and start over, going along with whatever catastrophe appeals to their imagination), tales of imminent doom are being made by a new and vast menagerie of players.

The stock market, for example, has more than a few, established and respected members readily acknowledging the imminent doom of the market. Some have even gone to the extreme of predicting the idea of owning stocks becoming extinct (or at least stocks owned by outside investors who are not actually working for the company). Considering the graft and corruption so rampant in the stock market and in the publicly-held companies' board rooms, this is probably an inevitable result. And if one then considers the basics of the Business Cycle (i.e. what goes up, must come down), then a recession or depression in the 1990s is inevitable. Not just possible, but guaranteed. A sure thing. This decade!

Worse yet, another aspect of the Business Cycle is that what goes up the highest and stays up the longest, precedes that which goes down the lowest and stays down the longest. Thus the 1990s are almost certainly going to see a very severe recession as a minimum. More likely is the distinct possibility of a major depression to make the nineteen-thirties look tame.[1]

But the inevitability of a looming worldwide economic disaster is very real, particularly when, among other things, the United States national debt may rocket up toward seven or eight trillion dollars (the current U. S. debt plus the current "contingent liabilities" – i.e. the money owed by the U. S. in the event of guaranteed loans from banks, savings and loans, FHA, VA, students, etc, failing). The only question is the extent of the disaster. Worse yet, such forecasts have not even considered recent predictions of changing weather patterns, where much of the rainfall moves to sea, causing yet another dust bowl.

---

[1] One current astrological prediction for the final bottoming of the stock market is October 7, 1991, when Neptune and the North Node conjunct in Capricorn, squaring the Sun, Moon, Mercury and Mars! Astrology does not predict whether or not the stock market will subsequently recover from this "Crash of '91."

In his book *Memories and Visions of Paradise,* Richard Heinberg has written:

> "Not only religious zealots but economists, social theorists, technologists, nuclear critics, population experts, ecologists and political ideologues agree that an unprecedented shift in man's world – whether catastrophic or beatific – is inevitable within the next half-century."

Today the pace seems to be quickening as predictors of doom seem eager to leap upon the end-of-this-world bandwagon. The only real divergence of opinion is whether the expectation is for Armageddon or the flowering of a new planetary culture built upon the ashes and complete with an unprecedented spiritual awakening (including most any scenario lying between these extremes). The more pessimistic of the lot tend to view the end of the millennium as the absolute limit for the culmination of all the horrifying trends. The more optimistic like to think of things changing for the better. This view seems the least defensible in that things almost never change for the better. On the other hand, the effective elimination of the IRS would surely usher in a Golden Age.

Manmade Catastrophes

Certainly, world problems tend to provide fuel for the doom and gloom teams. Mankind is now faced with a proliferation of major problems due to overpopulation, famine, disease, war, and man's own inhumanity to man. We also have specifics, such as the very real probability of a world debt and financial crisis (which would make 1929 look tame), the possibility of nuclear winter from too many bombs or nuclear reactors, starvation and famine in many parts of the world, and ecological disasters, ranging from the extinction of animals and other forms of life to the wholesale elimination of forests, croplands and natural habitats. On top of all this, AIDS (Acquired Immunity Deficiency Syndrome) has all the earmarks of a plague guaranteed to decimate the earth. (How, for example does one quarantine a disease with an incubation period of from one to ten years, a disease that is transmitted sexually and that opens up the victim for every known infection, plague, and/or virus, and a disease that continually mutates and thus tends to stay ahead of medical researchers looking for a cure?)

The problems seem overwhelming to say the least; but are we overdoing it? Are we over-reacting to our problems, and always seeing the worst? Perhaps. Psychologists believe that every generation prefers to see itself as the culmination of history. In this view, we may be simply attempting to justify our own self-worth, by ascribing to our age, some form of immense importance. That possibility, of course, exists by virtue of the fact that we like to think of our "times" as very significant.

The approach of the end of a millennium (as reckoned by our somewhat arbitrary calendar) seems to add fuel to the fire. But as Norman Cohn noted in his study, *The Pursuit of the Millennium*, fears and expectations of the end-of-the-world tend to show ebbs and flows through the centuries. We may be at nothing more than a crest in the wave, potentially the greatest eschatological wave of all history, but still one that is just a momentary upsurge in the predictable flow through time.

In 1971, Jay Forrestor, an MIT professor, disturbed his colleagues considerably with a paper entitled "Counterintuitive Behavior of Social Systems." In this thought-provoking paper, Dr. Forrestor used a computer model to combine the effects of long term trends in population growth, pollution levels, usage and availability of natural resources, and rates of capital investment; on variations in the quality of life. His computer model ran from the year 1900 through 1970 (in order to establish a base of known data) and extrapolated expected scenarios or trends to the year 2100.

Dr. Forrestor developed a series of scenarios, most of which caused severe gyrations in the quality of life and population beginning sometime in the years of 2020 to 2040. Only two of his published scenarios came close to the actual population increases actually experienced since 1971. In one of the more likely scenarios (based on its adherence to recent history), the population fell by 2045 to about 5 percent of the expected 2015 peak.[2] With better pollution controls and reduced pollution combined with this same scenario, the crisis was delayed by 20 years and reduced in its destructiveness – population fell to only about one third of its 2040 peak. The only scenario considered that yielded equilibrium in world conditions was an immediate leveling off of the population to that of 1970 levels. In the last two decades, we have virtually eliminated the possibility of this scenario.

Perhaps our time is, in fact, noteworthy . . . or at the very least interesting. There is an ancient Chinese curse which says: "May you live in interesting times." The present day would seem to qualify, but then other times would seem equally appropriate. For example . . .

Mankind has always maintained in its collective memory the myths and stories of humanity on the brink, where its insanity and recklessness have forced the vengeance of mother nature. Plato's description of Atlantis and its ultimate destruction is but one example of the end of a civilization run amok. Atlantis did not, according to legend, disappear because of the natural phenomena of earthquakes and tidal waves that just happened to come along and carelessly decimate Atlantis. Instead, Atlantis brought destruction on itself by pride, unseemly behavior, and wicked coveting. (That doesn't describe us, does it?) Plato has implied that Atlantis' destruction was intended by the Greek God, Zeus, to return the Atlanteans to the fold and restore their piety. The fact that the civilization was virtually wiped from the face of the earth does suggest that Zeus and the gang may have overdone it a bit. However, the end result was still due, supposedly, to mankind's own folly.

---

[2] Interestingly, the reduction in the population to 5 percent of what went before it, is reminiscent of Dr. Wambach's prediction for 2100.

Lemuria, another legendary land (but perhaps even more obscure than Atlantis), is said to have met its end for the same reasons. In fact it appears from Edgar Cayce's description that Lemuria was given more than one opportunity to recognize the inevitable, but in each case eventually fell into trouble, and ultimately was wiped out.

Natural Catastrophes?

The insistence of the myths and tales of lost civilizations being destroyed by the irreverence of its peoples should give us pause. Why must major, worldwide catastrophes be attributed only to the fault of man? Cannot volcanoes erupt without man somehow causing the ecologically devastating event? Are earthquakes, no matter how potent, the result of man's inhumanity to man?

In *Worlds in Collision*, Immanuel Velikovsky gives a scholarly account of near-collisions between the planet earth and the planets Venus and Mars, during historical times. Using modern physics and the so-called mythologies of ancient peoples throughout the world, Velikovsky explains the miracles of the Exodus, including the biblical passage:

> "And the sun stood still, and the moon stayed, until the people had avenged themselves upon their enemies. Is not this written in the book of Jasher? So the sun stood still in the midst of heaven, and hasted not to go down about a whole day." (Joshua 10:13)

Amazingly, Velikovsky's theories suggest that the sun did in fact stand still (i.e. the earth's surface, the floating plates, did in fact slip such that the sun appeared to stand still.) In the process of explaining this incredible historical fact, Velikovsky also called into question the chronology of Egyptian dynasties, earning him a great deal of fanatical and irrational responses from pseudo-scientists and narrow minded historians.

But noteworthy in Velikovsky's accounts is the lack of motive for the massive destruction occasioned by two planets in what could best be described as a near-collision. There appears to be nothing which tells us that "we brought it on ourselves." It was in fact a natural catastrophe, and not the result of heavenly displeasure toward man or a group thereof.

Mankind's Responsibilities

One might wonder why man is so eager to accept responsibility for natural calamities. If you are wondering this, then consider the alternative. If mankind is thoroughly good and doing all that can be expected of him (and her), and then the world is torn asunder by the random acts of nature, the implication is that the world and/or the universe is out of control, essentially, not a very nice place to live. For if the planet Venus wreaked havoc in 1500 B.C., what's to prevent a similar occurrence today? If Atlantis were "inadvertently" or carelessly wiped from the face of the earth, could we not suffer the same fate? And even after we've been good!? Clearly we could, and this prospect of an uncontrolled nature sporadically and randomly wiping out the good, the bad, and the simply ugly, is often more than egotistical man can tolerate.

The accrediting to mankind of worldwide disasters has two advantages. It certainly satisfies man's ego by implying that he can determine the cause of natural events on a massive scale. If by being bad, he can destroy his world, and, alternatively, by being good, save it, mankind must be a very powerful and important group. Maybe that's true. But don't count on it.

A second advantage of mankind's ability to cause disaster, is the potential for control by some of the doomsayers. Again we have the implication that if you don't straighten up and fly right (i.e. obey my rules) the world will be destroyed. The onus is on you (and others like you) to save the world. It's rather severe punishment for not adhering to what I think is right, but I have to revert to such extreme measures just in order to catch your attention.

Just as we might suspect the objectivity of those who threaten pain and anguish for their followers who do not follow every precept of the faith, one might also doubt the coming Armageddon. God, in fact, may not strike down the wicked and preserve the good, but may simply allow us to continue as before. While we may be facing the distinct possibility of worldwide catastrophes of unprecedented scale and from a variety of causes, our "being good" may have little or no effect in averting the crisis.

The Great Purification

On the other hand, traditions of peoples throughout the world tell of a time of "purification" and the "reawakening of spiritual man." The Hopi Indians believe that within the next twenty to thirty years, mankind will either destroy itself or transform itself into a new spiritual age. They also see famines and other natural catastrophes as one step in the Great Purification. Apparently, the world is about to shake, rattle and roll, despite mankind's action. Man's only choice may be whether or not to join in the spiritual awakening.

The Hopis are not alone. The Mesquakie Indians also see the need for massive earth changes in the process of cleansing the earth and returning man to his original state. The Tibetans go a step further and add political strife to a series of global catastrophes before man can enter into the new era of spiritual awakening. Interestingly the Tibetans also believe that man is now living at the end of a 26,000 year period of darkness. After waiting that long, it's no wonder that they are so eagerly searching for "the light at the end of the tunnel."

There are a multitude of predictions of the coming doom, as well as compensation for the true believers. From thirteenth century Japanese religious teachers to the founders of today's major religions, we have the same story of gloom and doom, followed by a time of peace, joy and second comings. The prophet Mohammed promised peace:

> ". . . when the Trumpet is blown with a single blast and the earth and the mountains are lifted up and crushed with a single blow.

"Then, on that day, the Terror shall come to pass, and heaven shall be split . . ."

Buddhist scriptures, being a bit less belligerent, have prophesied the future incarnation of Buddha, Maitreya:

"Human beings are then without any blemishes, moral offences are unknown among them, and they are full of zest and joy. Their bodies are very large and their skin has a fine hue. Their strength is quite extraordinary . . . And then (Maitreya) will with a perfect voice preach the true Dharma, which is auspicious and removes all ill. . . and leads to Nirvana."

There are now suggestions that Maitreya has now returned to earth and is living in London! Perhaps you caught his news release.

In the 24th chapter of Matthew, Jesus' disciples ask "what shall be the sign of thy coming, and of the end of the world?" Jesus' answer was:

"And ye shall hear of wars and rumors of wars: see that ye be not troubled: for all these things must come to pass, but the end is not yet.

"For nation shall rise against nation, and kingdom against kingdom: and there shall be famines, and pestilences, and earthquakes, in divers places.

"All these are the beginning of sorrows."   (Matthew 24: 6-8)

"Immediately after the tribulation of those days shall the sun be darkened, and the moon shall not give her light, and the stars shall fall from heaven, and the powers of the heavens shall be shaken:

"And then shall appear the sign of the Son of man in heaven: and then shall all the tribes of the earth mourn, and they shall see the Son of man coming in the clouds of heaven with power and great glory.

"And he shall send his angels with a great sound of a trumpet, and they shall gather together his elect from the four winds, from one end of heaven to the other."   (Matthew 24: 29-31)

Many would suggest that the closing decades of the twentieth century are the "beginning of sorrows," and admittedly there are noteworthy correlations. However, World War II might easily have been considered a more likely time for the end-of-the-world times and its associated tribulations. And with mankind being rather consistently at war, perhaps one should look for a substantial increase in earthquake activity to herald the coming of troubled times. This view of relying on nature's signals instead of man's is often the rationale for more modern predictions of impending doom.

It is noteworthy, however, that in the same 24th chapter of Matthew, Jesus repeatedly warns against false Christs and false prophets and being deceived by others claiming to be Christ. If we plan to seriously consider the text of modern day predictions, it might be well to keep in mind this warning of possible deception.

Exactly When?

Missing in most of these ancient prophecies are specific dates. If you're talking about next week, you are much more likely to have everyone's undivided attention; but if we're looking at decades or centuries, then perhaps we all have a bit more time to take care of last minute details. The world in 2100 may have only 5 percent of today's population, but if we're talking about something a century away, there would appear to be nothing to worry about. However, if Armageddon is only ten to twenty years in the future, perhaps we should listen to the possibilities a bit more carefully.

Warnings of Armageddon, based on the year 2000 or the end of the current millennium, leave something to be desired. On the one hand is the fact that most scholars believe that Jesus Christ was born in 4 B.C. (qualifying this statement as an oxymoron). This would imply the end of the world in 1996. More importantly, there is nothing particularly magic about the number 2000.

Mathematically speaking, the coming year 2000 is derived from a "base ten" numbering system. Such a numbering system is quite arbitrary, and, from a mathematician's viewpoint, a rather poor choice. A much better choice is base 8, which a computer uses with infinitely greater ease (actually a computer uses base 2, but base 8 is effectively two cubed). In the base 8 system, the year 2000 is actually the year 2400, obviously not a year to which we would attach particular importance. (For those who would suggest we have ten fingers - and thus implying the rationale of a base ten system - please note that in reality we have 8 fingers and 2 thumbs, i.e., the base 8 and base 2 systems. So there!)

On the other hand, the year 2000 is, approximately, the end of the Piscean Age (and the start of the Aquarian Age). While many modern predictions tend to rely on the year 2000 as the height of global changes, others find other dates. Some of these possibilities are even more noteworthy. For example:

Quetzalcoatl

The Toltecs and Aztecs of Central America include in their sacred traditions the prophecies given by a priest born about 950 A.D., whom they considered as the reincarnation of Quetzalcoatl. Quetzalcoatl was the Mayan God who at the beginning of the world taught his people the rudiments of agriculture, mathematics and theology. His priest, who was light skinned and bearded, prophesied that a man like him in appearance would come from the east in a canoe with huge wings, wearing a feathered plume and a coat that would shine like the sun. Upon his arrival, the white man would initiate a period of nine "hells," each hell being a 52-year cycle of darkness. At the end of the nine hells, there would begin a time of supreme cleansing and purification, when cities and mountains would collapse and civilization would be reduced to rubble by fire. After the Great Purification, the Christlike God,

Quetzalcoatl, would return to initiate a Golden Age.

In 1519, Cortez arrived on the west coast in a sailing ship (with white sails), wearing brightly polished armor and a plumed helmet. Montezuma, the Aztec emperor, immediately recognized the obvious fulfillment of the prophecy, and this fact explains in part how the relatively meager contingent of conquistadors were able to fairly easily destroy the Aztec Civilization. (It is left to the reader to calculate the first year of the supreme cleansing and purification, which will begin with worldwide destruction and end with the start of the Golden Age, i.e. 1519 A.D. + [9 hells x 52 yrs/hell) = —.])[3]

The Aztecs, at the time of Cortez, practiced human sacrifice on a grand scale, regularly made war with neighboring tribes just for the purpose of obtaining sacrificial victims (and for some, dying with honor), and in general were not the precise exemplification of what Christians would consider "nice" people. Whether or not this decline of the Aztecs into sin and loathing from 950 A.D. to the time of Cortez, is responsible for the Spaniard's arrival is not clear, but, for our purposes, the initiation of a Golden Age might be relevant.

It's all well to talk about the beginning of the end of the world in the immediate past, but are we ready to believe a prophecy made a thousand years ago? Surely Quetzalcoatl's priest could have been off a couple of years (if not decades)! If man has been slightly better than expected, have we bought some additional time?

Not if you believe some of the predictions.

Stars and Planets

The year 1991 is the end of the solar activity cycle, when solar flares and sunspots are expected to greatly increase in number and intensity. Many astrologers are now referring to this year as the "Year of the angry sun."

Not to be to left out, the planets may also be ganging up on us. According to many astrologers, the "start of it all" began on January 19, 1984, when Neptune entered Capricorn (the sign normally important to governments and rule makers). In 1989 Saturn joined Neptune in three separate conjunctions (Moscow might appreciate this timing). In December 1990, five planets conjunct in the constellation Capricorn. Such conjunctions, according to astrologers, will have major effects on the earth. Small wonder then that January 11, 1994 is considered to be of significance – seven planets will be in conjunction in Capricorn in what has been termed, "The Big Daddy!"

January 11, 1994! Mark it on your calendars, folks – you wouldn't want to miss out on the festivities!

Edgar Cayce's Predictions

We have already alluded to Edgar Cayce's predictions of the future and their implications. As a modern prophet, Mr. Cayce was quite prolific. For

---

[3] Hint: 1987. (Perhaps we'd better check Cortez's log again, just to make sure of his arrival date in the New World.)

example, Cayce spoke of the time period 1958-1998 A. D. in terms of physical changes. These included the western portion of American being "broken up", most of Japan going into the sea, Northern Europe changed in the twinkling of an eye, land appearing off the east coast of America, upheavals at the North and South Poles, eruption of volcanoes, and ultimately, a shifting of the poles – such that frigid climates will become tropical!

Instead of California falling off into the ocean, we have it merely being "broken up." Presumably New Yorkers will not be too "broken up" by this news, particularly in light of the fact that they may find new land off their coast for condominium development. Japan, on the other hand (not to mention northern Europe) may have greater cause for concern. On the plus side, this could greatly decrease the trade deficit with Japan.

Nostradamus

Nostradamus was the sixteenth century French astrologer we discussed in Chapter 13. Considering Nostradamus' rather incredible record of successful predictions, extending over a period of four hundred years, his predictions discussed here must be considered with some degree of credibility. At the same time, however, we should keep in mind that Nostradamus' cryptic style does not lend itself to unambiguous interpretations by different scholars!

John Hogue, in his book, *Nostradamus and the Millenium*, for example, makes the following interpretations of Nostradamus' many Quatrains, all of which might appear particularly relevant to the world's near term future:

1. The third "anti-Christ" (following Napoleon and Hitler) may already have arrived. (There are certainly plenty of candidates!)

2. A force of a million Iranians will sweep across Iraq all the way to Egypt, in the late eighties or early nineties.

3. The Jihad (holy war) will continue with the Iranians invading Macedonia, France, Italy and Spain by 1993 (starting a world war).

4. A Mediterranean fleet will be melted by a nuclear device ("a second sun") in 1994.

5. Russia is predicted to enter the war by an invasion that effectively supports the Islamic Jihad in the north, but in the final phase of the war (which last 3 years and 7 months) will reverse its policy and join the west to push back the Islamic invasion. "By 1999 the last war of the millennium is over, leaving the world in 'complete ruins and desolation'."

According to Hogue, Nostradamus also predicts "so vast a plague that two thirds of the world will fail and decay." Hogue believes that Nostradamus' plague may be AIDS. Great famines are predicted for the future as well, with potentially (according to Hogue) the "worst drought conditions in history by 1990 or 1991." As you might expect, Hogue uses Nostradamus to predict massive earth changes in the last decade of this millennium. Among the victims of the latter are first India, secondly Japan, and then Italy, northern and western Europe, western United States (broken into islands), east Africa, New York, Florida, et al.

The earth changes predicted by Hogue are only loosely based on Nostradamus, while the AIDS plague is somewhat better linked with the astrologer, even if the connection does require some rather subtle interpretations. The Jihad of the coming years, however, seems to have numerous Quatrains by Nostradamus which better support Hogue's interpretation of the prophecies.

The good news is that Nostradamus also makes predictions for the next two thousand years (albeit only a few), as well as the Age of Capricorn (4000-6000 A.D.) and the Age of Sagittarius (6000-8000 A.D.). Unfortunately, the latter ages appear to be off the planet, as the end of the world is slated to occur by a massive meteor crashing into the Aegean Sea sometime between 3755 and 3797 A.D. (But which should not affect this summer's vacation plans to Greece.)

Some of the more intriguing of Nostradamus' prophecies involve the Roman Catholic Church and, specifically, the various Popes during the last four hundred years. Even more noteworthy is the fact that Nostradamus' predictions agree in many aspects with an Irish priest, named Malachi, who visited Rome in 1138 A. D. and had a vision of the entire succession of 112 popes. Malachi's prophecies were unknown to Nostradamus, but both agree on most details and both have proven to be uncannily accurate, even to the giving of actual names.

Points of agreement, for example, include details concerning Pope Pius XII, John XXIII, Paul VI and John Paul I. The latter Pope (who reigned as Pontiff for only 30 days) was predicted by both Nostradamus and Malachi to be murdered by members of the Vatican!

> "The one elected Pope will be mocked by his electors,
> This enterprising and prudent person will suddenly be reduced to silence.
> They cause him to die
> Because of his too great goodness and mildness.
> Stricken by fear, they will lead him to his death in the night."

Hogue believes that the questionable financial dealings of the church were the cause of John Paul I's death, since this Pope might have reshuffled power in the Vatican because of financial questions.

> "He who will have government of the great cape,
> Will be led to execute in certain cases.
> The twelve red ones will spoil the cover.
> Under murder, murder will be perpetrated."

It is not yet clear if these deadly prophecies were correct. But both Nostradamus and Malachi agree that the next two Popes will be named Clement and, following Clement, Peter; and that Peter will be the last Pope of the Roman Catholic Church. While neither of these prophets may be correct, if the next Pope (after John Paul II) is named Clement, it might be wise to sell your stock in the Vatican.

Pole Shifts

The shifting of the poles is particularly noteworthy, and is expected to take place, according to Cayce, in the time period 2000 to 2001 A.D. A pole shift is substantially more important than mere earth tremors or limited volcanic activity. Shifting of the poles would result in immense tidal waves, extensive and abrupt changes in climate, whole sale submergence of continents, as well as massive and extensive earthquakes and volcanic eruptions. A pole shift involves nothing less than continental movements on a grand scale, and would cause massive destruction as the continents underwent convulsive shifts to new locations. The bulk of the earth might continue to spin, but the outer shell (crust) would be completely changed (in similar fashion to the continental shifts theorized by Velikovsky and his supporters in explaining the day the sun stood still).

The idea of the earth's crust shifting over a constantly rotating earth has also been discussed in *Earth's Shifting Crust* by Charles Hapgood and James Campbell. Hapgood is a professor of history and anthropology at Keene State College in New Hampshire, while Campbell is an engineer who helped develop the Sperry gyroscopic compass. Hapgood and Campbell noted that Antarctica has an off-center ice sheet with its center of gravity located more than 345 miles from the polar axis. The effect of this mass being off-center from the axis is akin to an unbalanced washing machine. Load a washing machine with a heavy rug in one section and you may very well see that machine "walk" all over the room.

An alternative view of the mechanism of the pole shift has been discussed in Allen W. Eckert's novel, *The HAB Theory*. The novel was in fact a dramatization of Hugh Auchincloss Brown's theory that the accumulation of ice at one or both poles could periodically upset the equilibrium of the earth's spin, causing it to tumble in space "like an overloaded canoe." Instead of the crust moving over a constantly spinning core, the entire planet would become involved. This is a noteworthy difference in that a crustal shifting might alleviate the unbalanced earth immediately and thereafter settle down. A tumbling earth on the other hand might continue to tumble for a substantially longer time.

The "HAB Theory" has some support in the writings of Dr. Thomas Gold, one of the world's most noted scientists, and in the book *Continents in Motion,* by Walter Sullivan. Gold has gone so far as to suggest that pole shifts have apparently occurred in the geologic past at intervals of millions of years, and as a consequence have brought about great changes in climate and life on earth.

Immanuel Velikovsky has described many of these changes in his books, *Worlds in Collision, Earth in Upheaval,* et al. While Dr. Velikovsky did not address pole shifts directly, his theories allowed for them as part of the general conflagration, as well as abrupt and major shifts in the continental plates. Importantly, Velikovsky's theories are based on catastrophic world changes occuring during historical times, specifically about 1500 BC.

Velikovsky has been viciously attacked by certain scientists since the publication of his first book in 1950, mostly in true Galilean fashion – science's method of burying one's head in the sand. His theories, however, have continued to flourish as new and significant findings have continued to support the theories and Velikovsky's detractors have failed completely to find flaws. The implication is that not only have there been massive earth changes in the past, but such catastrophic changes may have occurred during historical times and as recently as 2,700 years ago.

Credibility

The question of the exact mechanism of predicted pole shifts is probably of less importance than the question of whether or not we can actually expect such an event in the foreseeable future. One way of looking at such predictions is to consider the track records of the pertinent prophets.

In Edgar Cayce's case, we need to note some preliminaries. Cayce discussed in some detail the building of the Pyramid, the Sphinx, and a smaller Pyramid of Records. According to Cayce, an alleged Hall of Records, would be discovered in a pyramid of its own, lying between the Sphinx and the Great Pyramid. A sealed room of this pyramid would contain a record of Atlantis, including its early development, its first destruction, the subsequent changes that took place, a record of its activities, and the final destruction. Obviously the discovery of a hidden pyramid near the Sphinx would constitute a major verification of Cayce's predictions.

There is some indication that Cayce predicted the opening of the Hall of Records in Egypt and/or the rising of the temple of Atlantis during the 1968 to 1969 time period. The discovery of a hidden room had not occured by this time, however.

Cayce also predicted a variation in the polar star (Polaris) in relation to the lines from the Great Pyramid. Supposedly when this change becomes noticeable, there would be many more souls from the Atlantean and Lemurian Civilizations reincarnating. If one believes Shirley McClaine is from Atlantis and Ramtha from Lemuria, there could be some suggestion that this time is upon us. But this is perhaps greater speculation than Cayce's predictions.

In the final analysis, Cayce's predictions have not yet seen enough verification to allow us to make any assumptions as to the validity or invalidity of his other prophecies.

Nostradamus, on the other hand, has a "longer track record," and has had 400 years for events to either occur or fail to occur. His most famous quatrain predicted the death of King Henry II in 1559, and so accurate in the details of the jousting accident that killed Henry, that all of the bystanders immediately recognized Nostradamus' prediction (which had already become well known). We have already mentioned many of Nostradamus' previous successes in Chapter 13. However, the difficulty with Nostradamus continues to be the correct interpretation of his predictions.

The Earthquake Generation, by Dr. Jeffrey Goodman, provides an alternative set of catastrophic predictions, and the chance to evaluate their accuracy. Copyrighted in 1979, Goodman's book predicted a 20-year season of catastrophes beginning with the eruption of Mount St. Helens. Goodman has combined predictions made by a group of psychics and clairvoyants with geological and scientifically based data to arrive at some spectacular and very dramatic conclusions. His predictions for the year 2000 include:

1. A sudden tumbling of the planet, during which rotation ceases for several days,
2. Alaska becomes temperate and Florida becomes downright frigid [bad news for the orange crop],
3. New Zealand becomes the new land of hope and opportunity,
4. Land rises off the southern tip of India,
5. The western coastline of the United States established in Nebraska and Kansas,
6. Copenhagen "relocated as a safety measure,"
7. The U.S. undergoes severe economic setbacks
8. Jesus Christ returns with many helpers, and
9. Space people visit the planet to observe.

Goodman's book makes many more predictions for the future, but you get the gist of the situation. For the most part there will be little or nothing left; practically no area of the earth will be spared from the holocaust. But before you become too upset or concerned, it is perhaps worth mentioning a few of the predictions made in Goodman's book for the period 1980-1985, i.e. prior to the present time:

1. Palm Springs under water,

2. San Diego, Los Angeles and San Francisco destroyed,

3. Sacramento, Fresno and Bakersfield located on the new California coast,

4. Idaho with access to the ocean via a seaway opened up through Oregon,

5. New York City destroyed in part by a major earthquake, and

6. The U. S. government unable to help all of the stricken.

Goodman makes numerous other predictions for these years, but with the single exception of the inability of the U.S. government to help anybody at any time, none of the predictions for the time period 1980 to 1985 have come to pass. In other words, it's all wrong! So far.

A few diehards have pointed out that psychic predictions of the future have one inherent flaw. Inasmuch as time is virtually irrelevant in the space between lives, one should not expect any psychic to be terribly accurate with respect to the precise time scale for a predicted disaster. Obviously, this could be merely an excuse for bad predicting.

Catastrophism vs Uniformitarianism

It is important that we not dismiss predictions of disasters on the basis of arguments which say that natural catastrophes have not occured in the past on the massive scale envisioned by the psychics. Evolution, as taught in the schools today, tends to overemphasize the slowness and stability of evolutionary change. Everything is viewed as minute modifications spaced over long periods of time. There is substantial evidence that such slow, gradual changes are indeed in operation even today. However, there is nothing in this view of uniformitarianism that precludes an occasional catastrophe from completely changing the lay of the land.

Immanuel Velikovsky, in *Earth in Upheaval*, does an excellent job of documenting the evidence for catastrophism as a standard means of changing the earth and its inhabitants. The evidence for the occasional, very abrupt worldwide disasters is overwhelming to the extent that evolution must be considered as a combination of both uniformity and catastrophe. Uniformitarianism simply carries us from one catastrophe to another. Anyone who insists that catastrophism is a myth is burying his head in the sand.

Interestingly, when evolution is considered to be a combination of uniformity and catastrophe, we find potentially less conflict between its view of history and that of "creationist" theories. If major and abrupt changes are allowed within the evolutionary scheme (catastrophe is perhaps a misnomer, as all abrupt changes would not have to be viewed as catastrophic), then it is possible that certain elements of creationism and evolution would no longer be contradictory. They might even agree.

Wouldn't that be too bad! No more fun arguing with one another and shooting each other in the foot.

The New Age

Some sources have predicted that human egos will have been completely transformed by the year 2015 (Good luck!). In effect, man will no longer be isolated from his fellow man, but will have shed his fears, paranoia, and mistrust. In this view, man will continue to be an individual, but not one at odds with other individuals. In effect, the "rat race" will have terminated and everyone will be getting along splendidly. [4]

This is one of the views of the coming Golden Age. But is love and peace any nearer than wholesale disaster? Will there truly be a "Second Coming"? Edgar Cayce, has predicted the return of Christ to earth in this day and generation, although when queried as to the exact day, Cayce suggested that only the Creative Forces knew.

Added to Edgar Cayce's predictions are all manner of people assuring everyone of the coming age of love and peace, the end of pain and death,

---

[4] It is unlikely that there will be an awards ceremony for the winners of the rat race immediately following the event.

enlightenment for everyone, and the return to earth of Jesus, Buddha, and the rest of the Profound Teachers' Gang.

Ulterior Motives?

Unfortunately, some of these predictions also point out, that there will also be a time of judging as to who gets to live in the New Age and who doesn't. It is this added stipulation or fine print in the contract of some of the prophets of doom and gloom that makes the possibilities of the New Age less desirable.

Consider for a moment . . . Would a just and loving God set up a classic pass/fail situation for his beloved children, when the rules were not at all clear? Would he truly damn those who did not know what was expected of them?[4]

By the same token, would a loving mother tell her children to be good, and then note, "But if you're bad, I'm going to throw you out of the house so that you will starve to death!"

The trembling child might respond, "But mommy. What is bad and what is good?"

Mommy would then answer, "That, you have to learn yourself, through trial and error."

Good luck, kid.

If man was sent to earth to learn, to question, to develop his soul; is it now time for one big, single attempt at passing the entrance exam to heaven? Are all the previous incarnations so much smoke, if we don't manage to measure up this one critical time? Trial and error may be okay, provided that the consequences of an error on the first trial is not the elimination of any subsequent trials. With each incarnation, we learn more, and hopefully come closer to enlightenment. But with the deadline set, are there no more chances? Was free will just a temporary experiment that has run its course?

One would have to have a very low opinion of God to think that he has suddenly displayed uncharacteristic impatience and established a deadline for conversion to the party line. Peace and love are laudable objectives, but threats of missing the really big "bandwagon in the sky," cannot be condoned. Surely God had more in mind when he created free will than a momentary diversion at seeing what might happen.

One can always question the motives of those who would see a "parting of the ways" in a New Age, between the good guys and the ones with black hats. Clearly the control factor may again be present, where the good guys are earnestly attempting to convince the bad guys to shed their darkened headgear. To "sell the concept," a deadline has been established whereby today may be the last day the offer can be made. Sign up now or lose your best deal yet!

There is also the possibility that these particular proponents of a New Age may be primarily those people who are not making it in this age. If things are not going according to one's desires, one can always insist that things are about to change for the better. It may be comforting, but it is not self-evident to those who seem to be be doing just fine.

Benefits?

Before closing our thoughts on why have a cataclysm, we might ask one more possibly pertinent question: Is the coming cataclysm an act of mercy? Have things gotten sufficiently bad that God feels the necessity of dropping back ten and punting? Is the almost cyclical nature of periodic worldwide disasters an essential part of the plan?

Perhaps. One common belief making the rounds now, involves the concept of "Gaia." Gaia is the name of the Greek goddess who gave birth (without a male's cooperation!) of all the other generations of Greek Gods. Gaia is also the name now given to the earth, when the earth is assumed to be a self-contained organism of its own. The theory, accepted by many, is that Gaia is now clearing her throat, so to speak, and clearing out all of mankind's cluttered garbage. The idea is not quite that "It's not nice to fool Mother Nature!", but it's close.

A perceived benefit, therefore, is that Gaia is simply going through a renewal, and mankind may end up getting in the way. In this case, the environmental terrors of ozone holes, rainforest decimation, polluted water and air, and so forth, will be addressed in a rather abrupt manner. The fact that civilizations and cities may also have to go, is, of course, an unfortunate consequence.[5]

As we have noted before, many proponents of reincarnation have viewed our continuing reincarnations as a series of courses. Perhaps cataclysms are the ends of semesters where we have the opportunity to check our grades and ultimately urge ourselves to do better during the following school term. Or perhaps the new course, Cataclysm 666, is just another (albeit possibly advanced) course, that a large number of reincarnating souls have signed up for. Such a thing is possible, of course. But then again, anything is possible. Right?

We might also note the results of Helen Wambach's and Chet Snow's research into the future, as detailed in the book, *Mass Dreams of the Future*. Dr. Wambach's research, whereby the population of the year 2100 is only 5 percent of today's population, has a fair amount of statistical validity to it. On the other hand, the immediate future, when massive earth changes begin in 1996, after years of economic depression and massive hard times, was based on the future progressions of only six people. And of the six people, five were delirious with joy (i.e. they had died and gone to heaven). The person having the hard time, often cold and miserable, was the survivor! The old advice of there being "nothing to fear, but fear itself" is probably worth repeating. If we think of the possibility of massive, worldwide disasters wiping out 95 to 98 percent of the population, we can also view it as 95 to 98 percent of the population going to heaven quickly and with perhaps a great deal less of the pain occasioned by slowly dying in hospitals and nursing homes.

---

[5] As Martin Glass has recently noted, however, it may be that the cities ought to be destroyed.

If reincarnation is correct, then everyone planned to be on earth for Arma-geddon, and the ones not surviving, had already decided on this particular fate, prior to their incarnation! It can even be viewed that the ones who will be staying a while longer (and struggling through a great deal of basic survival), have also made their decisions before coming into this incarnation! There is thus no such thing as bad news, just our perception of it. We may indeed be living in very interesting times.

A rather staggering thought, but who knows? It might even be true!

Chapter 16:

Living with

Reincarnation

Thomas was a grandfather seven times over. His two sons had each had three delightful kids, two girls and four boys between them, and his daughter had a young girl named Stacey. Unfortunately, the boys and their families lived "halfway across the country," and Thomas had never been able to spend much time with his grandchildren . . . except for Stacey. Stacey and her mother lived with Thomas, and partly for that reason, Stacey had become very, very special to her grandfather.

Stacey's father had left his wife and new born child shortly after Stacey's birth. Thomas had welcomed his daughter and small girl into his home, and, being a widower and only 48 years old, he had happily become a substitute father for his youngest grandchild. The transition from widower to temporary daddy had been an easy one – Stacey had been an ideal child.

As a baby, she had almost never cried, smiled more than she slept, and had always greeted her grandfather's attentions with delight and glee. By the time she was three and a half, she had somehow managed to skip the "terrible twos," and had become the brightest gem in her grandfather's eye. She was everything for which a grandparent could ask.

Two months before her fourth birthday, Stacey was killed in a traffic accident.

Living with Death

Can you imagine how Thomas felt? In similar circumstances, how would you have felt? Think about that for a moment. How does one cope with the death of a young idyllic child?

One of the most fundamental questions that arises from theories of reincarnation and related aspects concerns the way in which our theory of reincarnation affects the way we live. In other words, what are the implications of this theory on our everyday lives? From the view-point of Thomas's loss, what can we say about reincarnation that can help a grandfather cope with the loss of a darling grandchild?

Bluntly speaking, there are only three possibilities for the grief that Thomas feels for the loss of his grandchild – two are positive and one is negative. The negative one is that Thomas is feeling sorry for himself and is grieving the loss to him of the joys brought by Stacey's love. It is definitely sad that Thomas has suffered this personal loss of his, but it is his loss and not Stacey's that he grieves for here. As such, our sympathy for Thomas has definite limits; i.e., self-pity is not acceptable in the long run.

Furthermore, reincarnation theory would suggest that Thomas and Stacey may very well have planned for this event in their lives, and probably more for Thomas' benefit than for Stacey's. Thomas, for example, has been given an opportunity to use this bitter and terrible experience and grow from it. He can allow the experience to cause him great unhappiness, or he can find ways to gain from the experience. Thomas can always choose the manner in which he will live with the death of his grandchild. Inasmuch as Stacey had previously given so much happiness to her grandfather, perhaps we should not grieve too much for Thomas.

The two more positive aspects of Thomas' grief is that he is grieving for the state of affairs that has ended a young girl's life. In effect, this more socially acceptable grief is for the fact that the young girl has lost her life. However, this fact of life and death is not necessarily sad. According to our theory of reincarnation, Stacey has returned to a blissful heaven. Why should we be sad about that? Isn't this a time for rejoicing on her behalf? According to the theory of reincarnation, it's definitely good news for Stacey.

Christianity and many other religions, that no longer recognize reincarnation as a viable theory, promise essentially the same positive end. Christianity, for example, tells of a heaven for Stacey (assuming that Stacey, by virtue of her exemplary but brief life, has qualified for entrance into heaven). Hell is also provided for, but hopefully, Stacey will not have to reside in that dark place. Reincarnation, on the other hand, removes any doubts about one's future destination (insomuch as one chooses to go there). While Christianity may provide only the possibility of good news, reincarnation assumes the good news to be the normal state of affairs.

The two views diverge even more, however, when we consider Stacey's youth. Here is a child who had less than four years of life. According to Christianity, this is indeed sad, for Stacey had only one life to live and ended up with a mere three years and ten months. For other children who may have had even briefer lives, the tragedy is greater. Where's the justice in a death for a child who dies at one month and before being baptized? It is indeed cause for grief.

Reincarnation sees it differently. Stacey was merely living one of many lives. She very likely planned her early death (or at least the probability of dying before her fourth birthday) and now can move on to other variations on life. Reincarnation takes the position that young Stacey was not shortchanged by an early death, but simply took the course in Dying Young at the local college of earth. Again, there's no cause for grief.

The implication, therefore, of living with reincarnation is that death is seldom cause for genuine grief. Perhaps a bit of self-pity, but minimal grief. According to reincarnation, death is but a mere transformation and a temporary one at that. Anything we missed the first time around we can come back for a second try. And if we make the same mistakes, a third try and so forth. Why else, do you suppose "history repeats itself?"

On Dying

The same train of thought can be used in dealing with deaths and tragedies of others. For example, when an airliner crashes, killing the crew and passengers, we can view the horror with considerably more calm. We may want to participate in a group effort to help send the bewildered victims into the Light (this is done in many cases by volunteer groups), but our normal sense of tragedy is considerably lessened. In fact, most of life's tragedies can be viewed in the same manner, whereby the pain and death afflicting both ourselves and others are viewed as aspects of the various courses in living in which we are enrolled in this incarnation. There are no errors in the universe – "misfortune" has been planned for its ultimately beneficial effects on the evolution of the soul.

In *The Bridge Across Forever*, Richard Bach thinks of the death and tragedies regularly reported by the media as nothing more than the comings and goings of adventuresome spirits with enormous power. Instead of grim horror, the evening news dealt with current classes, social investment opportunities, and the various challenges and gauntlets recently enacted. In his earlier book, *Illusions, The Adventures of a Reluctant Messiah*, he placed injustice and tragedy in a different context, noting that the end of a caterpillar was the beginning of a butterfly.

But please note, this is not fatalism. Death, suffering, destruction, etc., are not something to tolerate because in the end we all die. Quite the contrary. Ram Dass, in his book with Stephen Levine, *Grist for the Mill*, points out that we can eventually look back upon our lives of neuroses and suffering and realize life's perfection in bringing a person to a particular state in one's life. These authors see life as a paradox where on the one hand we are participating in an incredible melodrama, and on the other there is a great deal of suffering going on. They also note that when one is suffering, it doesn't help a great deal to say, "Hey, it's only an illusion, don't worry." Instead these two advocates note that even as we understand that there is real suffering in the world, it's nevertheless a perfect world, and that further our doing everything possible to alleviate the suffering is part of the perfection. They also claim that the the only reason to stay in the incarnation is to alleviate suffering and to bring others to a consciousness liberation or to God. In their view, life is hell and perfect at the same time.

If one believes in reincarnation and the blissful heavenly life in the bardo awaiting us after we have cast off our physical bodies, then death can no longer hold a threat over our lives. The elimination of any fear of dying can give immense comfort and provide us with a shield capable of deflecting any of the slings and arrows of outrageous fortune. Anyone who truly believes in the bardo described herein will have no fear of death. Such individuals cannot be threatened, coerced (upon pain of death), intimidated, or even cajoled, and thus can be very tough hombres! Certainly not ones to be scared to death.

This alternative view of death as something to accept, also raises some disturbing questions. At what point do we continue to exert extraordinary efforts to keep someone alive? How far do we allow our medical practitioners to conduct Herculean efforts to prevent a loss of life, when there is little hope for recovery? Should there be limits to the preservation of comatose patients?

This book cannot answer all of the questions posed in these pages, but the implications of accepting reincarnation theory demand that such questions be posed and that answers be sought. Feel free to begin seeking the answers on your own.

Finally, the reincarnation view of death suggests a strong reason for knowing *how* to die. Westerners are not known for spending a great deal of idle time thinking about dying and such is not the intent here. Rather, it is to suggest, that anyone and everyone come to terms with the death experience. If you know to look for the white Light (no matter what!), you will be well on your way to the promised land. If you remember to avoid the fanatical and emotional ties to earth and how to let go and depart this earth for the Light, you will be able to avoid being earthbound or worse. And if you understand the process of death and dying, you may even be able to help others find their own way to the Light.

Swimming can be a delightful sport, but it is always more fun if you know how. When you die, it's truly sink or swim time. Knowing how to swim (or die) is infinitely preferable to sinking.

Bardo Decisions

Did you choose to be born? Were you reluctant or expectant? Did you actually choose the mess you find yourself in today? In any case, if you believe that your soul did in fact make all the critical decisions and planned for the coming life by choosing parents and environment, then you have to accept responsibility for your bardo choices (as well as your choices made during the incarnation).

By selecting this probabilistic future, you have eliminated any justification you may have had for exhibiting jealousy, envy, covetness, etc. You are suddenly responsible for your lack of talents, money, friends, etc., in that you chose the specifics for yourself (and for a purpose!). We have and are precisely what we chose in the bardo state (and to a lesser extent, what we choose while incarnated). In that state, with clear understanding of the plans of other souls as well, we made our decisions and there is precious little that happens in this life that we can blame on others.

Has someone recently hurt you? Were they just being a bad guy, or did you bring it on yourself? Not, did you act like a seeming victim, but did you specifically choose to be hurt? Some would advocate that the choice is always up to you and to you alone. You have free will, you can do whatever you want to do, including being hurt by someone else . . . or, you can choose not to be hurt! In many cases, it's a question of how you perceive it!

Obviously, this is a massive charge on your responsibilities. Life's events are what you bring upon yourself. Your responsibility is what you choose to do with them.

This view is quite prevalent in reincarnationist thinking. Its major characteristic is that it places all responsibilities for each soul's action directly on that particular soul. Fate cannot be blamed on others. This may be disconcerting to some, but it's an inevitable implication of the concept of our choosing our own fates.

A related aspect is that when hardship befalls you, you can avoid dwelling on the problem and consider instead, how you can benefit from the hardship. Sounds a little bit like the "power of positive thinking," no? Perhaps so, but if we have chosen our probabilistic destinies while in the bardo, then we also probably chose this particular hardship and, more importantly, we chose the hardship for a specific reason. Think of it as a challenge we placed in our life paths in order to learn some valuable lesson.

A rather mundane example is Clyde, an entrepreneur trying to start a new consulting business. After months of nice growth in the business to where he was finally at the break even point, our enterprising consultant was notified of a 40 percent increase in his office rent. The normal reaction would be anger, review of the lease agreement in haste, the threat of a possible lawsuit, and a great deal of emotional upset. Clyde, on the other hand, having become a believer in the theory of reincarnation, took it calmly. Instead of fighting it, he immediately considered if it was time to move the business. Thinking about it, he realized that he needed less office space and could save on other expenses as well. The very next morning, he met a friend of his who had just leased office space and was looking for someone to sublet an extra office. The extra office was perfect, Clyde would be able to cut his office expenses in half, and suddenly, his business was in the black. A business friend of his is still fighting vainly the rent increase.

Decisions While Incarnated

Not only do we plan in the space between lives the experiences and events that come to us in the incarnation, but because of free will, we can actually do some very impressive ad-libbing in the here and now. There appears, for example, to exist in the universe some basic and very fundamental laws. One is that "Like attracts Like", or "The Law of Attraction." Simply stated this "law" says that if you are constantly thinking about a hot fudge sundae, and in fact, are becoming quite emotional about it, you will soon receive a hot fudge sundae! Really! And it's guaranteed! Note, however, that it makes no difference if you earnestly want one, or for diet reasons, are earnestly trying to avoid one! You still get it. It's like the universe does not understand "no." The key is whatever you're dwelling on, will eventually be attracted to you. Importantly, this can include health or sickness, prosperity or poverty, safety or rape; depending entirely upon what your mind and emotions constantly concentrate their attentions.

A corollary to this "attraction law" is that you have the free will to decide precisely what you want (in other words, your chance to ad-lib like crazy!). At the same time, you can avoid "negatives" by simply concentrating on the positive alternative. The universe is quite clear on this: You can, in fact, create your own reality. This simple fact derives from the abilities of your mind and soul, the fact that you're created in the image of God (and therefore have the creative abilities of God), and the fact that the reason you're here in this incarnation (among other things) is to create. (More on this in the next chapter!)

Given that you understand how things come about in your life (through your attracting them), and that by deliberate decisions you can specify what you want to attract, it might appear that you pretty well have it made. However. There is one other aspect of which you should be aware. Other souls have the same privileges! And more than any other challenge in our lives, the one that counts is the requirement that we *allow others* to create and attract the experiences and events that they decide upon. This additional "Law of Allowing" appears to be fundamental and very, very necessary!

Possessions

No, we're not talking about your new boat. We're talking about attached entities hooking on to you or your loved ones.

With reincarnation we recognize the possibility of an entity attaching itself to a living being. One of the many implications of this idea is that we should know how to avoid such parasitic attachments. Good mental health is always an effective way, and some proponents would also include a careful watch over your aura (that strange shimmering surrounding your body and which acts as sort of an esoteric immunity system). Nevertheless, there is always the possibility of your letting your guard (or aura) down, at least, occasionally. Such moments of weakness may occur in traumatic emotional states, sudden injuries, and so forth.

Being aware of the possibilities of possession can always reduce the likelihood of becoming possessed and, in the event of actual possession, knowing or suspecting you're possessed will allow you to get depossessed. The choice is yours, but generally it's better to shed excess luggage before you attempt to soar with the eagles. (But then again, perhaps you prefer to run with the turkeys.)

Extra Capabilities

If the many aspects of reincarnation theory are correct, we can expect to be able to, among other things, heal ourselves of many afflictions. We may want to use medical professionals for most situations, but we can contribute to our own cure and not depend entirely on modern medicine.

Through meditation, dreams, and possibly extrasensory powers we can accomplish wonders. Epileptics, for example, can often reduce the number and intensity of their seizures through routine meditation, while, at the same time, not giving up the beneficial aid of prescribed medications. Individuals with emotional problems can often discover underlying meanings and possible solutions to their difficulties. We can each control, to a large extent, our mental and physical health by preventive means and self-help. We may also be able to help others.

Just don't try practicing medicine without a license. That might be thought of as "attracting" some very unpleasant experiences!

As mentioned previously, we do want to keep in mind the limitations on helping others, which are imposed by an acceptance of reincarnation. This generally accepted implication is that we should not impose our help on someone who does not want it. We can't expect to eliminate all the suffering – if for no other reason than that suffering might be a part of another soul's evolution. And we can't always help others by doing it ourselves. Instead, we can better help them by teaching them to help themselves.

The possibilities for growth are immense, and the techniques for achieving growth include a multitude of diverse and unique capabilities. We can potentially do everything from starting a day on a more positive note, to taking a quick tour of Saturn's rings in an out-of-body state. Reincarnation, far more than any other view or philosophical theory of life, allows for a vast menagerie of ideas and capabilities. While many philosophies impose limitations and rules, reincarnation loosens existing constraints and provides a host of unlimited potentialities. In a manner of speaking, the sky's the limit.

Love

What's this? Are you suggesting that we actually have to love one another? No more fun in flushing others down the drain? No more the thrill of victory as we trip our opponents and surge ahead? Just as we were savoring the possibility of excellent health and out-of-body experiences, you expect us to suddenly think in terms of others? Surely you jest!

The fact of the matter is that you're free to do whatever you want, including being unloving. Life's not nearly as much fun that way, but you still have the choice.

Kurt Vonnegut tells a particularly appropriate story of an alien visiting the earth and becoming fascinated with the story of Jesus Christ. The biblical story was so intriguing that the alien began to study the gospels in detail. But then our ET investigator began to realize that somewhere along the line, the religions of the world had missed the point. This became such a major concern to the alien that he actually went to the trouble of writing a new gospel, one in which the point would be more self-evident.

The main difference in the alien's gospel was that Jesus had not been born the son of God, but in reality, the ordinary son of a carpenter and his wife. There was nothing miraculous about the birth, no star of Bethlehem, no wise men from the east – just a normal delivery. But as Jesus grew to manhood and beyond, he began teaching, accomplished all of the miracles told about in the other gospels, and, in general, gave us the same inspiration of his life. The only difference in the alien's gospel was that Jesus was just an itinerant preacher with a lot of good things to say, but nevertheless a preacher with absolutely no connections with higher authority. It was what he knew and not who he knew that counted.

When Jesus had accomplished all of the miracles and given all of the teachings, he ended up on the cross and was near death. But just before he died, God came down from on high and announced that God was adopting Jesus as his son. Suddenly, Jesus now had connections! The Romans, Pharisees, and all of the other bad guys had started out crucifying some poor ordinary fellow with no important connections whatsoever, and ended up crucifying a Christ with a direct line to God!

The implication seems clear. One must be careful about treating badly or, alternatively, not taking care of, some bum who apparently has no connections. There is always the chance that this same bum will suddenly come into connections with the most high. Cheat someone or pass by on the other side of the road, and you may find you've done it to a recently adopted son of God. Wouldn't that be a bummer? That's the sort of thing that could spoil your whole day.

Jesus, in Matthew's gospel (Matthew 25: 40, 45), said:

> "And the King shall answer and say unto them. Verily I say unto you, Inasmuch as ye have done it unto one of the least of these my brethren, ye have done it unto me.
>
> "Then shall he answer them, saying, Verily I say unto you, Inasmuch as ye did it not to one of the least of these, ye did it not to me."

It's easy to love someone who is kind and beautiful. It's not so easy when they're ugly, thoughtless, antagonistic, and downright belligerent. Loving the "least of these" can really be a challenge, but it is just one of the challenges posed by a belief in reincarnation.

But how, exactly, does one love? Considering the potential for misuse of the word, "love", perhaps we should define it a bit more clearly. Scott Peck, in his bestselling book, *The Road Less Traveled*, provides what is perhaps the best definition of love: "The will to extend oneself in order to nurture one's own or another's spiritual growth." If you apply this definition to all your acts of "love" which are extended to others, you may be in for a rude awakening.

What you have called love, may instead be based upon a desire to control (basically fear of the lack of control), to elicit gratitude, to possess, etc., etc. If you really want to know about love, read *The Road Less Traveled*. If you don't really care about love, read the book twice!

Tolerance

Proponents of reincarnation tend to have notable tolerance for the growth and beliefs of others. This may derive from the idea that karma and successive reincarnations will always ensure justice, and that, therefore, there is no major hurry for such proponents to work actively ensuring that everyone gets whatever they deserve. Neither are "quickie" conversions essential. Everyone can live and let live.

Such a viewpoint is even extended to helping others. An almost fundamental tenet of proponents of reincarnation is that one doesn't "help" another unless asked. As was noted before, praying for someone is not necessarily in their best interests. If they ask for help, you can rush to help with total enthusiasm. If they don't ask, don't help! Everyone is almost always better off, if they are, at least given the chance to solve their own problems – particularly if that is the very reason they are here. If you solve their problem, they may have to make the trip to earth again. By tolerating their idiosyncrasies, you may save them a long and arduous trip.

Of course, if someone is drowning and appears incapable of calling out, you might not want to wait for them to ask for help.

War and Peace

A larger scale corollary to this point is in the earnest quest for peace on earth. Peace is a laudable goal, but the means by which it is achieved is equally important. There is every reason to believe that the end (peace) may not justify the means (how some have advocated the achievement of peace).

Why? Consider the following. If in the bardo state, we all plan for our next lives, then it is reasonable to assume that much of the pain and anguish, the war, the poverty, the famine, and the other traumas rampant upon our globe, were planned for in that space between lives, at least as possibilities. Our future probabilities have already been set and for, ostensibly, very good and important reasons.

If someone now finds a way to enforce a peace, they will end up violating the free will of others who are attempting to come to terms with their own lessons from the past or present. An enforced peace may deny the opportunity for others to settle their karmas, learn from the changes that they can bring about (by their own free will), and impose help where it has not been requested.

In C.S. Lewis' classic, *The Screwtape Letters*, the devil tells why he prefers peace to war. In war, all sorts of noble and honorable acts are committed (not the sort of things that sends men to hell). Men and women make all manner of sacrifices on an almost daily basis, relationships are intensified (usually for the best) and in the ultimate gesture, some give up their lives to save their friends ("Greater love hath no man than that he give up his life for another"). Peace, on the other hand, is a time when people slowly become bored and begin to look for diversions at whatever level of morality ("Idleness is the Devil's workshop.").

Peace is still an honorable goal to work toward, but if the process of seeking peace violates basic principles, then the end result will not be worth the achieving.

Unconditional Love

Do-gooders, rushing in where wise men fear to tread, are, according to many reincarnationists, doing no good. A possessive or controlling love is no love at all. One person solving the problems of the world is doing a disservice to all those who need to be about the business of solving their own problems. One can respond with help whenever it is asked for, typify by their own good example, make available teachings and healings, offer their unconditional love, but one must NEVER legislate help and require people to accept help.

Note the qualifier on the word love: unconditional. Love has a severely limited value, if the extension of it includes attached strings. For love to be unconditional, there must be nothing that obligates or controls the recipient. Unconditional love does not infringe upon the free will of others.

Self-Reliance

Clearly the implications foisted upon us by the existence of free will and souls in the bardo planning their own futures, are extensive and far reaching. When we stand before our advisors and counselors, participating in the instant replay of our last incarnation, the questions will not be what happened to us, but how we reacted to events. It will be our decisions, not that of others, that we will subject to our own self-judgment. If self-reliance is a privilege we seek, then why should we attempt to deny others the same opportunity for self-reliance? After all, self-reliance is merely the ability to exercise free will. The tolerance of another's self-reliant nature is equivalent to allowing them to exercise their own free will.

Is this reasonable? Can anyone live this way?

Perfection is hard to obtain (primarily because everything is changing, including whatever defines perfection). Thus we seldom expect to find anyone totally self-reliant with the wisdom to allow others to seek the same notable goal. However, if there is a common characteristic of the true believers of reincarnation and all its related aspects, it is that they seek to direct their own lives without the seeming necessity to direct the lives of others. This is important, because you really can't have love without tolerance (i.e. continuing forgiveness).

Relationships

Accepting reincarnation has some profound effects on our personal relationships whether they be with spouses, children, parents, friends, acquaintances, or even people we "chance" to meet in the street. With a multitude of lifetimes behind us, we invariably meet up with those to whom we may owe a debt (or vice versa) or to whom we need to "complete a relationship." Perhaps you shot your brother in a previous life and that same entity which was your brother in that lifetime is now your child in this one. If that child, understanding all the implications, can turn to you and say, "I forgive you," all may be well. If not, you may have to resort to other means to finish what your soul has started.

Soulmates may be nothing more than unfinished relationships. The intensity of lovers or married spouses only places a greater need for dealing with the karmic ties. If you deserted your wife in a previous life, leaving her in dire circumstances, you may find this time around an entity who is looking for compensation. But do you now have to marry her and this time stay married till death parts you? Possibly. It would depend on what was needed. If you married her and then managed to complete your relationship with her, you could conceivably divorce her and move on to other relationships.

Divorce tends to be a tricky subject, which may be a result of Jesus' teachings against divorce. However, if one recognizes the reality of the age in which Jesus lived, His teachings would be better understood. It is important to realize that at the time of Jesus, a man could divorce his wife with a word and toss her out onto the street. The woman would typically end up with absolutely nothing. For the female, divorce was a disaster. Jesus taught against divorce for obvious reasons. It was, to say the least, catastrophic for the woman.

Because divorce today does not always have to be disastrous for either party, it's entirely possible that Jesus would not view modern day divorce as an absolute and inherent evil. If one views divorce as the return of free will to two people, divorce can take on all the attributes of good. Some proponents of reincarnation and related thinking believe that divorce is justified when one spouse is restraining the other from spiritual development. It may be that any severely limiting feature of a marriage can constitute justification for divorce. Sometimes it may very well be that the relationship is complete, and it's simply time to move on.

There are a multitude of ways to complete a relationship. Mutual agreement is nice, but in some cases it may be enough for someone to simply (or not so simply) come to terms with any lingering hate, anger, desire or other attaching emotion. If someone, for example, has done you a great disservice (and is unlikely to apologize), you may be able to complete the relationship by forgiving and forgetting the trespass. It is not enough to simply agree not to seek revenge – one has to extend unconditional forgiveness and truly eliminate the upset feelings. This usually takes time and some extension of your own effort, but the alternative is a return incarnation, when you may have to deal with that entity again. Wouldn't you rather forgive the S. O. B. now, and avoid him like the plague in a later incarnation?

The Tao of Pooh

Winnie the Pooh is one of the classic characters of fiction. Written in 1926 by A.A. Milne, the fuzzy little bear with a yen for honey has captured the hearts of millions. However, would you believe that Pooh may also represent an ideal in how to live one's life?

In Benjamin Hoff's book, *The Tao of Pooh*, the little bear's true heritage becomes clear. The wise old owl is shown to think too much, the clever rabbit to be much too calculating for his own good, piglet too hesitant, and Eeyore just too fretful. But Pooh, wandering through life without a care, letting his intuition roam, gathering his honey wherever he may find it, seems to be living life just right. Pooh just is.

The Tao (pronounced dao) is not easily summed up in a few paragraphs. Better you read *The Tao of Pooh* yourself and allow a fuzzy little bear named Pooh to enlighten you. Suffice it to say for now that the Tao suggests that we are better off if we cease our clever tampering with the nature of things, shift our thinking with the left brain to experiencing with the right brain, and return to simplicity. Go with the flow, so to speak. This same point is beautifully illustrated in the handwritten preamble to Richard Bach's *Illusions, The Adventures of a Reluctant Messiah* (another book, particularly worth reading).

The Tao may not necessarily be the best way of living. It may be more a means of avoiding growing pains. If one avoids any attempt at achieving things, one will seldom fail. Wading through life with the single-minded desire to avoid making waves is not likely to be a significant learning experience. And learning may be what it's all about (see chapter 17). The Tao seems to provide for a means of achieving the easiest living, but such is not necessarily the best tactic for a developing soul.

Besides, can you visualize yourself patterning your entire life after the example of Winnie the Pooh? Really?

Lighten Up

Making one's primary goal in life the search for honey may not appeal to the average intellectual, but some advocates of reincarnation and related thinking do have a tendency to take this laissez faire attitude to an extreme. If something good happens to them, then obviously somebody on high is taking care of them, but if something bad happens, it's obviously designed to build character. It's a win/win situation – the perfect sort of thing for optimists.

There is something to be said for the idea of easing off and taking life as it comes (and not necessarily as it is preferred). In Tom Robbins' book, *Jitterbug Perfume*, the ultimate piece of wisdom appears to be: "Lighten up." Don't take the day-to-day happenings of life so seriously that you lose sight of what's really important. Try to keep in mind what the forest looks like when you're wandering from tree to tree. Or perhaps running into trees.

In this respect, meditation (and/or prayer) may help keep things in perspective. Considerable comfort can be derived from meditation, and it seems likely that regular meditation can also develop introspection, directed thought and understanding. All of these aspects are fringe benefits of living with reincarnation. There is also the potential of dreams. Taking note of dreams, for example, may provide a lot of good hints for planning a life. Richard Bach, in his book, *The Bridge Across Forever*, suggests that one could program self-directed dreams and specify the form of your enlightenment from dreams. Seems like a straight forward way of accumulating information.

Why Are We Here?

Ultimately, reincarnation theory allows us to answer the all important question of: "Why are we here?" Without understanding the answer to this basic question, all of our theories of life and living are built on sand. It is thus time to attempt to find an answer that can provide the essential foundation.

For this effort, however, we will defer to chapter 17.

Chapter 17:

Choices

A fundamental (if not simplistic) purpose of philosophy is to provide the ready means by which choices can be made. The establishment of some basic principles to live by allows for consistent and more easily obtainable decisions. Instead of taking the time to completely analyze every situation that requires a decision, philosophy allows us to set up guidelines to which we can always resort whenever the need arises.

Religions offer a convenient set of rules and principles for anyone who has neither the knowledge, the time, the inclination, nor the mental capacity to develop and evolve their own set of principles. As such religions can be thought of as prepackaged philosophy, something you might be able to pick up at the local supermarket, thus making it no longer necessary for each individual to thoroughly contemplate what is best for that individual. Independent thinking is not necessary. As a matter of fact, religions have actually been known to discourage their followers from independent thinking.

Religions also offer the convenience of understanding and predicting the actions of others. If everyone else subscribes to the same set of rules and principles as yourself, then you can generally anticipate what their actions and reactions will be. In effect, this allows you greater control of your interactions with others and, consequently, is highly sought after. On the other hand, someone who believes in a different set of principles (or worse yet) his own unique and custom designed set of rules, is the type of person who cannot be easily anticipated and thus poses a possible danger to others. Such a person appears to be acting without known controls.

People who profess to follow a particular religion, may have moments when they question specific rules or principles laid down by that religion. As long as the religious rules work, everything is fine, but if there is a "crisis of confidence," if somehow a portion of the philosophical base does not appear to accommodate a person's evolving picture of themselves and their universe, then that person may feel the necessity of making slight or major changes in her or his religious beliefs, or even disregard them altogether.

The key is to provide a set of basic rules or principles, that allow a person to consistently and quickly arrive at day-to-day decisions. Without such a base the individual may meander from decision to decision, as if staggering from too much alcohol.

In Chapter 16, the implications of reincarnation and related psychic phenomena gave us a few clues as to what might be thought of as rules to live by. However, we only briefly considered some of the possibilities, and clearly did not evolve any basic rules. What is needed is a more fundamental principle or principles, that can be used as the basic criteria for all of our choices – choices that are, inherently, a result of having free will.

The Principle of Karma

Karma seems a logical choice for a decision-making principle. If the goal of living on the earth plane is a reduction in karma, one can then make decisions on the basis of whether or not such a decision will increase or decrease karma. Furthermore, if one does not eliminate karma, one supposedly has to return to earth until he does. We not only have a set of rules, but a means to enforce them. Better yet the enforcement agency is the universe, as opposed to the possible arbitrariness of human agencies.

One of the disadvantages of karma as a decision-maker is that there is within societies no consistent view of karma. One can view karma as "an eye for an eye," a law of more flexible compensation, a law of cause and effect, or a personal view of balancing one's own books. Some might even ascribe to an "instant karma," where one's actions and decisions are immediately reflected back – a "one day at a time" view. (Such a view has the advantage of not worrying about what you did before as, theoretically, you have already paid the price for your indiscretion.)

Karma appears to be defined very much in the eyes of the beholder, in effect, a "custom karma." As such it constitutes a rather poor choice as a decision-making criteria for two reasons. In the first instance such a view does not allow others to easily predict another's actions, a somewhat antagonistic situation. Secondly, a custom-designed karma is open to easy manipulation in times of stress or inconvenience. It is definitely not a set of hard and fast rules.

Karma has other flaws. What about "good karma", the type where you do something good for someone else? One view of karma is that you must receive compensation in return, but if you have to return to get your just desserts, then the problem in exiting the Wheel of Life becomes an attempt to achieve "zero karma." The best way to accomplish this is simply withdrawing from all contact with others. If interacting with other souls implies the likelihood of causing karma (either good or bad), then such interactions should logically be avoided.

Such a view tends to have numerous flaws. Withdrawal from contact with the rest of humanity would appear to be less than beneficial in contributing anything to the world, in learning anything from the world, and more of an attempt to just exist without having a purpose in life. Trying to find your Higher Self is a good idea, but if done exclusively, there's not a whole lot of reason to be here. To some degree it automatically pre-supposes a belief in the Fall of Man, and that our only purpose is to find our way home. Rather a pathetic set of circumstances, when you think about it.

Evolution of the Soul

One of the more consistent themes in reincarnation theories is the Journey of the Soul. We find ourselves on a Wheel of Life, reincarnating over and over again, trying on each attempt to further the evolution of the soul. Contrary, and sometimes in addition, to the choice of karma as a principle for our decision-making, we have the principle of the soul's evolution.

Sounds good, but what does it mean? What are we expected to gain by our routine returns to earth? How do we evolve? How do we grow? Must we search for suffering and pain, must we tread the straight and narrow, or can we throw caution to the winds and do whatever comes naturally? Are we faced with the classic, "no pain, no gain," or is God's plan for us a great deal easier? How do we make life decisions and for what purpose?

Learning

In *Illusions, The Adventures of a Reluctant Messiah*, Richard Bach views our purpose in life as essentially to learn and have fun. That's it? To learn and have fun? That's all we need do? As you may have guessed, there are a great many proponents of this idea.

The concept certainly has appeal. Searching for knowledge and enjoying the ride sounds both philosophically and scholarly sound, while at the same time, being attractive to the masses. And there has to be a whole slew of ways to do both. Clearly God has been more than considerate in providing this playground for our edification and enjoyment. We can learn our way around and avoid boredom at the same time. Perhaps, on our return to heaven, we should do as the playwrights do, and say to God, "Thanks for the use of the hall."

However, it may not be quite that easy. Ram Dass takes a slightly more involved view. He argues that you're not here because of some mistake or fall from grace, but in order to be human. He advises you to be in the world, only not of it; take the curriculum and doing begrudge the fact that you're still in school. The modern guru also suggests that freedom is gained by overcoming suffering, and that which freaks you out is precisely what you need to work on. He cautions you, however, not to get trapped in the want of doing good or become involved in what might be called a spiritual materialism.

Enlightenment and Identity

Learning can be thought of as a search for enlightenment, a knowing and understanding of all things. Certain aspects of reincarnation imply the ideal wherein we seek to find ourselves, to understand our Higher Self, and to become enlightened.

However, our identity is in large part based on what we know, what our opinions and prejudices are, the unique way in which we view the universe. But if one becomes enlightened, i.e., begins to understand all things, then our opinions converge to what all other enlightened entities believe (i.e. the ultimate truth). Enlightenment thus implies a loss of identity.[1]

Is this a good idea? Do we want to seek enlightenment if reaching such a goal automatically assumes a loss of identity? Maybe we're not ready for enlightenment, at least not in its ultimate form. Why have an ego, if the goal in life is to eliminate it? As a reason for our being, it does not seem to have a great deal of appeal.

This is particularly true if enlightenment turns out to be nothing more than learning what is already known. If we are part of God, if we someday return to the bardo where we will have access to all that is known, why struggle to learn our lessons now? We already know the truth; we've just temporarily forgotten it while we take a holiday on earth. Enlightenment of what is already known would appear to be a complete waste of time.

Finite and Infinite Games

An appropriate concept in this regard is the fundamental differences in finite and infinite games. A finite game is one with boundaries. These boundaries imply rules, and include time and space limits. When the game is over, the game is over. The confines of the boundaries limit the range of play. Change may be allowed within the confines of the game, but even change has limiting rules. Enlightenment in this sort of game, therefore, would just be learning all the rules, limits, and boundaries.

On the other hand, infinite games have no boundaries. They cover all time and space, and more importantly, they are forever changing. The rules of the infinite game must change as well. In fact, one could view a finite game as one played for the purpose of winning, while an infinite game's purpose was for the play itself. In this way, a finite player consumes time, while an infinite player generates time. Thus enlightenment in an infinite game is ever changing, a goal that is never quite reached.

This concept of finite and infinite games carries with it a very significant implication in that, if the universe is infinite, it must be changing. There is no other alternative. Any limit on change is a limit on the infinite – a contradiction in terms.

An Infinite Universe? Is the Universe Infinite?

Good question. Just don't expect a final answer; especially if everything is constantly changing.

---

[1] The ultimate truth or the final answer, according to Douglas Adams (in his trilogy, *The Hitchhiker's Guide to the Galaxy*), is 42. Adams is still working on the final question, but it appears that it may be: "What is 6 times 7?"

Philosophically, an infinite universe seems preferable. Why limit ourselves or anything about us? Why limit God? Why place upper bounds on what the universe can become? There appears to be no good, defensible reasons to limit the universe in terms of either time or space. There may be a beginning, but we need have no end.

Is there any evidence to suggest a finite universe? Perhaps. One such speculation is due to Olber's paradox. This paradox assumes the universe is infinite and populated with galaxies in a homogeneous fashion. If this assumption is correct, then the sky should not be dark at night, inasmuch as the infinite galaxies would make the night sky infinitely bright. The "solution" to the paradox comes under the following possibilities:

1. The amount of matter in the universe is finite, i.e. the basic assumption is wrong. (Note, however, that this still allows space to go on forever, and the amount of matter in the universe can change),

AND/OR

2. There is a beginning of time, i.e. some of the light has not yet reached us. (Note that this does not imply an end to time).

Aside from this possible physical limitation there appears little to suggest any need to establish universal limits. In fact, the limits implied by Olber's paradox do little to modify the possibility of change. If this is the case, the universe can be relied on to change. So why is this latter point important?

This prelude of finite and infinite games is meant to introduce the idea of the essential requirement of a changing universe. For if the universe is constantly changing, then the answers we seek must also change. Hopefully not so fast that we can't progress in our understanding, but fast enough so that we will always have to seek new answers. In other words, a soul can never rest on its laurels, its enlightenment, and/or its worldly understanding. Because of this, there can be no hard and fast answers given in this book (or anywhere else, for that matter). We can only tally the points and perhaps point in the direction of future questions. If you take away nothing else from this reading, remember that there are no final answers, only the continuing need to question. (Sorry to have to be the one to give you this bad news.)

Creation of Knowledge

Equally important to the idea of an infinite universe, is the concept of free will. If the universe is changing and evolving, it follows that one means to accomplish this universal evolution is to allow all souls the free will to create. It's more efficient that way.

Why else, for example, would God give us free will, knowing that we could use it for evil? What's the trade off? What was there to be gained by such a rash act, if the gift of free will also carried with it the possibility of major variations in the direction of evil?

The simplest answer is: Free will allows for each soul to create!

If we are made in the image of God, can we be less than creative? Is the reason that we do not remember our past lives or the bardo, or know the future with any degree of certainty, due to the fact that we would then be less creative and simply follow some preplanned and predetermined program? Determinism eliminates any spontaneous creativity. Likewise, planning is inherently limited by prior knowledge. Too much planning and we reduce the possibilities of unforeseen events and the resultant potential for creativity and a changing universe.

By our experiences on earth we can create knowledge; we can learn from all our many defeats and relatively fewer victories. The purpose of all these souls incarnating and reincarnating over and over again may very well be to increase the sum of knowledge in the universe, to create knowledge, to create knowing. Perhaps God is learning as well! Perhaps God dispensed free will to the masses, because He knew that they would try anything and everything, and thereby create whole new realms of knowledge.

One theological assumption is that God is omniscience. If so, then he knows all there is to know. However, the assumption of God's omniscience does not necessarily imply that God also possesses knowledge that has not yet been created. And without new knowledge being created, God could become, if nothing else, slightly bored. As a part of God, one might object to a situation where we can only look forward to enlightenment, a joyous homecoming, and ultimately, boredom. On the other hand, the idea of creating knowledge as our goal in the Wheel of Life provides us with a concept whereby we can have a positive and useful purpose in the universe. We may be "reversing entropy," by the very creation of information.

The Last Question

The idea of "reversing entropy" is beautifully told by Isaac Asimov in his short story, The Last Question. Dr. Asimov begins by describing a brief scene where two slightly drunk technicians ask the very latest in modern technological and very large scale computers how entropy of the universe can be reversed. The only reply they receive from the very sophisticated computer is: "INSUFFICIENT DATA FOR A MEANINGFUL ANSWER."

The story then proceeds into the future in successive jumps with various people asking the same basic question and receiving the same basic answer. In each jump into the future, however, the computer has become progressively more complex, advanced and accessible to mankind. At one point the entire earth is devoted to the computer while mankind begins to roam the stars. Then the computer becomes self perpetuating, repairing itself, adding and remodeling as needed. Eventually the computer transforms itself into another dimension, but always in contact with mankind to aid and assist mankind as he explores the universe.

Eventually the ultimate fate of the universe becomes all too apparent to mankind. While the computer provides all of the needs of mankind, the apparently irreversible flow of entropy makes it very clear that the physical universe is dying. Mankind begins to devote itself to collecting data for the computer so that the computer can finally have "sufficient data for a meaningful answer" to the all important question of how to reverse entropy.

But the answer always turned out to be the same, "THERE IS AS YET IN-SUFFICIENT DATA FOR A MEANINGFUL ANSWER." Eventually all of mankind and the universe die, leaving only the computer to exist in some sort of hyperspace. The computer, however, does not cease to exist, because it had not completed its calculations for the unanswered question. It has all the data from the universe now but has to spend a timeless interval correlating the data in order to find the answer to the last question. Only when this is done can the computer cease to function.

Finally the computer solves the question. Unfortunately, there is no one to whom the answer could be given. Instead the computer decides it has to give the answer by demonstration, such that it will thereafter be obvious to all concerned. The computer thinks about the demonstration, organizes the program and then says: "LET THERE BE LIGHT!"

And there was light.

The intriguing aspect of Asimov's story is that the computer had accumulated all the knowledge from the universe during the "lifetime" of the universe. And using this as a base, programmed another universe and initiated it as a demonstration. What Asimov does not mention, however, is that the subsequent universe was built upon all of the knowledge in the preceding one. Thus, it may be that succeeding universes are progressively greater or more sophisticated, always benefitting from the previous ones.

Individual evolutions of souls may also be viewed in this light. Each lifetime may be able to take advantage of lessons learned in prior lives and thus progress ever further. Instead of a "wheel of life," the soul may be involved in a "spiral of life" in which the loci of the spiral is constantly progressing.

Good and Evil

But in our unceasing search for knowledge, can't we learn a thing or two by dumping all over someone else? If I blow your brains out with my new shotgun, won't I learn something from the experience? Won't you learn something? Like for example, not to be around me when I've got a shotgun?

Is there good knowledge and evil knowledge? Is the manner in which we gain knowledge, inherently good or evil? Does God have any clear preference on how we learn our lessons? Why bother to possess free will, if the only choice for good is to submit your free will to a divine will? Free will is not free if there is a gun at your head, ready to go off at a wrong choice. Free will implies that we can create our own individual good.

All philosophical positions require assumptions. If we assume we have free will, if we assume the responsibility for our decisions and choices and act accordingly, then, in the event that we are correct in choosing free will, we will have prepared for such an eventuality. If on the other hand we assume determinism, and it turns out we're wrong, we could be in BIG TROUBLE! As one sage as pointed out:

> "If you bet on the Gods, and they don't exist, you lose nothing. But if you bet against them, and they do exist, you lose everything."

For our purposes, it seems less risky to assume free will and that we can make choices in this incarnation for good or evil.

Is the distinction between good and evil limited to the fact that it is perhaps tougher to be good? Are we back to the "no pain, no gain" concept? Do we need evil in order to create love? Is bliss boring? Do we contribute more to an evolving universe by being good? Is there really any distinction between good and evil?

Richard Bach reflects the feelings of many reincarnationists when he argues that suffering and death are only from consent of the victims. In effect, the only distinction between good and evil is what makes us happy. And inasmuch as all beings are divinely selfish souls, they can be expected to live in their own best interests (and with no exceptions)!

There seems little doubt that all human motivation derives from what that soul considers to be in its own best interests. We may give gifts, but we do so because it affords us status, it obligates others (even if only a "thank you"), it makes us feel good (even if given anonymously), or a combination of all three. We may even give up our life, but in our own best interests and because it is what we want to do.

However, the flaw in this view is that it does not include why we are here. It's all well and good to say that we're here for our own purposes; that there is no good or evil. But how are we to use such a principle to make decisions, to choose between alternative possibilities? And what about children? Do we owe them anything, or did they choose us because they knew we would ignore them?

If in fact, "everything balances," or if some form of karma exists, then such concepts presuppose the existence of good and evil. How can you balance good and evil if they do not exist? Is good and evil purely in the minds of the beholder, or is there a more fundamental nature to these fundamental concepts?

It seems as if a refusal to acknowledge the existence of evil in the world, would constitute the "Joe Cool" approach – a pseudo-sophisticated approach to avoid real, concentrated thought and the possibly inevitable commitment to wage forces against evil.

Choices

Free will implies choices. Choices are the means whereby knowledge is created. In effect every choice allows a slightly different experiment or potential scenario. The more choices, the more we learn. Conversely, if something limits our choices, then it limits our ability to learn, and if our purpose on earth is to learn or create knowledge, any imposed limitation on our choices would constitute a barrier or a lessening of our ability to accomplish our life's purposes.

Let us assume that God's purpose defines good. God gave us life and free will and then sent us out to accomplish His goals. We constitute His agents on earth and were sent to create. As long as we assist in accomplishing God's ultimate purpose, we are accomplishing good. If God's purpose is creating knowledge, then we do good by creating knowledge and allowing its creation. In other words, good is removing or decreasing limitations on the sum total of our ability to create knowledge.

Evil can be defined as denying or limiting others in their free will to choose. If the sum total of choices in the universe is reduced, the sum total of potential knowledge is reduced. On the other hand, increasing another's range of choices is good. They can now create more knowledge and assist in achieving God's purpose.

Why does evil exist? Why didn't God arrange for good only, and leave evil to the philosophers? We might also ask, as Scott Peck has done in People of the Lie, "Why is there good in the world?" One possible answer is the need for both.

Implications of Good and Evil

The implications of this view of good and evil are truly immense. Suddenly, reincarnation theory combined with the idea that we're here to create good, love, and knowledge from our choices, can be applied to our day-to-day lives. Steal from a man, for example, and you limit his choices – therefore, stealing is evil. Murder is even more limiting and is thus a greater evil. Giving someone a gift may increase their choices and is therefore good. But note that if we seek to limit their choice by our giving, the gift becomes evil. Expecting gratitude or compensation in return would turn an otherwise good gift into an evil one. Only if we increase their choices, and the sum of choices in the universe, will a gift be good.

Keeping someone alive by extraordinary means (such as in a comatose state) when they may be ready to die and proceed with their plans for reincarnation, would by this definition be evil. Possessive love is evil, because it limits the recipient. On the other hand, a gift of unconditional love is good, because it does not limit, and hopefully may increase the potential for greater choice. Abortion may or may not be evil, depending upon several factors, including whether or not the soul of the fetus had planned to be aborted as part of his or his mother's experiences in life. The possibility of a conflict with the fetus' "right to be born" and the mother's "right to choose" is superseded by the belief that both made the choice while in the bardo state, and by the fact that evil would be determined by the sum total of the choices of the mother and embryo's soul.

Karma may be thought of as deriving from the sum total of knowledge gained by all choices, not just one. If your choices limit the choices of other souls, then the sum total of knowledge may be limited and thus your choices may be wrong. Evil may be nothing more than denying or not allowing others their right to choose.

Organized Evil

An essential question in defining evil as limiting choices is whether or not there is an "organization" attempting evil in the world, i.e. does Satan and his legions of demons exist? Has mankind, in effect, with his powers of creating, created The Prince of Darkness and a supporting host? Why not? If man can create alter personalities, entities like Phillip (Chapter 10), psychosomatic illnesses and health, then it seems likely that mankind can create demons. Why should any form of limits be imposed in an infinite universal game? The existence of free will always implies the possibility of creating evil, as well as good. The duality of good and evil, in turn implies the reality of exorcisms, a natural corollary to the existence of demons.

It is noteworthy that no one who has ever seen a full scale exorcism has, thereafter, doubted the existence of Satan. Even a few observations of demonic depossessions can convince virtually any skeptic that demons exist.

Lucifer and demons may very well exist then, if only due to man's free-willed imagination. Surely the cumulative effect of man's centuries-long fear, loathing, and thinking of an entity called Satan is bound to produce something!? With all of the thoughts directed in his direction, Satan may very well be the Prince of Darkness, even if he has only recently ascended his throne.

In effect, collective fear may very well have created organized evil, which perpetuates itself with continuing fear and deception – deception of the weaknesses of evil, as well as the deception of what constitutes good and/or evil.

A precise definition of organized evil is made difficult by its mysteriousness and vagueness. But this is in itself, a part of its definition. As Mary Kay Rae has noted, in her discussion in Whirling Darkness:

> "Central to the existence of 'evil' is deception – not merely in its extreme, overt or easily identifiable forms, but in all the slippery, confusing gray areas between the polarities of evolution and disintegration, where most of us make our choices (or forfeit our right and ability to make those choices). What better way to hide the existence of something than to make it hard to define? Alternatively, naming something (i.e. identifying or defining it) is the first step in mastering it."

Scott Peck has defined evil as a force, within or without humans, whose purpose is to kill life. Evil is thus about killing – killing of the body as well as the spirit and the various essential attributes of life (sentience, mobility, awareness, growth, autonomy, will). In Scott Peck's book, *People of the Lie*, the ramifications of evil and its presence in our lives is well documented. It is one of those unpleasant concepts, but one of those essential ones we need to learn, if we are to create good in an evolving universe.

Other Implications

Many proponents of reincarnation advocate the necessity of subduing one's ego. But this may not be a good idea. For ego allows for unique choices (i.e., unique gains in universal knowledge). Ego is therefore good, unless the effect of ego is to limit others or for that matter, limit yourself. Evil is when the ego's choices infringe upon the sum total of choices of yourself and others. Ego can be just free will, and free will cannot be evil in and of itself, even though its manifestations (choices) can be. Ego, therefore, like most things has its inherently good aspects, but also carries with it the possibility that it can be used for evil purposes as well.

Therapy can be thought of as helping another person to have choices. Therapy may eliminate roadblocks, mental hang ups, and all manner of constricting external controls. For example, when you are angry with someone, that person controls part of your life. Release the anger, and they no longer have any control over you. (Besides, why would you want to spend any of your valuable time thinking about someone with whom you were angry?)

Is vegetarianism a means of allowing choice to other souls? In other words, do ducks have souls? What about carnivorous animals – are they evil? If wolves keep the caribou herd fit, are they evil? Are there degrees of choice?

Unwarranted control is the principal form of evil. Entropy implies that the universe moves away from control and toward chaos. Yet, in chaos or confusion, there is more opportunity for creating love. Control is, therefore, anti-entropic and thus, a violation of universal law.

Love

Perhaps even more important than knowledge is love. In the thirteenth chapter of Corinthians, we have: ". . . but the greatest of these is love." Christ and other major religious figures always established love as the primary commandment.

Raymond Moody, in *Life After Life*, reports that his subjects have stressed the importance of two things in life: Learning to love other people and acquiring knowledge. Dr. Moody goes on to stress that the whole idea of life is to cultivate a unique and profound love, while at the same time, acquiring knowledge.

Love is certainly the most potent force around. Love begets love. Love (like hate) is omni-directional and cannot be directed, limited, or controlled; it recognizes no boundaries and tends to gently run amok. It is instead a state of being, one that can constantly change in intensity and which has no upper limits.

Good is anything that increases choices, which in turn, then allows for the creation of more knowledge and/or love. Greater creation in an infinite universe then implies infinite creativity. On the one hand, hate is limiting, while on the other, love is non-limiting.

According to John Sanford, in The Man Who Wrestled with God:

> ". . . man is different because man has the gift of consciousness with its power of self-reflection. We are not an unconscious part of nature like other forms of life. We have the gift of psychological discrimination and moral responsibility, represented in the story [Adam and Eve] as the power to discern good and evil. We can choose alternatives in life, and our consciousness, with its wonderful, dreadful freedom, separates us forever from nature's paradisiacal wholeness.
>
> "For without evil, without choice, without the opposites in life, no moral or spiritual growth is possible, and evidently the development of man's soul and spirit is of more value to God than his mere happiness."

Our grand principle of reincarnation, therefore, may be that we are here on this earth to create love; to act as transformers, creating love from the raw materials of physical experience. And with free will, we can make the choices which will increase the sum total of love in the universe. Reincarnation thus becomes a progression from being one with God, going out into the world in order to create love, then returning to God; hopefully having increased the love in the universe, recognizing our mistakes and planning for our next attempt, and then once again, reincarnating in a universe seeking more love. The grand plan, according to this theory of reincarnation, is the creation of love, whereby the universe is greater at the end than at the beginning. Is the increase in knowledge to be gained in our lifetimes nothing more than an increase in our ability to create love?

Why not?

Chapter 18:

Theory of Reincarnation

and Paranormal Phenomena

It's time to consolidate what we have learned into a theory that includes re-incarnation. We will begin with certain philosophical assumptions, outline a basic theory of reincarnation, and then include several corollaries.

The Assumptions

1. The universe is infinite, evolving and increasing in the dimensions of omniscience as God and all entities of God existing in physical and non-physical forms, learn, love, create and experience the varied aspects of the universe. The reason for a universe (The "Why?") is to allow for the increasing omniscience of God and the evolvement of all of God's entities. (This does not necessarily imply an infinite material universe, but rather a universe that has no boundaries or limits on either time or space. Specifically, it is a universe that increases with time.)

2. As entities of God, mankind exists as one aspect of a Divine Plan which provides for an increasing omniscience of God, through cycles of learning, loving, creating and experiencing. Mankind exists as discrete minds experiencing the universe in discrete ways. Each mind is independent and yet connected, and incarnates as discrete beings through an evolving series of lifetimes. Each mind has free will, in both the incarnated and disincarnated states, constrained only by the free will of others and the universal physical and metaphysical laws.

3. God is just and thereby justice constitutes a basic building block of universal law (which in turn, implies the existence of good and evil).

Reincarnation

The mind is immortal, nonphysical, and capable of all things attributable to an entity of God. The mind is distinct from and essentially independent of a physical brain and/or physical body. Analogous to spirit or soul, the mind is the essence of the entity of God. Through a series of incarnations, the mind joins with physical bodies in order to experience the universe through the sensorium of different bodies. In this manner, the mind learns, loves, creates, and experiences, contributing to the increasing omniscience of the universe. Each successive incarnation provides greater evolvement for each mind and therefore greater potential in that mind's contribution to the increasing omniscience.

An essential element in the physical incarnation is a loss of memory, which prevents the mind, while incarnated, from remembering the Divine Plan. Thus the lost memory allows for random, chaotic, and creative actions or thoughts, which are external to the Plan. Without such deviations from the Divine Plan, the execution of the Plan would be limited to the pre-conceived Plan and thus no new knowledge or increase in omniscience would be achieved. The unique, unplanned events occuring during each incarnation (within the framework of the Divine Plan) are the main reasons for incarnation. Reincarnation allows for even greater deviations by extending the previously attained mental, physical, emotional, and spiritual states from prior lifetimes, into a continuing series of lifetime situations and thus provide for a higher potential level of contribution by each succeeding lifetime.

The reincarnational cycle is initiated at birth, continues as the physical body grows, experiences, and eventually dies. At death, the mind leaves the physical body, relinquishes all sensory aspects of that body, and continues to exist as a discrete mind, independent of any physical body. Because of free will, the mind may continue to exist in this disembodied state (as a phantom, spirit, ghost, etc), attach to the physical bodies of other incarnated minds, or may go into the "Light." The Light is a return of the mind to the Host of other minds and the collective body of God.

In the Light the mind reviews its past incarnation (learning from the experiences) and begins planning for its next incarnation. This planning is coordinated with other minds, the overall divine plan, and with guides or counselors. Guides or counselors consist of minds of higher evolvement and include the mind's Higher Self. The Higher Self is the aspect of the mind that does not incarnate, nor take on physical form, but remains connected to the Host of other minds and available to the mind for direction in the mind's purpose during a physical incarnation.

While in the Light, the mind has access to all of the accumulated knowledge of the universe, the Divine Plan, and the individual plans of other minds. As a non-physical being, the mind is free to move without restraint in space. The mind is also aware of the past, present, and probable future. Time exists for the mind while in the Light (as well as when incarnated), but poses less of an apparent barrier or constraint due to the mind's knowledge of the course of universal events. Time exists in the physical as well, but is more dominant due to the lack of foreknowledge of planned futures.

Traditionally, the availability of the accumulated knowledge of the universe is contained in the Akashic Records. Carl Jung and Rupert Sheldrake describe similar concepts to which they refer, respectively, as the Collective Unconscious and Morphogenetic Fields. In all cases the essence of each concept is the availability (under the proper conditions) of universal knowledge, including the continual input from current experiences.

Planning by the mind while in the Light is done within the confines of pre-planned events and tendencies, such that when the mind again incarnates, information on the planned events and tendencies is available. Occult sciences, such as astrology, provide an outline of these pre-planned events and tendencies; thus an individual mind in the Light can plan its next incarnation around specific astrological events. In this way an individual can choose an astrological natal chart in order to specify the psychological makeup desired for the coming incarnation and to provide structure in the lifetime with respect to "external" events. Thus, astrology can be used as a means of communication between the pre-incarnated plan and the mind during its incarnation. Astrology represents a "script" in which "ad-libs" are possible (but only within the context that "The show must go on.")

Once the next incarnation is planned, the mind may join the physical body at any time while the body is in the womb or at the moment of birth. The mind may also depart the physical body while it is still in the womb or, later, after the birth. Such separation of the mind from the physical body is termed "out-of-body" and may occur frequently in the dream state. The mind may go out-of-body while in other meditative states, but such conscious out-of-body's are less frequent. During the out-of-body state, the physical body achieves its maximum repair and recovery of physical problems.

During an out-of-body state, a "silver cord" maintains the connection between mind and body. The silver cord has no apparent limitations in length or elasticity and does not constrain the mind while out-of-body. The physical body requires the silver cord connection with the mind in order for the body to rejuvenate and resist decay. A severing of the cord is equivalent to death, in that the mind no longer provides the essential motivating forces to the body's rejuvenation and resistance to decay.

Mind/Body Connections

The mind connects to the physical body through two primary methods. The mind receives information from the physical body by telepathy. Essentially the mind telepathically reads the brain by "tuning into the particular frequency" of that brain. The brain, in turn, acts as a repository for the sensorium of the body. The mind directs the body through the use of psychokinesis. The mind essentially directs all physical activity by willing the brain to make it so. The telepathic and psychokinetic connections of the mind and body allow for the mind to exist independently of the body, but also allow for the possibility of other minds (such as those in an earth-bound state) exercising control over the body as well.

The mind has access to the Akashic Records, Morphogenetic Field, or

Collective Unconscious by telepathic means. Much of this information is obtained through the individual subconscious (particularly in regards to the development of bodily growth).

Disease, illness, and accidents are directed by the mind for its evolvement and possible guidance. Such directions may derive from when the mind was in the Light, or during an incarnation. Just as illness is psychosomatic, so is healing. The mind directs the body through the brain and the immune system, directing the establishment of illness or wellness.

Healing may deal with past lives. Reincarnation allows the mind to connect with a variety of bodies. At the same time the memories of different incarnations (specifically those memories which represent unresolved problems) may continue to influence the mind (and indirectly the physical body of the present incarnation). The memories of each incarnation (during, as well as after) are stored in the morphogenetic field. The mind has access to these memories and certain memories will be more accessible because of the similarity of vibrational frequencies between the accessing mind and the memory. Therefore, some of the memories will represent past incarnations of the mind which is accessing the memories, but some of the memories will be of other mind's past lives (but which have relevance to the mind's current incarnation, due to similarity in vibrational frequencies). In addition, the intensity or amplitude of the vibrational frequency will affect the accessibility, with trauma and unresolved problems having greater intensity than resolved issues.

Communications

Just as the mind can tune into the memories of other minds in the morphogenetic field, the mind can also tune into another mind's current thinging, i.e. telepathy between minds. The mind is capable of reading the physical body's brain/sensorium to which it is attached by means of similar vibrational frequencies. When two minds are operating at similar vibrational frequencies, the two minds can share information through the use of the same telepathy that the mind uses to gather information from its physical body. The degree to which a "mind-reader" is capable of "reading another mind" is the degree to which the "mind-reader" can "de-tune" its own frequency and open its brain to the vibrational frequency of the reader. The greater the intensity or amplitude of the information (or feelings), the greater the accuracy of telepathically transferring information from one mind to another.

The ability to communicate telepathically with other minds derives in part from the inherent connections between entities of God. The sensitivity of this connection to others can be overridden by the greater intensity of the sensorium of the physical body, i.e. subtle variations in thought from telepathically communicated information can easily be overwhelmed by the physical senses. In an out-of-body state the sensorium of the physical body can be greatly diminished (except for "emergency callbacks") and thus the mind, while out-of-body, can receive much more information telepathically. (Physical senses can also interfere with the reception of information from the morphogenetic field.)

Information can reach the mind while incarnated and in its physical body through the subconscious. Dreams, hunches, sudden insights, and intuition provide means for information to be given to the mind through the subconscious. Connections between the subconscious and conscious can be made by the mind's willing the conscious to reduce its sensory input and "listen."

Guidance for incarnated minds wishing to understand the Divine Plan (at least in part), is provided through such means as intuition, I Ching, channeling, astrology, numerology, Tarot, etc. Intuition and channeling may be accomplished through connections to the Morphogenetic Field, Collective Unconscious, Higher Self, or other aspect of the Light. Grace plays a part in that subtle guidance from the Light may sometimes protect the incarnated being from problems. Such guidance, however, can be modified to a greater or lesser degree by the mind's ego, and can effectively reduce the accuracy of the communications to zero.

Detours

The transition at physical death into the Light can be interrupted for numerous reasons, including: strong emotions of anger, fear, jealously, resentment, guilt, remorse, strong ties of possessive love, confusion and disbelief in an afterlife, and perceived needs. Perceived needs include (but are not limited to) addictions to drugs, alcohol, material assets, and/or other people.

In the event a mind does not make the transition, it becomes "earthbound", essentially still emotionally/mentally attached to the physical plane. Earthbound entities may follow one of several paths. One path is to become a ghost or phantom (which is usually associated with some specific location relevant to its last incarnation). Poltergeist incidents arise from the mind of the earth bound spirit exercising its psychokinetic ability to affect physical happenings. This psychokinetic ability is more pronounced when the earthbound mind is more closely associated (emotionally and otherwise) with the physical surroundings (such as a "haunted house").

A second path is for the earthbound entity to simply wander in the plane between the physical plane and the Light. This may include detours to what the mind may visualize or conceptualize as hell, purgatory, or simply an empty, gray space. Such wandering earthbound entities may slowly come to understand their predicament, but typically require earthly and/or heavenly assistance.

A third path for an earthbound entity is to attach its mind to another physical body. Just as a mind uses psychokinesis to direct the activities of its physical body, other minds may use the same psychokinetic ability to direct another's physical body. However, because of the variation in vibrational frequencies between the earthbound entity and the physical body to which it attachs, the ability of the earthbound entity to control the physical body may vary from virtually ineffective control to almost total control. The control ability of the earthbound entity also depends upon the degree to which the resident mind allows such control (either consciously or unconsciously). A strong mind in its own body can nullify much of the control of its physical body by an attached earthbound entity, but a weaker mind (or one which is heavily distracted, unaware, etc) can lose control to the point of having large parts of its life blanked out. Any mind can also consciously welcome an attaching earthbound entity – through mutual love, the attraction of talents sought by the host mind, or for almost any other emotional, physical, or mental reason.

The mind's ability to guard itself against the onset of an attachment is in its aura, essentially its immune system against external psychokinetic control of its physical body. The aura's ability to act in this way depends upon the host mind's emotional, physical, and mental condition (all interconnected). Drunkenness or drugs can reduce the ability of the aura to defend the body from intruding earthbound spirits or other forms of attachment. But also sudden shocks, illness, accidents, any abrupt changes, voluntary invitations, strong and essentially unhealthy emotional ties to others, etc, can result in weaknesses in the aura, such that earthbound or other entities may attach themselves to the physical body.

Purposes

Minds are not incarnated in order to analyze or attempt to understand all the intricacies of such things as *I Ching*, Sabian Symbols, esoteric writings, and so forth. All such knowledge will be known when the mind reaches the Light. Instead, minds are here to create, contribute and add experience and love to the universe. Joseph Campbell, in *The Power of Myth*, thinks of such creations and/or contributions in terms of heroes, leaders, and visionaries:

> "If your private myth, your dream, happens to coincide with that of the society, you are in good accord with your group. If it isn't, you've got an adventure in the dark forest ahead of you."

Campbell goes on to describe these heroes and heroines:

> "They've moved out of the society that would have protected them, and into the dark forest, into the world of fire, or original experience. Original experience has not been interpreted for you, and so you've got to work out your life for yourself. Either you can take it or you can't. You don't have to go far off the interpreted path to find yourself in very difficult situations. The courage to face the trials and to bring a whole new body of possibilities into the field of interpreted experience for other people to experience; that is the hero's deed. The hero's sphere of action is not the transcendent but here, now, in the field of time, of good and evil – of the pair of opposites."

These heroic contributions utilize the physical, mental, and emotional, as well as the spiritual (the attributes of the incarnated state), to achieve something more than is realizable in a discarnate state. With the lack of specific knowledge of the Divine Plan, each mind is thereby allowed to create unique and heroic acts of love. With such creations, the universe increases in omniscience.

The Will of God includes the random and the chaotic, and allows for creativity, uniqueness, and specifically, the creation of love. In *Emmanuel's Book*, it's stated this way:

> "The separation from God
> began a journey of love.
> The individuating consciousness seeks,
> through the experience of human reality,
> to know itself fully and completely
> so that it can return to the Oneness
> with a greater light and a greater understanding.
> This adds to the reality of the Oneness
> for all things are in a state of continual expansion
> and creation."

It is left to the reader to complete the theory . . .